Teaching College Freshmen

Bette LaSere Erickson
Diane Weltner Strommer

Teaching
College
Freshmen

Jossey-Bass Publishers • San Francisco

TEACHING COLLEGE FRESHMEN
by Bette LaSere Erickson and Diane Weltner Strommer

Copyright © 1991 by: Jossey-Bass Inc., Publishers
350 Sansome Street
San Francisco, California 94104

For sales outside the United States, please contact your local Simon & Schuster
International Office.

www.josseybass.com

Library of Congress Cataloging-in-Publication Data

Erickson, Bette LaSere, date.
    Teaching college freshmen / Bette LaSere Erickson, Diane Weltner
Strommer.
       p. cm.—(The Jossey-Bass higher and adult education series)
    Includes bibliographical references and index.
    ISBN 1-55542-310-8
    1. College teaching—United States. 2. College freshmen—United
States. I. Strommer, Diane Weltner, date. II. Title.
III. Series.
LB2331.E76   1991
378.1′25′0973—dc20   90-46069
                                       CIP

TCF Manufactured in the United States of America on Lyons Falls
Turin Book. This paper is acid-free and 100 percent totally
chlorine-free.

JACKET DESIGN BY WILLI BAUM

FIRST EDITION

HB Printing   10 9 8 7 6 5 4

Code 9112

The Jossey-Bass
Higher and Adult Education Series

Contents

ix

Preface

Each year, thousands of college faculty teach courses taken by more than three million freshmen. Widely acknowledged to be the critical college year, the freshman year is also the one in which the greatest student need confronts the least institutional support. Although recent reports on higher education stress the importance of the freshman year as the time when institutions succeed or fail at incorporating students into the academic community and at engaging them in their own academic development, the instructional needs of freshmen have been largely ignored.

Increased competition for a reduced number of eighteen-year-olds has changed the academic climate, however, for few institutions can afford the rapid loss of one-fifth or more of those students so recently—and at such expense—recruited to their campuses. A new focus on freshmen is thus a major trend in higher education today.

To date, however, most efforts to strengthen the freshman year have focused on the periphery of academic life rather than on its center: the freshman classroom. Any serious efforts to improve the freshman year must involve faculty and must focus on the main events—teaching and learning in courses and classrooms.

Unfortunately, information that might motivate and guide faculty to reconsider freshman instruction remains scattered in places faculty are unlikely to visit. Although freshmen present unique instructional challenges, none of the available books on college teaching specifically deals with instruction for freshmen. *Teaching College Freshmen* fills this gap by describing today's freshmen, then taking an inside look at the freshman classroom and its needs. While our characterization of the freshman year and our recommendations for teaching practices draw on research and theory, our emphasis throughout is on the concrete, the practical, and the applied.

Audience

We have written this book for several groups. It is, of course, primarily for college and university faculty who teach freshmen. Beginning college teachers, whose first teaching assignments often include freshman courses, will find that we address their immediate teaching concerns while providing a general introduction to college teaching and learning.

Teaching College Freshmen is equally valuable for experienced professors, and especially for those assigned to teach freshmen after a period of teaching upper-level or graduate students. Even the most talented teachers are easily overwhelmed by the diversity among freshmen, bewildered by their different needs and reactions, and baffled by the discovery that teaching practices that have served them well in other undergraduate courses fail miserably in freshman courses. To these faculty, we offer a synthesis of the research on freshmen and help in adapting teaching practices to meet freshman needs. We are particularly conscious of faculty concern about high failure rates in freshman courses. We explicitly address the issues that such high-risk courses raise and suggest a variety of strategies for reducing failures while maintaining high standards.

Finally, although *Teaching College Freshmen* is intended primarily for college teachers, it is also an important resource for faculty development personnel, department chairs, deans, and other administrators whose responsibilities include ensuring quality in undergraduate programs and supporting faculty efforts to improve instruction. The needs of freshmen differ from those of other undergraduates and place special demands on faculty who teach freshmen—demands that have implications for institutional planning and educational policies.

Overview of the Contents

The three main parts of the book reflect our three major concerns: to understand the students themselves, to present effective teaching practices, and to provide practical suggestions for dealing with some of the special challenges presented by freshman classes. Part One portrays freshmen and the complexities of their lives to lend insight into who they are, why they behave as they do, and what instructional support they require. Chapter One begins with a backward look at high school and its influence in shaping expectations and habits, examines the changing nature of the freshman class, and describes the attitudes, values, and goals of entering freshmen. Chapter Two depicts the day-to-day reality of freshman life and the demands of adjusting to it. Chapter Three summarizes the research on student development and learning styles that we judge to be most relevant for faculty who teach freshmen.

Part Two describes teaching practices that both challenge and support freshmen. Chapter Four examines the goals of freshman courses, offers some working definitions for the types of learning frequently stressed in them, notes the ways freshmen are likely to interpret the challenges, and previews some implications for selecting teaching methods and developing testing procedures. Chapter Five deals with preparing a syllabus and meeting the first class, two crucial activities for getting a course off to a good start. Chapter Six suggests several techniques for helping freshmen learn from lectures. Active involvement by students—the key to remembering, understanding, and thinking—is the focus of the next two chapters. Chapter Seven describes several methods for getting students involved in class, provides examples from different disciplines, and offers advice on how to use these methods in freshman courses. Chapter Eight highlights a variety of assignments designed to encourage student involvement outside class. Chapter Nine focuses on the evaluation of student learning and proposes changes in our traditional methods of grading, both to meet the special needs of freshmen and to adhere to good measurement practices. The questions faculty ask about grading are addressed in Chapter Ten.

Part Three explores some of the special challenges of teaching freshmen. Chapter Eleven offers techniques for reducing student anonymity, increasing involvement, and evaluating learning in large classes. Chapter Twelve suggests a variety of contexts and strategies for advising freshmen and providing individual, personal support. Chapter Thirteen addresses the need in virtually all first-year courses to reinforce the development of basic skills in reading, writing, mathematical reasoning, and critical thinking. We recognize that good teaching in freshman courses is especially demanding. In the final chapter, Chapter Fourteen, we suggest some ways colleges can support faculty and faculty can help themselves in accomplishing the difficult tasks we propose for them.

While we hope that faculty will read the entire book, it is intended to be divisible, a tool to pick up and use as need or interest arises. Part One provides the framework, but the chapters in Parts Two and Three may be read separately. While we do not underestimate the amount of time and attention good teaching demands, we also do not think that faculty need be overwhelmed at the prospect of improving teaching practices. We hope that our readers will initially select one or two ideas of interest, try them out, and return for more a semester or a year later. Over time, the cumulative effect of making small changes will greatly enhance freshman learning.

We have omitted much. We would have liked to pay more attention to the needs of diverse groups of freshmen, and we regret ignoring honors students. When we talk to our colleagues about teaching college freshmen, however, we find that it is the 90 percent—or more—who are *not* honors students who most challenge faculty. Our intention is to foster the learning of these students. We also would have liked to find or invent a more satisfactory word for *freshman*. We considered and rejected *first-year student* and *fresh-person* as having rather different connotations and as being too unwieldy for general use.

Acknowledgments

Many people have contributed to this book. We are grateful to the Jossey-Bass Higher and Adult Education Series editor, Gale Erlandson, for her enthusiastic support throughout this project. Our colleagues at the University of Rhode Island, particularly those who have been teaching fellows in the Instructional Development

Program or faculty advisers and staff at University College, will recognize some of their ideas and strategies. Sandra Pearlman shared her expertise on learning assistance; Barbara Roberts, on learning disabilities. Drafts of some chapters were reviewed by Everett Harris, Eugene Knott, and Sarah Rockett. Glenn Erickson reviewed each chapter, and his suggestions helped sharpen our views. Virginia Gordon of the Ohio State University read the chapter on advising. Our husbands, Breck Peters and John Strommer, supplied humor, a sense of balance, and editorial skill. Faculty involved in the Freshman Project of University College deserve special thanks: Jayne Richmond for her leadership; John Stevenson, Richard Sullivan, and Ruth Waldman for provocative conversations.

By sharing their hopes and plans for their freshman year and a year later candidly telling the stories of their experiences at colleges as diverse as Duke University, Hampshire College, the Community College of Rhode Island, and the University of Delaware, a special group of young people reminded us of what making the transition from high school senior to college freshman was really like. We thank those graduates of South Kingstown High School for the quotations used here. For frankly relating her experiences as an older freshman, we also thank Mary Raymond. Unless otherwise noted, all students' comments are from students at the University of Rhode Island, many in response to surveys of freshmen conducted by University College.

Our principal debt is to the faculty. As practitioners creatively developing their craft, they have taught us much of what we know about teaching and learning. We are especially indebted to the following faculty members for contributing examples and ideas included in this book: Judith Boss, Winifred Brownell, Allan Cain, Lois Cuddy, James Fasching, Frank Heppner, Wendy Holmes, Don Kunz, Stephen Letcher, John Montgomery, Lynn Pasquerella, Breck Peters, Yngve Ramstad, Eric Schoonover, John Stevenson, and Jacklyn Vittimberga.

Teaching College Freshmen began when a dean concerned about freshmen and their learning happened into an instructional development program and found someone who knew more about teaching and student learning than she thought could be known, even after years of classroom and administrative experience. The authors wish to emphasize that just as they have learned from one another during a decade of personal and professional friendship, so too this book is in every way a joint project.

This book is dedicated to our former freshman, Erik Strommer, to our future freshmen, Willey Erickson and Jae Elizabeth Strommer, and to our colleagues, the faculty of the University of Rhode Island.

Kingston, Rhode Island   Bette LaSere Erickson
December 1990   Diane Weltner Strommer

The Authors

Bette LaSere Erickson is an instructional development specialist in the Instructional Development Program at the University of Rhode Island. She received her B.A. degree in English (1967) from St. Olaf College and her Ed.D. degree (1975) from the University of Massachusetts, Amherst. Erickson is an authority on instructional methods and course design. She has published articles on faculty development programs and on teaching techniques. She has conducted numerous workshops and seminars at colleges and universities throughout the country and has had extensive contact with faculty in a variety of disciplines. She was a founding member of the Professional and Organizational Development Network (POD Network) and also served as its executive director.

    Diane Weltner Strommer is Dean of University College and Special Academic Programs at the University of Rhode Island. She received her A.B. degree in English (1963) from the University of North Carolina, Chapel Hill, and her M.A. degree (1965) and Ph.D. degree (1969), both in English, from the Ohio State University.

    Strommer's recent research activities have focused on advising, learning assistance, and administrative units for freshmen, and she has consulted and given presentations on mentor programs, advising as teaching, and University Colleges. She is the founding president of the Association of Deans and Directors of University Colleges and Undergraduate Studies. Her publications include articles on education and feminism, on teaching writing, on faculty involvement in advising programs, and on University Colleges, and a book on a seventeenth-century masque, *Times Distractions*. Strommer frequently gives presentations at the National Academic Advising Association's national conferences and at the annual conference on the Freshman Year Experience. She was a faculty fellow in the Instructional Development Program at the University of Rhode Island in 1983–84.

Teaching
College
Freshmen

PART ONE

Understanding Freshmen

If undergraduate education is to be improved, as higher education's critics insist it must, that improvement will largely occur in the college classroom. Effective teaching of undergraduates begins with freshmen, and we think it begins with understanding them. To aid in that understanding, Part One delineates some of the most significant aspects of freshman lives, as students and as learners.

The factors that make today's freshmen different from their predecessors are the focus of Chapter One. There, we look first at the high schools in which habits of mind are shaped and preparation for college takes place, then at the societal factors and demographic forces altering the nature of the freshman class, and finally at the values and aspirations of the new freshmen themselves. In Chapter Two, we describe the college environment during the freshman year, a year that presents myriad adjustments and transitions for the student, a virtual cacophony of distractions from academic life. In Chapter Three, we present a summary of research on student development and learning styles. This research reveals some of the reasons that teaching freshmen poses particular quandaries and provides a context for the instructional strategies that we discuss in Part Two.

1

From High School
to College:
The Entering Freshman

Overhear a conversation in the faculty club that begins "they don't" or "they can't" and the odds are better than even that freshmen are the topic of discussion. "They can't read." "They can't write." "They can't do simple math." "They don't study." "They don't come to class." "They don't participate in discussion."

Such concern, even despair, about the state of undergraduates' minds is of course not new, as these comments from a 1928 study of undergraduate life suggest: "The general level of intellectual interest among undergraduates is low. The collective life is not characterized by intellectual curiosity and intelligent discussion. . . . A small minority are sincerely interested in all their academic work; a large minority do not put their hearts into any of it; while the great mass are genuinely intent upon only a few of their subjects, commonly the more practical ones, and apathetic toward the rest" (Angell, 1928, p. 2). While such reminders are consoling, it is clearly not enough to say that few students have ever been fully involved in academic pursuits or that most have submitted to education primarily for its utilitarian value. Although students have probably never quite met our expectations, by always being somewhat reluctant to engage in intellectual challenge or less than perfectly prepared to work on a college level, something *has* changed. There is something different in kind as well as degree in today's high school senior who believes school "is kind of like a job you don't like; it's like washing dishes," but nonetheless intends to go to college (Mingis, 1987, p. 6).

To know how to teach them, we must understand our freshmen better. We must have a clear-eyed view of who they are, where they come from, how they have been instructed, what values they hold, and what their expectations and goals are. While no golden age of undergraduate learning ever existed, nor have freshmen ever been as committed to learning as we sometimes recall through the rosy glow of memory, the sense most faculty share that today's freshmen are different from their predecessors, more disengaged, and more difficult to reach and teach, is probably accurate, even at highly selective institutions.

High School, a Backward Look

Several recent reports help to explain that perplexing difference we note in many of today's freshmen (Richardson, Fisk, and Okun, 1983; Powell, Farrar, and Cohen, 1985; Sedlak, Wheeler, Pullin, and Cusick, 1986). Some of the most insightful work has been done by a research team at Michigan State's Institute for Research on Teaching. Their report, based on both field studies and extensive reviews of the literature, is primarily concerned with high schools and "the nature of the relationship between educators and their students and the extent to which students are actively engaged in the learning process," a relationship they believe is "the most fundamental variable in the educational process" (Sedlak, Wheeler, Pullin, and Cusick, 1986, p. ix). Their work confirms what many of us suspected: many of our students do indeed come to us less well prepared than they once were. The problem of academic standards in the high schools of the 1980s, they find, was "one of low academic achievement in the vast majority of schools, even in wealthier small towns and suburbs" (p. x)—a problem, that is, that cannot be blamed on a changing student body, on higher high school graduation rates, or on wider access to college. It is too widespread.

Their findings not only confirm our suspicions, but also suggest the extent of the challenge facing higher education. Their summary of the research concludes that "according to virtually ev-

ery objective and subjective criterion presented in the recent literature, high school students today achieve less academically than
their predecessors of 20 years ago. . . . They enroll in fewer challenging advanced basic academic courses and in more introductory,
service, and personal development classes. They spend less time on
homework and more time working and watching television. High
school attendance rates have worsened. Over the past decade the
U.S. graduation rate has declined in excess of four percent. Adolescents' higher-order reasoning and interpretive skills have weakened.
High school students are more visibly disruptive, less committed to
high school, and less engaged in academic activities. They appear
to care less about their educational experience and have come to
invest their time, effort, and attention elsewhere" (p. 2).

Although students with an intrinsic love of learning still
exist, of course, as well as those whose belief in the extrinsic reward
of being a top student compels their engagement in learning, Sedlak
and his colleagues conclude that "the disengaged population probably exceeds two-thirds of the total number of high school students
nationwide. Perhaps two-thirds of those intending to enroll in institutions of higher education do not have to concentrate on challenging academic coursework to be admitted, even to the better
public universities" (pp. 9–10). Such findings are echoed in *The
Shopping Mall High School* (Powell, Farrar, and Cohen, 1985),
which argues that for most students high school is a place for
"hanging out," much as they would in a real mall after school, for
these students sense that neither college admission nor classroom
success requires a high level of academic involvement.

Students are not responsible for their culture, and it does
little good to blame them for their deficiencies. Like most of us, they
do not go out of their way to make life difficult for themselves
without cause. If, however, we are to succeed in enabling these
former high school students to learn as new freshmen, we must
understand the environment that most recently taught them what
and how to learn. In describing that environment, our intention is
not to blame. Our society has a history of thrusting its failures and
inadequacies into the school, then closing the door and walking
away, ignoring what has been left inside. We owe our understanding and support to high school teachers who have often coped in

imaginative and significant ways with the results of integration and mainstreaming, the declining influence of church and family, and the increasing prevalence of drugs.

The Course of Study

High school was more laid back. I had my credits, so I took gym, cooking, stuff like that.

—Freshman

I wish I had paid more attention to my math courses and had taken chemistry. I could have prepared for college a lot better.

—Freshman

High school graduation requirements are governed by the Carnegie Unit, which represents, at minimum, thirty-six weeks of study in classes that meet four or five times weekly in periods of forty to sixty minutes. Some high schools require as few as sixteen units for graduation; others, twenty. Eighteen satisfies the admission requirements even of selective colleges. Given that six or seven time slots per day are available for classes in a typical high school schedule, however, many students virtually complete graduation requirements by the end of their junior year, often leaving only senior English and perhaps physical education or health for their senior year. While some students do rigorously prepare themselves for college by taking advanced chemistry or physics and advanced placement or other courses for college credit, others slide along with electives like Independent Living Skills.

Within the broad requirements set by the state, local school districts usually determine what constitutes a high school education. For graduation from high school with a valid diploma, the usual basic requirements are three years of English, two years of social studies, one year each of mathematics and science, and a course in health education. In addition to and sometimes replacing academic subjects (classified by the College Board as those in the six areas of English, arts and music, social sciences and history, foreign and classical languages, natural science, and mathematics), students take electives and personal service courses such as driver education. One study based on transcripts and schedules from 1964 to 1981 suggests that during the 1960s and 1970s high school students began the pattern of taking more of these personal service and development courses and fewer basic academic courses and so received a less rigorous academic education (Adelman, 1983). Other high school courses are quite specialized, like the college courses they imitate. This growing tendency toward narrower subjects is quite likely connected to teachers' duplicating their own undergraduate experience in the major. At best, a course thematically linking poetry, drama, and the novel may substitute for a broad survey of British or American literature. At worst, so may a course in the Poetry of Rock Music. "Few high schools," the Sedlak study group concluded, "offer a coherent academic program required of all students" (1986, p. 43).

Some slight evidence exists that more rigorous college admissions requirements in the 1980s may have had an effect on what high school students study. The *1988 Profile of SAT and Achievement Test Takers* reports an increase in the average number of units of study of academic subjects in high school from 18.2 to 18.3. While that minute change is insignificant by itself, the study also reports the encouraging sign that the percentage of test takers reporting twenty or more units of study of academic courses (that is, an average of five courses for each of four years) increased from 34 to 36 percent (The College Board, 1988, p. iv). Other data reveal, however, that student interest in personal service and development courses remains high. Students surveyed as a sample of those listed in *Who's Who Among American High School Students* (1988) include only one academic subject among the five courses they wish had been available in high school, a group including College Selection/Preparation for College Life (50 percent), Personal Finance (32 percent), Comparative Politics (28 percent), Suicide Prevention (24 percent), and Drug and Alcohol Abuse (21 percent).

Even when students are prepared for the freshman year by the standard of having taken an adequate number of academic courses in high school, the transition is rarely smooth. The content of a high school course seldom meshes logically with the freshman course, and titles on high school transcripts provide few clues about actual course content. Senior College Math, for example, could be the second half of Algebra II, pre-calculus, or a general review. Many colleges now regularly subject incoming freshmen to a battery of placement tests for the very reason that high school transcripts do not reveal what a student might actually know.

From the student's perspective, on the other hand, many of the courses studied during the first college year appear similar to those taken in high school, at least superficially, and they are often subjects about which students already have strong feelings. Because freshmen anticipate college as the place where they can finally pursue their own interests, they greet the familiar course titles with a sense of disappointment and, often, with their attitudes toward the subjects already formed by high school experiences.

Teaching Practices

I never had a class before when the teacher just stands up and talks to you. He says something and you're writing it down, but then he says something else.

—Freshman

My biggest challenge during my first year was learning how to play the game, so to speak, of the instructors' expectations and note-taking strategies. Wasn't too bad, though.

—Freshman

The lack of engagement in academic work, the lack of caring that so many freshmen bring with them from high school, is particularly troubling to college faculty who themselves are deeply committed and engaged, and probably were so even as freshmen. Evidence is mounting that students' disengagement, their passive learning, their lack of caring begins early, is reinforced in high school and, all too often, in higher education as well. In the view of this research, as Theodore Marchese (1985, p. 6) puts it, "institutions and cultural realities conspire to induce in students an expectation that classroom demands will be kept at a tolerable (low) level, and that 'the system' is such that teachers come to acquiesce."

While the reasons that students become disengaged from learning are complex, several researchers strongly suspect the process begins in late elementary school, where children work in isolation at their seats and where teaching is defined as the transmission of bits of information and learning is defined as memorization (Sedlak, Wheeler, Pullin, and Cusick, 1986; Goodlad, 1984). By high school what is operating in many classrooms is "a complex, tacit conspiracy to avoid sustained, rigorous, demanding inquiry" (Sedlak, Wheeler, Pullin, and Cusick, 1986, p. 5), a bargain between student and teacher. When it is set at a low level, the essential features of the bargain identified in the studies by Sedlak and his colleagues include: "relatively little concern for academic content; a willingness to tolerate, if not encourage, diversion from the specified knowledge to be presented or discussed; the substitution of genial banter and conversation for concentrated academic exercises; improvisational instructional adaptation to student preference for or indifference toward specific subject matter or pedagogical techniques; the 'negotiation' of class content, assignments, and standards; and a high degree of teacher autonomy in managing the level of academic engagement, personal interaction, and course content" (p. 7). Learning is the price paid for a "more comfortable and less troublesome" relationship between students and teacher (p. x).

The personal relationship and genial banter that constitute part of the "bargain" help to explain why students are so concerned about establishing personal relationships with college faculty. We sometimes feel that students want us to serve as surrogate parents, but, more likely, high school seniors' often expressed hope that college faculty will provide "the same sort of individual attention that was received in high school" is rooted in genuine anxiety about their ability to perform according to strict and impersonal academic standards. Rather surprisingly, the one area in which some students expect college and high school to be alike is in this relationship with the instructor. As one student put it, "I expect that college will be similar to high school in that one has the ability to have a close rapport with one's faculty; I expect it to be different in every other way."

High school seniors acknowledge that their standards and motivation—how much they study to prepare for a class, whether they cheat on a test, whether they read an assignment or a text—depend primarily on their relationship with a teacher, the bargain in possibly its most benign form. The brightest of the college-bound high school students, in particular, are likely to enjoy a great deal of personal attention from high school teachers, and the absence of that attention excuses everything from not doing homework to cheating. Teachers who notice them, who pay attention to whether they do their homework, for example, are more likely to elicit hard work and high ethics in classroom behavior. "I'd feel so guilty cheating in chemistry after all Mr. Mac has done for me," one student remarks. But another responds, "Yeah, but Mrs. Brown just doesn't care, so it doesn't matter what you do in her classroom." Most revealing about these comments, both positive and negative, is the total irrelevance of the subject matter. Most astonishing is the interpersonal basis of morality, an ethic based on the amount of attention paid by the teacher. Since high school classes are small by most college standards and allow for personal interaction, one wonders what will motivate those students who find themselves in classes of 200 or more.

In its less benign form, the bargain substitutes for learning altogether. One researcher reports that in a number of classrooms observed, content had entirely disappeared; "in more than a few cases, there did not seem to be any subject matter other than cordial relations" (Cusick, 1983, p.53). The operation of the bargain is also implicit in this student's report of his study habits: "In math, a group of us just go to the teacher and ask for examples. He always gives us examples of the same stuff that will be on the test, so we never have to study for that. In English, just read the notes, and the teacher goes over everything in class. Except for Spanish. I study about half an hour a night for that, but not every night." All too rare is the engaged student, the one who comments, "If I want to learn something, then I get involved in it and do it."

Students in the typical high school classroom expect that any assigned reading will be "gone over" in class, which is to say that the teacher provides a gloss, highlighting important points, meaning those likely to appear on a test. An *A* student recently accepted by a highly selective private university brags that in high school he never read the text and never took notes. "I just listen very, very carefully in class," he claims, "and I can learn everything I need to know." While more than just paying attention is required for success in many high school classes, students often report that they find little need to read texts or to do more than memorize terms, facts, or formulas. In high school, tests are frequent, covering relatively short spans of material, and "learning" is often just another word for memorization. Like much else associated with school, bright students find homework "very easy, very dull, very redundant, just doing the same thing over and over," and comment, "I try to tell myself it's good for me. Other times, I don't bother; I just do it without thinking or don't do it at all."

Frequent testing on brief bits of material with few, if any, cumulative examinations; problem solving that does not progress to greater degrees of difficulty and other homework that is sheer busywork; lack of the need to read relatively difficult material; and glossing by the teacher—these are common practices that ill prepare students for college. High school seniors talk about the need to study more when they get to college, just as virtually all entering freshmen expect to put more effort into academic work in college than they did in high school. Many wish they had selected more difficult high school courses and had experienced more challenges. But despite these sentiments, it is not always clear what students mean when they talk about working harder. On the one hand, most incoming freshmen at one state university expected to study only three or fewer hours a night to earn a solid *B* average; on the other, they are often acutely, even painfully, aware they lack some of the essential skills for academic success, with fewer than 10 percent rating their skills as excellent in note taking, preparing for tests and quizzes, reading comprehension, understanding lectures, or time management (University of Rhode Island, 1988).

Often, of course, the desire to "do better" or "work harder" is insufficient. The ingredients for effective study are simply not there. Doing more becomes rather like trying to make a badly flavored soup taste better simply by cooking it longer. It is perhaps not so surprising therefore that two of every five freshmen (40.5 percent) in 1989 indicated that a "very important" reason for deciding to go to college was "to improve my reading and study skills," up from 22 percent in 1971 (Astin, Korn, and Berz, 1989, p. 54).

If the clock could magically revert to the high school years, many freshmen say they would spend more time on reading. "I wish," one student writes, "I had read textbooks. In high school, I could get good grades—mostly *A*'s—without reading much from the textbook. In college there just isn't the class time available to cover all the material, so you must do plenty of outside work, which includes reading the textbook." For whatever reason, today's freshmen are overwhelmed by the quantity of material they must read. It is also true that many learned to be very successful academically in some high school courses without reading assigned texts. One senior, graduating with high honors, reported her discovery in her first year of high school that reading an assigned book in English class just got in the way of doing well on the tests. She performed much better by reading the Cliff or Monarch notes, since they dealt with those matters tested; reading the actual book often confused her by providing too much information. In making possible these and other strategies for learning, we have indeed been selling students short.

While we cannot hold students accountable for the failures of society or our educational system, we can avoid perpetuating such practices. There are some disturbing signs that the habit of disengagement and the making of implicit bargains have already moved into higher education. Shortly after the publication of the Carnegie Foundation report, *College,* its author Ernest Boyer reported in an interview that in the classroom, "overall, the picture is not bright. . . . Students are eager to get a good grade, but they're not caught up in the excitement of learning. We found on many campuses that a 'bargain' had been struck between teachers and students that goes like this, 'If you don't hassle me, I won't hassle you'" (Marchese, 1986a, p. 15).

At some institutions, particularly community colleges, rising costs and declining availability of financial aid, among other factors, have increased the numbers of the worker-student. The worker-student, who typically began combining the two roles in high school, works longer hours in college than did previous generations of students, frequently off campus and at jobs unrelated to academic work. Students who are more worker than student have an impact on the classroom, where we often accommodate their needs in ways that ultimately ill serve them, as a study by McCartan (1988) documents: "In addition to teaching more classes at night, faculty with working-student populations find themselves assigning less reading between classes. Because working students find it difficult to schedule library time, faculty assign more textbooks instead of original source documents. Many faculty take pains to compile and duplicate 'readers' of essays and articles for their students, knowing they are unlikely to read materials placed on reserve in the library" (p. 16). McCartan notes that perhaps most "disheartening," as one faculty member put it to her, "is the revelation that there is 'astonishingly little reading of assignments beforehand'" (p. 16).

In response, we reconcile ourselves to summarizing what was in the assignment while students busily scribble down notes. We find ourselves relying more on tests and quizzes and less on research papers and fieldwork assignments. On commuter campuses, "faculty are reluctant to assign group projects or form study groups since students have difficulty arranging times when they can get together outside of class" (McCartan, 1988, p. 16). These faculty, in short, have imitated their high school counterparts and entered into an implicit bargain with their students, one that virtually guarantees reduced academic expectations and students' disengagement from learning.

The Rhythm of the Day

The toughest thing for me in college is juggling. I mean having a full class schedule and its exams, problems, homework, and classwork. A long work week with its problems and conflicts. Family conflicts from the home front and long distance. Social life withering into nonexistence, and the loss of some good friends.

—Freshman

Time, high school style, does not at first seem to have changed very much over the years. Class days are still controlled by periods, begun and ended by ringing bells, with brief respites for study hall, phys. ed., and lunch. New freshmen, used to having virtually every minute of their days controlled, feel very anxious when confronted by the relative freedom of college life. As one upper-class orientation leader reports, "They are very much frightened. Suddenly they don't have someone telling them what to take, what to do, where to be. I'll say, 'What do you want to do?' and they'll say, 'I don't know.' The thought of having choices is frightening." Let loose from the imposed controls of high school, students often find their new freedom hard to limit. Time Management, a popular workshop or short course on most campuses, is high on the list of skills freshmen say they need to develop, even freshmen at the most selective institutions.

But if some students come to college used to a rigidly controlled schedule of classes and activities, others have had a very different experience. Bowing to student pressure, many high schools now allow students to depart early from school to go to work. Seniors, particularly, who have often completed many of the required courses for graduation, may spend surprisingly little time in school. The pattern of working while going to school, which has so increased over the last decade, is established in high school. The proportion of employed males aged sixteen to nineteen enrolled in high school increased steadily from one-third in 1960 to nearly one-half by 1977; young women increased their participation in the work force from 22.6 percent in 1960 to 39.1 percent in 1977 (Sedlak, Wheeler, Pullin, and Cusick, 1986, pp. 59, 60).

According to the High School and Beyond project (a U.S. Department of Education longitudinal study of high school seniors in the class of 1980), not only have "the labor market participation rates for adolescents increased over the past generation, but students work a startling number of hours. Three out of four senior males surveyed who worked, for example, were employed at least fifteen hours per week; . . . nearly one-half worked half-time (20 hours or more). Young women worked only slightly fewer hours: 70 percent worked 15 hours or more" (Sedlak, Wheeler, Pullin, and Cusick, 1986, p. 60). More recent data suggest that "76 percent of [high school] seniors are likely to be in the labor force at any given point in the school year" (McCartan, 1988, p. 13).

This trend, which seems to coincide with the growth of the fast-food industry, signals a widening gap between students and their schools and a reduction in time available for any high school activities. Most important from the perspective of higher education, the worker-student has established yet another pattern to interfere with involvement in college and in learning.

The Changing Freshman Class

> In class, I sat down and smiled at the young man sitting next to me. He looked at me and said, "Oh, my God, this is just like going to class with my mother." And I burst out laughing and said, "Yes, and you'd better wear your raincoat, too." And he kind of laughed, and that was the end of it.
>
> —An older freshman

The average faculty member turns fifty in 1991, putting his or her own freshman year experience over thirty years in the past. The cumulative effect of the changes during that time is dramatic. In recalling the differences between the mid 1980s and his own college days thirty years earlier, Aubrey Forrest (1987, pp. 39–40) summarizes some of the factors that altered the course of higher education and changed the nature of the freshman classroom:

- Enrollment in higher education increased 400 percent to the present 12 million students.
- The number of eighteen-year-olds nearly doubled.
- The high school graduation rate increased from 50 to 75 percent.
- The proportion of high school graduates going on to college increased from 25 to 60 percent.
- The proportion of college students older than twenty-five increased from 20 to 40 percent.
- The proportion of women students increased from 34 to 54 percent.
- The proportion of freshmen enrolled in at least one remedial course went from near zero to 35 percent.
- The proportion of freshmen who had enrolled in at least one

college credit course while still in high school went from near
zero to 13 percent.

- The proportion of freshmen who delayed entry into college
from high school grew from a small percentage to 33 percent.
- The proportion of all college students attending college part
time grew from 23 to 42 percent.
- The percentage of freshmen who expected to work at least part
time while in college grew from a small percentage to 40
percent.
- The proportion of bachelor's degree recipients who took more
than four years to complete a degree rose from 30 to 55 percent.
- The proportion of all college students who would be characterized as full-time students, living on campus, and age eighteen
to twenty-two fell from a majority position to 17 percent.

Colleges at different levels and in different areas of the country feel enrollment pressures and the impacts from our changing
population differently, but the direction of the change affects everyone. Increasingly fewer institutions will resemble the homogenous
college of the 1950s; rather most will need to find ways to accommodate to what Harold L. Hodgkinson calls "the changing face of
tomorrow's student" (1985b; also see Hodgkinson, 1983 and 1985a).
The college class of the first decade of the twenty-first century is
already in kindergarten where values, attitudes, learning styles, and
skills are now being shaped. As Hodgkinson and others point out,
that kindergarten class contains more minority and poor children,
more with just one parent, more with teenage mothers, more from
families with limited English ability, more who have never been
read to, more who have not even learned to tie their shoes.

Over the next twenty years, majority students will decline
from 83 percent to 72 percent of all high school students. We will
have, in sum, "fewer suburban, middle class, majority students and
more inner-city, lower-socioeconomic, minority students in the
prime college-age years" (Estrada, 1988, p. 18). The population of
white middle-class children is actually declining now, while the
population of all minority students continues to grow. America's
black population is projected to rise from 26.5 million today to 44
million by the year 2020, while Hispanics will increase from 14.7

million today to around 47 million by 2020, due to higher birth rates and immigration. The trend is clear: "In 1970, minorities accounted for about 13 percent of 18- to 24-year-olds. But by 2000, they are projected to make up more than 30 percent of that age group and nearly 40 percent by 2025" (Fields, 1988, p. 27). One-third of the nation will soon be members of minority groups, and all but Asian Americans have far lower college-going rates than whites.

The "model minority" stereotype attached to Asian Americans, the nation's fastest-growing group of college-goers, ignores the striking diversity within a group that includes recent Vietnamese, Laotian, and Cambodian refugees, Pacific Islanders, Asian Indians, Koreans, and second- or third-generation Filipino, Japanese, or Chinese Americans, among others. It also denies the academic needs of many of these students. We seldom realize that "for 60 percent of all Asian American students, English is a second, often barely learned tongue" (Lou, 1989, p. 16) or that they are often "excluded from or overlooked in educational opportunity programs" designed to serve minority students (Suzuki, 1989, p. 17).

While finding new ways to attract and retain minority students is the major challenge and opportunity for higher education, we also need to adapt to the changes that have occurred in majority students in recent decades. What to an earlier generation seemed peculiar, even revolutionary, became normal for the next: family instability, a new, less protective attitude toward children, and a culture increasingly dominated by television (Winn, 1985, p. 20). Day care is a normal experience even of the middle class. There are now, in Hodgkinson's terms, many more " 'latch-key' children, and children from blended families resulting from divorce and remarriage" (1985b, p. 38). Colleges will continue to enroll more women students than men and increasing numbers of disabled students. An increase in those with learning disabilities is likely, due in part to the increased number of children born prematurely (Hodgkinson, 1985b, p. 39) and to earlier identification of those disabilities.

Most of our colleges and universities will intensify the effort to diversify our campuses by welcoming more students from all these minority groups because both we and the nation need them. On the one hand, the nation's population of young people is getting smaller and the survival of all but the most selective institutions depends on their ability to attract and retain new populations of students. On the other hand, and more important, higher education has traditionally been the most significant means in our society for upward mobility, and so our success in educating all our citizens is a matter of national urgency.

Whether they are majority or minority, all students today have been shaped by societal factors that alter their approaches to learning and pose new problems for the teacher of freshmen. Both the instability of families and the influence of television probably have a negative effect on children's learning, particularly on their ability to read and comprehend substantial quantities of written material (Winn, 1985, p. 18). Given free time, most students prefer watching television to reading. While many children still do grow up within "the protective confines of a stable family, playing, reading, and learning in an orderly, sequential fashion," probably enough of them to continue "to fill the classrooms of our most selective and elite institutions of higher education," new and different kinds of students who come to us less well equipped with basic skills are enrolling in the majority of our colleges and universities (Winn, p. 18).

Even so, quality need not be the price of access; the two are not mutually exclusive. As the report of the National Governors' Association reminded us in 1986, "Access without quality is a cruel deception, while quality without access is betrayal of the cherished American ideal of equal education opportunity and the belief that it is important to educate all children" (quoted in Lenth, Zuniga, and Halcon, 1989, p. 11).

Attitudes, Values, and Goals

In college, I hope to gain the ability to deal better with people different from myself. I also want to become a better student and concentrate more time on my education. I would also like to dye my hair blonde.
—New freshman

The new freshmen are nervous. They say, "Kim, what's your major?" I'm a finance major. "Is finance

good, is that a good major? Are you going to get a
good job with that?"

—Orientation leader

Perhaps more than any other generation of college students,
today's freshmen bring with them varied expectations, goals, values,
and attitudes. In seeking the similarities within a generation of
college students, we must not ignore their many individual differences, differences between the older student fulfilling a lifelong
dream, the minority student seeking to improve equity, the first-
generation college-goer fulfilling more a parent's dream than her
own, the gifted student developing a major talent, and the lacka-
daisical student drifting into college because he cannot find a better
place to be. Campus differences exist as well; students at the most
selective campuses are quite different from those at the local community college. Nevertheless, we can make some general observations about the students entering in the early 1990s.

One goal is virtually universal. Students want preparation
for careers and they want assistance in helping them learn whatever
is needed so they can make it as "successful" adults in what they
persist in calling "the real world." Besides the perceived decline in
basic skills, the area of change of most concern to higher education
is this apparent shift in students' values, a shift documented by the
largest empirical study of college students in the United States, the
Cooperative Institutional Research Program (CIRP) at UCLA.
Sponsored by the American Council on Education, CIRP has collected and published data annually since 1966 on some 1,300 institutions and a total of over seven million students (Astin, Korn, and
Berz, 1989). Their questionnaire includes about forty values items.
Analyses of answers to questions about these items have shown
trends over the past several decades toward increasing materialism,
concern over an uncertain economic future, and a movement away
from traditional liberal arts interests into occupationally related
major fields (Astin, Green, Korn, and Schalit, 1987).

Being very well off financially, for example, was an essential
or very important personal goal for 75 percent of the freshmen
surveyed in 1989, compared with 44 percent in 1967. In 1967 almost
83 percent of freshmen said that developing a meaningful philos-

ophy of life was an important or essential goal compared with only about 41 percent of freshmen today (Astin, Green, Korn, and Schalit, 1987; Astin, Korn, and Berz, 1989). Astin commented in 1987 that "the life philosophy item reached its lowest point in the history of the survey, while student support for 'being very well off financially' reached its highest point" (Astin, Green, Korn and Schalit, 1987, p. 8). In 1988, a record 72.6 percent noted that "making more money" was an important goal of their college attendance while gaining "a general education" was important to just 60.1 percent, compared with a 1977 peak of 71 percent (Astin, Green, Korn, and Maier, 1988); 1989 saw little change.

Whether these students have become pragmatic and materialistic to a fault, as some critics claim, or whether they simply reflect the norms of their culture and are realistically assessing their future is a matter of debate. According to a fairly recent Gallup poll (Gallup 1985, pp. 45–46), the public's belief in the importance of education has grown every year since 1978, but for most it is important primarily because of its value in getting a job (52 percent) or because it leads to a higher income (18 percent). For the general public, then, colleges are worth attending because they lead to greater job opportunities and financial rewards for their graduates. Parents, too, increasingly seek practical benefits from a college education, perhaps because of their own anxieties about economic stability, perhaps because of their desire to see a return on a major financial investment (Krukowski, 1985, p. 25). In 1988 an all-time high of 78.2 percent of the freshmen were dependent on family support for meeting college costs, up 10 percent since 1980—a shift directly attributable to the decline in federal aid.

Are our students intrinsically more materialistic, more success oriented, than students in the past, or are they simply responding to a realistic assessment of their true economic position? The researchers involved with the longitudinal study of youth known as "Monitoring the Future" observed that young people's "hopes and plans still fit rather well into the 'American dream' of marriage, children, and material well-being," but they "have also seen some evidence of increasing concern about attaining that dream. The last few [high school] graduating classes have placed increased empha-

sis on job status, income, and opportunities for advancement"
(Bachman, Johnston, and O'Malley, 1986, p. 232).

Since the earliest days of higher education in this country,
students have expected that a college degree would lead to a job. But
jobs have become more specialized, now requiring not only particular degrees but also particular sets of courses at a particular grade
point average before a student can even gain an interview as a prospective employee. Our success in educating a higher and higher
percentage of our population has led to prospective employers' developing increasingly narrow sorting devices. Chief executive offi-
cers of companies, themselves educated in a different era for a
different job market, speak eloquently of the value of the liberally
educated man or woman, but their recruiters on campus rarely grant
interviews to English or philosophy majors, much less hire them.

This is not a confident generation. Some freshmen are jus-
tifiably anxious about their ability to duplicate the middle-class
lifestyle of their parents; others wonder if they will achieve it. Many
of the questions freshmen raise suggest that insecurity. Implicitly,
they ask, "How can I learn what I will need to know in order to
survive, when I'm uncertain about what survival in adult life
involves?"

While their concerns superficially appear to be overridingly
economic and connected with selecting the "right" major and the
"right" field of study, they have not abandoned the traditional
idealism of the young. Preparing for economic security may be their
most important goal in college, but it is not their only goal. As one
student says, "While at college I would like to learn how to be an
elementary teacher. But at the same time I would like to learn about
being independent and an adult. I'd like to learn if I can change
anything about the world." And freshmen still ask the traditional
big questions: "I want to learn as much as I can. I will take any
useful knowledge about the world and its mysteries—the largeness
of the universe, the smallness of the cell. Is there heaven, hell, or
what?" "What is the meaning of our existence?" "I wonder how to
fulfill my purpose morally." "How can I be happy?" "How can we
make ourselves better people?" "How do we stop nuclear war and
world hunger?" They know the world is a "messed-up" place, that
universal peace remains elusive, that the global environment is

threatened, that values are askew, that we face challenges and threats almost beyond comprehension. They wish to make it better or, at the very least, to understand it better. While, as Arthur Levine suggests (1989a), today's freshmen may not be as pessimistic about our collective fate as the generation of the early 1980s, they are less personally confident. Their image of "the world," that outside themselves and their immediate community of family and friends, is of something not only unknown and rather scary but also hostile and irrational. Some therefore look more inward than out; they are eager to develop themselves, to become more mature.

New freshmen often express as well an unrealistic notion of the scope of what can possibly be learned in four short years. They come with high hopes of finding answers to the questions of their lives: "I would like to learn how to develop myself as a person and prepare myself for a career. I want to find out what I want to do with myself for the rest of my life." "I would like to learn how best to lead the rest of my life so I will be happy and successful." "I want to learn about people; I would like to learn more in order to have stronger knowledge about the world and what it's all about."

As they approach the beginning of their freshman year, students have many goals for college. Like all of us, their goals range from the trivial to the profound: beginning freshmen wish to become more outgoing, more intellectual, more decisive, better able to deal with people different from themselves, more understanding of others, more respectful of different values and beliefs, but firm enough to maintain their own. So while today's freshmen certainly want to develop vocational skills and prepare for a career, they also want to contribute to the larger community and help to resolve the major issues of our time. They are keenly aware as well of what they have yet to learn. "You must ask questions," one sophomore advises a freshman, "because sometimes professors think you know something when actually we know hardly anything at all."

The context from which our freshmen emerge has major implications for instruction, and even though we cannot remedy all aspects of it, we need to understand it. Although we recognize that adult freshmen need a faculty sensitive to the multiple roles of adults, their anxieties, and previous educational experiences, most freshmen continue to be recent high school graduates. Many freshmen are imperfectly prepared for college work both in the content areas and in the development of skills; more of them combine employment with study; their backgrounds and experiences are more diverse; more are disengaged from learning and the institution; and many lack confidence in themselves as learners: these are among the realities of contemporary higher education.

The freshmen year is transitional. It is the year in which old contexts and habits are shed and new ones emerge; so while freshmen need the benefits of an understanding faculty, they need even more a faculty who maintain high expectations for their performance and avoid striking a bargain with them. While we need to be sensitive to the inadequacies and anxieties that accompany many of our freshmen, we must be equally sensitive to their potential to meet our highest standards.

2

The First Year: Coping with Challenges and Changes

As the foundation on which the rest of the college experience is built, John Gardner has argued at annual conferences on the Freshman Year Experience, the entire freshman year should be treated as a deliberately designed period of transition into higher education, a time to support, welcome, and attempt to assimilate the new members of our community. Whether we liken it to culture shock, to a rite of passage, or to basic training, this year marks not only an important transition from secondary to higher education but also determines whether students will complete a baccalaureate degree. In a 1986 speech Theodore Marchese (1986b, p. 15) summarized why the freshman year is pivotal:

> First, new entrants into higher education have high expectations that college will be different, exciting, challenging, and personally rewarding—that it will fulfill the "freshman dream." These, then, are the students who are most open and receptive to the *best* that a college can offer. Second, the year is a time when many critical attitudes are going to be set, especially attitudes towards self in relation to college. Third, it is the year in which critical decisions are often arrived at as to a major, a life-style, an occupation, a living

24

arrangement or indeed, of whether or not to remain in college. Fourth, given existing curricular arrangements, it is the year in which basic skills and orientations will be formed, or not formed, very much determining what will be educationally possible in the succeeding three. And, fifth, given current attendance patterns, the year has increasingly become a major sorting point on the educational ladder: many have access to the year, but far from all will continue beyond it.

Because the freshman year is so crucial to students' entire undergraduate experience, it is important for us to understand how students experience that year outside of class as well as in it. Being more aware of their transitions, of the multiple adjustments students must make in their first year, of the many issues with which they struggle enables us not only to make appropriate connections and to draw on the freshman experience in class but also to understand how important it is to focus students' attention on their academic work. Students need help, in short, in concentrating on the foreground of their academic life against the demanding, noisy background of the rest of campus life.

Being a Freshman

In college you have so many things to do and so little time to do them. You have classes and homework. You have meeting people and hanging out. You have work.

—Freshman

Despite an average age of twenty-six, the vast majority of today's freshmen were born in the 1970s. Events still powerful in many faculty memories—the Vietnam War, Watergate, the landing on the moon—are as remote to freshmen as World War II, Teapot Dome, and the flight of the Wright brothers. While today's campus life appears similar to that of other decades of this century, complete with the revival of interest in dormitory living and in fraternities and sororities, the similarities are illusory. Much has changed.

The recent hand wringing and criticism of campus life imply that there once existed a real-life community of studious young, sitting worshipfully at the feet of their faculty by day and discussing great ideas late into the night, no doubt while sipping tea. While we cannot return to such a golden age, for it never existed, much of what passes for campus life is indeed unfortunate, if not deplorable: the real as well as administrative division between academic affairs and student affairs, the general deterioration of dormitory life and other signs of lessening civility, the increasing abuse of alcohol and ugly incidents associated with that abuse, rising evidence of racism, sexual harassment and acquaintance rape, corrupt athletic programs, and the separation of faculty from virtually every aspect of student life outside the classroom. But freshmen are far less distressed by these problems than are critics of higher education. Like any other college generation, their experience of college is what they know, college as it is today. Unlike faculty, they have no earlier image to recall.

For freshmen, the arrival at college signals both an achievement and a stressful transition. At orientation, one student described a fairly common set of goals this way:

> In college I'd like to break out a little, expand my horizons. I want to change my study habits; meet and make many new friends; mature a little more and become used to the idea of being away from home. I hope I'll also have fun.
>
> —Freshman

Virtually all students come with two objectives: to achieve academically ("to do well in class," "to handle the academics") and to succeed socially ("to make friends," "to have fun," "to meet new people"). At least in theory, all agree about the centrality of "academics," but to them what goes on in class is only part of college. As Moffatt notes in *Coming of Age in New Jersey,* an anthropological study of students at Rutgers, college is "also about independence, freedom, autonomy" (1989, p. 28). Making new friends,

meeting people, living with a roommate, maturing, learning how
to be independent, learning new ways to relate to the family at
home, even coping with such matters as doing laundry or balancing
a checkbook—almost everything for the freshman is new, a first.
College is—and was—about coming of age, the place, Moffatt notes,
"where you went to break away from home, to learn responsibility
and maturity, and to do some growing up. College was about being
on your own, about autonomy, about freedom from the authority
of adults, however benign their intentions. And last but hardly least,
college was about fun, about unique forms of peer-group fun—
before, in student conceptions, the grayer actualities of adult life in
the real world began to close in on you" (pp. 28–29).

Except at very small institutions, the organization of the contemporary college makes it almost certain that students and faculty
live in ignorance of one another's lives and that the two seldom see
the same institution. What is true of Moffatt's students at Rutgers
is true elsewhere. Just as freshmen rarely understand that faculty
have responsibilities beyond teaching, so even universities that conduct research on virtually every subject seldom know much about
their students beyond broad, general demographic data. Those who
examine the lives of freshmen with care or attempt to follow their
academic schedule, like faculty in a special program at Rollins College who take courses as "master learners" (more about this program later in this chapter), find student life unexpectedly stressful
and difficult and admire students' ability to thrive in an environment so often inhospitable as the college campus.

Starting Out

> Looking around, they all seem to think that everyone
> but them has it on the ball. There's an incredible com-
> parison going on, and everyone else is better at every-
> thing than you are.
>
> —Orientation leader

Once in his life as a participant observer in the Rutgers
dorms, Moffatt passed as a "cryptofreshman," experiencing some of

the "impersonality and hassle" typically dealt to brand-new freshmen. He describes the experience:

> I took an English test and a math test. A graduate student administering one test told us to watch out; he knew we were all "programmed to cheat," he said. The room for the other test was, like the gym two nights before, over a hundred degrees in the late-summer heat. I theorized to myself that the long lines and other procedural ordeals of orientation at Rutgers were the modern functional equivalents of the older, suppressed practices of student hazing, an inadvertent way in which the bureaucracy, rather than the upperclassmen, now bonded us together in mild solidarity as common fellow sufferers.
>
> I attended student-life orientation and listened to local samples of American psychobabble: "Ask yourself, 'Who am I?' 'Where am I going?' 'What are my relationships like?'" I went to talks on professional and peer counseling, on student health, and on financial aid. And I sat through academic orientation, where the dean of the college told us we were a "select group" (a small exaggeration), an assistant dean of instruction reviewed the complex details of course scheduling and rescheduling, and the dean of instruction delivered what were to be the only official remarks I heard during all of freshman orientation in 1977 on the meaning of college as a place of learning [1989, p. 12].

Despite the best intentions of orientation leaders, typically upperclassmen, to depict the institution as a warm and welcoming place, this first experience of college heightens the anxiety of many freshmen. They have been tested and placed and may have been found wanting. This incident reported by an orientation leader is not rare: "I had two or three girls who came out of placement exams almost in tears saying, 'I'm never going to make it in college. I can't even do this stupid entrance exam.'"

Such freshmen suffer from "background shock" and an assault on their sense of who they are, what they know, and whether coming to this college or to college at all was the right decision. They have probably been told that only 50 percent of them will graduate—maybe fewer. Confronted with the price of textbooks, many worry whether they will have enough money. They have been warned about AIDS and wonder how they will fulfill their fantasies of a sexual college life. If they live on campus, they are worried about their roommates, whether they will get along, whether they will help to smooth the way to new friendships or prove a hurdle. If they commute, they are worried that they are not living on campus. If they are black, Hispanic, Asian, Native American, handicapped, older than the norm, or otherwise in any way different from the majority, they are probably more conscious of that difference than at any other time in their lives. If the institution is of any size—and most freshmen do attend large colleges and universities—their ID number has replaced their names as their identity, heightening their developing sense of alienation in a strange and bureaucratic environment.

Quite possibly, they have just found out that they must complete a general education program before they can take courses in the major in which they have the greatest interest or that the one class they were particularly eager to take is already filled. Already, before they have attended their first class, they may suspect that college will not quite match up to their expectations. It is not always the most auspicious of beginnings.

Expectation and Reality

In my mind, the university was a hotbed of intellectual activity. I was in search of the stuff of the mind, in search of the intellectual and the frontiers of human thought. After all, I thought, the university was the place where people were in the honest, innocent pursuit of knowledge. I found boring, unstimulating classes, professors and T.A.'s who put me to sleep and didn't give me the attention I needed. They didn't play

the muse. They didn't seem to care about students
at all.
—Student quoted in Schoem and Knox, 1988, p. 55

This student realized that his expectations were unrealistic,
that he was looking for a "passive education, wanting to be enter-
tained and catered to, desperately needing the attention and recognition [he] had received almost daily in high school." At the major
university he attended, he was not spoon-fed anything, but had to
seek, actively, the education he wanted. "No one asked *me* questions. If I didn't say anything the whole semester, *they* didn't care!
I felt light-years away from my professors and T.A.'s" (Schoem and
Knox, p. 55). Faculty often comment on students' passivity and, at
times, their expectations that we will actively rescue them from
whatever academic morass they have managed to slip into. This
expectation of a continued dependent style of learning is a by-
product of the hidden bargain described earlier. Freshmen at all
levels of ability need help in developing expectations that are at
once high, appropriate, and realistic.

The greater the discrepancy between what freshmen expect to
happen as a result of going to college and the reality of what occurs,
the more stress they experience. Some degree of "freshman remorse"
is common, but some students find so much they withdraw. Students on very small campuses may feel stifled; students on large
ones, ignored. A study at one university found, ironically, that students who had the highest expectations—for example, making a lot
of close friends, finding many people to date, and enjoying exciting
and challenging classes—were more likely to leave the institution
than those whose expectations were lower and more realistic (Ruddock and Wilkinson, 1983, p. 13). Researchers at another university
found that while 86 percent of their freshmen believed at orientation
that they would have the same academic record in college as they
did in high school, only 43 percent retained that belief just two
months later (Lemoine, 1988).

Faculty who teach freshmen orientation courses are often
struck by how rarely students talk about their academic work. More
than twenty years ago Joseph Katz (1968) noted that "it is the sphere
of their private lives, rather than academic pursuits or public con-

cerns, that receives the lion's share of the students' attention" (p. 15), and students today still measure their freshman year to a great extent by their success in meeting their expectation for a rich social life. At the end of the year, freshmen at the University of Montana reported that their most rewarding experiences were, in order, meeting new people and making new friends; learning "new things about myself, various disciplines, and the world"; being on "my own and responsible for myself, changing my lifestyle"; and having the chance to become involved in new activities (Corak, 1984).

Adapting to Change

I would not like to change for the most part, but I feel
that to go to an entirely new place and start all over,
it is almost impossible not to change at least a little
in all areas.
— Freshman

The great challenge of the freshman year is learning to manage change, to adapt. While a student may say, "I want to break out a little and expand my horizons," adapting to something new virtually every day can be extremely stressful. In the space of a week, for instance, a new freshman may have to share a room for the first time in her life with one or two total strangers, write his first check, find her way around on an unfamiliar campus in an unfamiliar town, select his courses and prepare a schedule, learn a whole new set of policies, procedures, and rules, and decide whether to drink at the fraternity beer blast.

Undergraduates assume that college should neatly balance work and play, "academics and college life" (Moffatt, 1989, pp. 286, 287). To succeed academically, many anticipate they will have to study harder, change study habits, take school more seriously. They accept that grades are critical, that they are the way faculty, friends, parents, and prospective employers measure, appropriately, academic success, that they are the dividend for hard work and tuition. Despite their noble intentions to study hard, however, many freshmen barely know how to begin. As Moffatt observed (1989, p. 288), "Non-honors students had to learn how to *really* study for their big

classes. The crunch often came after first midterms. *C*'s and *D*'s??!!
So, sitting around in the lounge with a book open was not really
studying. Reading something through quickly did not make it
stick. Listening to lectures without taking good notes was not
enough. Most freshmen made adjustments. Sometimes friends
helped, but more often the novices figured out new study routines
for themselves."

The three distinct styles of studying that Moffatt observed
seem fairly universal. What he calls the grind studies steadily and
hard throughout the semester, and perhaps approaches the ideal of
"two hours out of class for every hour in class" often recommended
at freshman orientation. The blow-it-off, who usually manages to
slide through, loafs all semester, compensating with intense cramming and sometimes with all-nighters around exams. Like the
blow-it-offs, the middle of the roaders alternate between lives of
leisure and hard work, but fluctuate less dramatically. They may
study one to three hours a day three to four days a week, then work
harder as exams approach (Moffatt, 1989, pp. 293–295). Fewer freshmen would embrace the strategies of the blow-it-offs or even the
middle of the roaders, however, were their instructors to test frequently or to provide other types of frequent feedback.

Besides learning a new approach to study, selecting or con-
firming the choice of a major is the major academic task of the
freshman year. Despite their career orientation, many new students
have very little knowledge about the field they have selected as a
major. When Louisiana State University asked new students to indicate how much they knew about their intended major, only 8
percent felt they knew "a great deal" (Lemoine, 1988). Two months
later that percentage had increased to 14 percent, still very low. The
Louisiana State University study confirms what many in higher
education already know anecdotally: majors are often selected with
virtually no knowledge of the field and for the flimsiest of reasons.
When able to do so, as they often are at liberal arts colleges, many
freshmen elect to enter as "undecided majors." The increase in the
number of students who enter college without having selected a
major and in those who change their minds (or are forced to do so
by closed programs) may reflect increased anxiety about the need to
make a *correct* choice. Sometimes students' changes in major are a

kind of trading down, a move from something more difficult to something easier, a move, say, from engineering to business (Moffatt, 1989, p. 287).

Freshmen also need to adapt to new ways of teaching and different classroom norms. At most universities and even at smaller colleges the separation between faculty and students has increased steadily throughout this century. Even at small institutions, classrooms can be impersonal, as these comments indicate: "At my old school, all my classes were discussion oriented, not lectures." "In high school teachers take their time and explain it. Here they just lecture. You teach yourself more in college." "There are different rules from high school. You can come in late, cut class." Large classes are often anonymous, which is comforting to some freshmen: "There are 125 students in that class, so no one notices whether you're there or not." Another says, "I love large classes; I'm anonymous; I can hide."

Some freshmen quickly find their own motivation to become involved in classes: "You pay more attention in college because you're paying for it," comments one student, and another, "I'm interested in the class because I selected what I wanted to take." While some are eager to take charge of their own education, others find it difficult to shift responsibility for learning from the school or the teacher to themselves. Others want to study and learn, but not what is offered in the freshman year. Impatient to specialize, they do not find the liberal arts core or a general education program relevant and view those courses as another irrationally imposed set of requirements, something supposedly good for you like liver or brussels sprouts, but not very tasty and certainly no substitute for the main course.

From a freshman's perspective, the first year runs at two speeds. Whatever difficulties it may present, the academic life is predictable, dull, often boring. But the social life runs fast, unpredictably, often out of control. It seems harder to manage, at least initially. Making new friends is a challenge to many students because, as one freshman observes, "You've been with the same people since kindergarten and then you're not. So how do you make friends? I don't remember. Everything in high school is so comfortable." While students today may be a lot "tougher and less innocent than previous generations" (Gibbs, 1988, p. 62), college life often presents new and difficult choices. Alcohol and, to a lesser extent, other drugs remain "an omnipresent lure made more enticing than ever as stress levels soar" (Gibbs, 1988, p. 62). One freshman states her dilemma: "I didn't hang out with people who drank in high school. College is a different story. It's almost impossible to find people who don't drink." "Having fun" or "partying" usually means drinking and often little else, with the drinking frequently to disturbing excess, making Saturday nights in the dorms "pretty gross" and sometimes scary. Deciding how and whether to retain high school boyfriends and girlfriends and negotiating the constantly changing rules of the mating game under the shadow of AIDS make the "fun side" of college rather less lighthearted than it once appeared to be.

While older adolescents may seem more adult and worldly wise than those of a decade or two ago, they are not immune to homesickness. Leaving home may be particularly painful for the growing number of freshmen whose families are torn by separation or divorce and whose departure for college may mark the end of arrangements for home ownership, joint custody, or residence in the same town for both parents. Anecdotal evidence suggests that "freshman-year divorce" of parents is also an increasingly common phenomenon, with freshmen often cast in the role of confidant and even caretaker of one or both parents, a role they are ill equipped to handle. Virtually all young students find that Thanksgiving and Christmas vacations mean negotiating new rules, new relationships at home. Older students, particularly women, may confront a different set of obstacles at home. "Of all the older students I've met," one woman notes, "I probably have the best situation. I have support at home to do this. My family isn't dangling financially waiting for me to finish. . . . I've met women who are struggling to survive through this period because they must do it in order to get a job. And I've met a lot whose husbands are dead set against it and make it very difficult and feel very threatened."

Time and Its Management

The major difference [between high school and college] is time. You have so much free time on your

hands that you don't know what to do for most of the
time.

—Freshman

Managing time is a concern of virtually all freshmen. Familiar with the high school practice of frequent, specific deadlines for
assignments, many college students struggle with developing their
own pace for reading texts and writing papers, with structuring
their own time in class and out. In the middle of October one
freshman reported that she had mislaid her course syllabi so she had
no idea what assignments were due; she assumed that her professors
would remind her at the appropriate time. Another wrote, "It's hard
to budget my time to be social and do work because nobody is
making me do my work." But for many freshmen the concern for
managing time stems not from lack of responsibility or inability to
plan appropriately but rather from structuring the right balance of
activities. While some do not know how to occupy long hours of
unstructured time, others race through their days frantically, overwhelmed by their responsibilities.

The pattern frequently established in high school of working
while going to school continues in college, and most evidence suggests that a part-time job, particularly one on campus, has a beneficial effect on academic performance. A recent study conducted for
the Washington Higher Education Coordinating Board, for example, suggests that students who work fifteen to twenty hours per
week tend to perform *better* academically than students who work
less than ten hours, more than twenty hours, or who do not work
at all. Several studies conclude that students who work have a
higher course completion rate than nonworkers (McCartan, 1988,
p. 16). One interesting finding from a study of five universities is
that students who work watch less television: 51 percent of those not
working disclosed watching at least three hours a day versus only
34 percent of those who worked (McCartan, 1988, p. 16).

Despite such optimistic findings, however, many fear that
the rising cost of higher education forces increasing numbers of
students to work longer and longer hours, that "studenthood" as a
period of life is rapidly disappearing. Along the continuum of student to worker, some faculty find the balance shifting so that class-

rooms are increasingly filled with those who are more worker than
student (Whipple, 1988, p.14). A 1990 study reports "a real increase
in student employment" of traditional college-aged students over
the last two decades, with 62 percent of students of all ages now
working (Hexter, 1990, p. 5). While employment for twenty hours
a week is the average for full-time students, almost 20 percent work
thirty hours or more, and 10 percent work thirty-five hours or more.

Rarely do students' lives on the job and in the classroom
connect. The 1988 report *A New Vitality in General Education*
observes that while "much student time is taken up by paid jobs,
. . . explorations of student work experience have rarely been the
focus of classroom activities" (Association of American Colleges,
1988; p. 32). The increasing numbers of student-workers may encourage the building of bridges between the work setting and instruction (McCartan, 1988, p. 20), giving students needed practice
in integrating what they learn and applying it to real-life situations.
Such connections will be easier to make with adult students or
seniors who have technical, managerial, or professional employment, however, than with traditional college-age freshmen who
find employment in service jobs, in food service, sales, and clerical
positions (Hexter, 1990, p. 5).

The stress and pressure caused by lack of time that many
students report may also be due to the pace of the academic year
itself. Serving as a "master-learner" in a Community of Learners
Program at Rollins College, Professor Roy Starling spent a semester
as a student. He discovered that it was not a good trade, concluding,
"We rush students, feverishly, through the art gallery of education.
At the beginning of the term, we fire the starting gun, telling them
that in fourteen weeks [at Rollins] they will have had rewarding
learning experiences in four, sometimes five, classes" (1987, p. 3).

One of the first lessons Starling learned (and, he reports, kept
learning and relearning throughout the term as a master-learner) is
that "the students aren't really 'ours'; they are merely working us
into a cluttered, hectic academic and social schedule. The experience of the first week of classes demonstrated clearly the false echo
that students sound throughout their academic careers: the professor's 'You will learn' answered by the student's 'I will survive'"
(p. 4). Each course is presented as the most important. Starling

recalls, "In the first week as a student, I went to my first class, was told the requirements for that course, and was warned that it wouldn't be easy. In the second class, we did some group work . . . and went over the course requirements. We had to walk through rain to get to the third class and found the room's air-conditioner set at somewhere near the igloo level. Wet, cold, tired, and with enough (we thought) to do already, we listened to another set of requirements: daily assignments, short papers, a long paper, seven novels, and a good share of reading on reserve at the library" (p. 4). Like previous master-learners at Rollins, Starling found that "there were times when the workload was so heavy that it was impossible to complete in the time allotted, much less complete it with energy and imagination" (p. 4).

How we spend our time signals, of course, our priorities, so how freshmen spend their time can be a good measure of their involvement academically and in campus life. It is therefore useful to a campus (or a faculty member) to determine what students do with their time. One way is to follow Moffatt's lead and ask students to fill out simple time reports. In the middle of the semester he gives students this assignment: "Please tell me, as precisely as possible, what things you have done, and how long each has taken, since this time twenty-four hours ago." On those reports, 60 to 70 percent of the students indicated they studied about two hours a day. Another 10 to 15 percent, typically those in the most difficult majors, studied more—up to six or seven hours a day—and the rest, about a quarter, "hardly studied at all on a day-to-day basis, but relied on frenetic cramming before exams" (1989, p. 32).

Fitting In

It's easy to veg out in your room. I know you can't expect people and activities to come to you, but it's hard to be independent and assertive. I want to be involved in the school, but I don't know how.
—Freshman

How freshmen elect to spend their time suggests the kind and extent of involvement they have with the college, how well they are fitting in. While more than 80 percent of college-bound seniors still graduate from public high schools enrolling fewer than 500 students (The College Board, 1988), since 1950 most colleges and universities have grown steadily larger, with the average enrollment of all institutions expanding by 25 percent in the fifteen years between 1970 and 1984 (National Institute of Education, 1984, p. 11). As colleges have grown and become more bureaucratic and complex, freshmen accustomed to a smaller scale find it more difficult to locate a niche, to feel they fit in. Although some schools have instituted strong systems of support for freshmen, on most campuses freshmen are expected to assimilate themselves to the ongoing system as quickly as possible. Nothing much has changed since the Hazen Report of 1968. Then as now colleges can be criticized for doing little, if anything, to maintain the curiosity of freshmen, to stimulate their interest, to expose them to intellectual experiences, or to involve them in college activities (Hazen Foundation, 1968, p. 31).

Although freshmen clearly understand the need to find their place academically as well as socially, the first priority of most is to make new friends with whom to "hang out." Most do so surprisingly quickly and engaging in "friendly fun," as Moffatt (1989) calls it, occupies much of their time outside class. Most colleges report a distinct decline in participation in more formalized extracurricular activities. On our campus, for instance, only 8 percent of the freshmen reported some degree of participation in student clubs or student government in an informal survey taken in 1989. Although freshmen often mention the need to take part in extracurricular activities with great earnestness, as if it were a faintly pleasant duty, their preference during nonworking hours is clearly for more private and casual fun with their peers—parties, pickup games or intramural sports, rock concerts.

Finding a circle of friends and becoming accepted can be particularly difficult for students who do not quite match the campus norm; disabled, minority, international, gay, and older freshmen may all feel particularly alienated and isolated. For minority students and many international students, the painful disparity between their college life and home life may increase their sense of isolation. Trying to live in two worlds can be exceedingly difficult.

As Marcus Mabry, a black student from New York attending Stanford, writes, "The ache of knowing [my family's] suffering is always there. It has to be kept deep down, or I can't find the logic in studying and partying while people, my people, are being killed by poverty. Ironically, success drives me away from those I most want to help by getting an education" (1988, p. 52).

For minority students, particularly those from disadvantaged backgrounds, the connection to college is often tenuous. They are less likely than majority students to have successful graduates in their immediate or extended families, less likely to have heard that they were expected to be successful in college from others (or to have had strong, long-term expectations for themselves), have fewer previous on-campus experiences, and have fewer peers to help them in exploring and adjusting to their new environment or in fitting in (Attinasi, 1989).

Although Moffatt reports that during his association with the dorm at Rutgers, blacks and Puerto Ricans "lived reasonably amiably among their white peers all year long," he also notes that the minority students did all the adjusting. "They were swamped," he comments, "by the white majority on an 'integrated' floor," and they "lived on the floor in terms of the white majority. None of them were 'threatening.' None of them made much of her or his black or Puerto Rican identity" (1989, p. 141). Another study reports that "the social environments of the large, predominantly white, public universities . . . were problematic even for well-prepared minority students" (Skinner and Richardson, 1988, p. 39). Minority freshmen may find social support only off campus. Institutions that expect all adjustment to be on the side of freshmen "limit the range of minority students they can serve responsibly to those who . . . resemble traditional college-goers" (p. 42).

Along with this ever-present assumption that minority students can and will conform to the majority, the past several years have seen a disturbing resurgence of racially and ethnically motivated violence and conflict on a number of campuses, demanding that colleges pay serious attention to the climate for minority groups (Green, 1989). While middle-class white students usually know they ought to appreciate diversity, they are in fact often frightened by it, a fear especially apparent as it relates to homosexuality, since being openly homophobic is more socially acceptable to peers than is fear of blacks, Hispanics, or Asians.

Typically, therefore, minority freshmen experience an unusual degree of stress as they attempt to fit in, to accommodate, the gay student concealing his or her homosexuality, the black student acting white. In the classroom, faculty create the climate. We know, for instance, not only that overt faculty prejudice "can result in inappropriate racial or ethnic remarks in class or in lowering the performance of alienated or discouraged minority students," but also that "unconscious assumptions that minority students are unable to perform up to par may become self-fulfilling prophecies" (Green, 1989, p. 115). Subtle behaviors or different treatment—like calling on students more or less frequently, not asking students the same kinds of questions, not paying the same attention—can create what Hall and Sandler first identified as a "chilly classroom climate" for members of minority groups and women (Green, pp. 114–116; Hall and Sandler, 1982, 1984).

Older students, too, need sensitive understanding. As one observes, "Faculty could be more tuned in to the fact that it's not that easy; you're balancing a lot of responsibilities. With age some people find it particularly difficult to admit they need help. Faculty could ask if they need help. And not make up impossible rules. I had one professor who said from the beginning that there would be absolutely no excuses for missing an exam. If you miss an exam, you get a zero. I hardly ever miss class. But my initial reaction was, what if something happens at home?"

The classroom may be key not only to the successful academic assimilation of freshmen, but, interestingly, to their personal growth as well. One somewhat surprising finding of a study designed to determine the benefits of college attendance was that "academic integration" had both direct and indirect effects on freshman-year reports of personal growth (Terenzini and Wright, 1987, p. 266). Finding a niche academically, fitting into and succeeding in classes, may have more influence on personal growth, this study suggests, than does fitting in socially (p. 268). The authors conclude, "Students' integration into the academic systems of an institution may be as important to their personal growth as to their academic and intellectual development. These findings suggest a potential need to rethink campus and departmental orientation programs, many of which focus on introducing students to social, rather than academic, aspects of the collegiate experience. The results also have important implications for faculty members who foster academic integration as they advise students. . . . Finally, the results suggest a coherence and integrity in the developmental process: experiences that we think promote students' academic or intellectual development also appear to influence students' personal growth" (p. 270).

Staying In

> I think adults are aware of the fact that things go wrong but kids don't believe it. During my freshman year I was ready to drop out and somebody said why don't you go see someone in counseling. I thought that if I can't handle my own problems, I shouldn't be here in the first place.
>
> —Sophomore

The dropout rate in American higher education has not changed much in the last hundred years. Over the past twenty years, the rate of graduation nationally has been roughly 40 percent in four years, not quite 50 percent in five years. Not surprisingly, rates of degree completion are highest at the most selective institutions (about 95 percent at Harvard or Notre Dame) and lowest at community colleges (under 20 percent at some inner-city schools), but even at the state universities, which educate the majority of our nation's college students, attrition is often 50 percent or more. Low rates of degree completion for virtually all minority groups except Asians are of particular concern. Voluntary withdrawal is four times as frequent as forced dismissal, and departure in the first year accounts for almost 50 percent of all attrition (Tinto, 1988a).

The old sorting strategy of "educate the best, shoot down the rest" no longer seems reasonable in light of what we know about student development and the national need for educating an increasingly heterogeneous society, but the current and burgeoning interest in the phenomenon of dropping out more likely grew out of self-interest than social need. As institutions confronted the shortage of eighteen-year-olds during the last decade, a new concern for retention and "enrollment management" surfaced. Retention research yields the expected generalization that institutional environments, student satisfaction, and dropout rates are linked, though the causes for departure from college are complex, even for a single student.

Although we have long known that the dropout rate is highest for freshmen, until recently few researchers have attempted to determine whether the reasons freshmen withdraw are any different from those of students at other points in college. It now appears that they are. According to Vincent Tinto, who has studied attrition extensively, the "forces that shape departure during the first year of college, especially during the first six weeks of the first semester, are qualitatively different from those that mold departure in the later years of college" (1989b, p. 443).

Drawing upon Van Gennep's anthropological theories, which concern the rites of passage to adulthood and becoming a member of the adult community, Tinto suggests a similar process for freshmen. To join the college community, they must successfully negotiate three major stages: separation, transition, and incorporation. Virtually all students must to some extent separate from their past, from membership in the communities of home and high school, experiencing "some form of parting from past habits and patterns of affiliation" (p. 443). This often disorienting process creates stress, stress so severe for some students that they cannot remain in college.

Different groups of students may experience the passage through the three stages differently. Commuting students who have less need to separate from their past may find moving into college initially less stressful and persisting easier, but because they are less likely to be incorporated into the college community, they are more inclined to drop out later. Whatever the specific cause, difficulty in adjusting to the academic or social life of the college—either in its formal or informal aspects—can lead to withdrawal (Tinto, 1988b, p. 448). Some degree of success at fitting in in both areas is necessary for full acclimation to college life and persistence to graduation, but academic integration is central.

The centrality of academic success for the freshman is highlighted by other studies on student attrition. These studies emphasize that the academic variable with the strongest influence on students' decisions to withdraw or remain is their academic performance in the very first semester, performance as reflected in first-semester grades (Guskey, 1988, pp. 69–70). That is not surprising, given the persistent pragmatic notion among undergraduates that grades come first. When they get good grades during their first semester, freshmen feel that they are making it, they fit in, they have adjusted to college life. Students who do poorly in the first semester, however much they may rationalize their academic performance to others, are aware that for some reason they have not met the institutional norm. It is likely, as Guskey notes, that "the vast majority of these students will see themselves as less talented, less skilled, and less academically able than their classmates . . . and [will conclude] that their decision to enroll was, probably, an error in judgment. Hence, they feel isolated, apart, and are likely to withdraw" (p. 70).

Other researchers have observed how vital early academic success is to women and to members of minority groups. In their study of minority students at predominantly white institutions, Skinner and Richardson report that "when their academic performance fell below their high school average, they were 'devastated,' 'depressed,' and 'obsessed' with a fear of failing their families and their communities. Terribly embarrassed because they had never needed help before, they were reluctant to seek academic support" (1988, p. 40). Without strong campus support systems in place from the beginning of the freshman year (or before), many minority students have little reason to remain when college life proves an ordeal or even when they receive one failing grade. Making the grade is confirmation of one's membership in the college community, affirming that one is indeed a college student by right, not by accident. All too soon, some freshmen feel they do not belong.

Climates for Learning

The atmosphere is exhilarating and I find the school
an exciting place to be. It has reawoken my personal

interest in studying and school which I lost in high
school.

                    —Freshman, quoted in Holdaway
                        and Kelloway, 1987, p. 55

Creating optimal conditions for learning in the freshman
classroom is the subject of the second part of this book. But as
members of the college community, we encourage faculty to keep
a weather eye as well on the climate of the rest of the campus. The
sum total of the daily environment affecting students, faculty, and
staff, the campus climate embraces everything from the college's
emphasis on students—or on research—to the condition of the dormitories and ease of parking, from the availability and skill of advisers to the smile given (or not) by a secretary in the bursar's office.
And it all has an impact on freshmen, on the extent to which they
are aided and supported in making the difficult transition from
home to campus, from school to college. Campus life, like the classroom, has a profound influence on student development and student learning and requires no less than the high expectations we
hold and standards of excellence we maintain in the classroom.

Throughout the 1980s critics of higher education drew increased attention to the significance of the freshman year. In its 1984
report *Involvement in Learning: Realizing the Potential of American Higher Education,* the Study Group on the Conditions of Excellence in American Higher Education called for "front loading"
of services in the freshman year to "improve student retention rates
by utilizing the key levers of student involvement" (National Institute of Education, 1984, p. 25). By assigning greater resources to
serving first-year students, the authors argued, institutions could
follow other recommended steps, including the support of first-year
classes that provide opportunities for intense intellectual interaction between students and instructors, large classes taught only by
the finest instructors, and an advising system that maintains regular
contact with students and provides access to a stable body of well-
trained advisers including faculty, administrators, and peers (1984,
p. 25). Researchers observe that the freshman year—particularly the
first six weeks—is the critical determinant of ultimate graduation
(Noel, Levitz, Saluri, and Associates, 1985).

If we understand students' critical need to find a niche socially and to experience early academic success and if we are aware of the difficulty the college environment can pose for freshmen, especially women, minority, and adult students, we are better able to become sensitive to student needs and concerned for the conditions necessary for their academic success. Faculty who understand what freshmen are going through are, in short, in the best position to put those events in a larger context and to help students focus on the academic aspects of their freshman experience.

3

Learning Styles and Intellectual Development

The gap that separates students from their faculty in the freshman class is not simply a product of the social and cultural forces described in the first two chapters. Many freshmen learn in ways different from their faculty, and they differ from one another. Even though we all realize on some level that people learn in different ways, most of us follow the intuitive inclination to teach our students just as we were taught and to teach them as if they all learned in exactly the same way. When we confront their differences in concrete terms—on course evaluations, for example—we are surprised. The following comments written by freshmen enrolled in the same course reveal how dramatic the differences are.

> I find the course very interesting. [The instructor] insists on group discussions, which I find to be an outstanding method of learning. He also provides demonstrations in many of his lectures, which makes the concepts we are studying easier to visualize. I've learned a lot and I can honestly say it's the best course I've ever had.

> I felt that I didn't learn half as much as I should have. Going to class was a waste of time. . . . For the first time in my life I became *very* apathetic toward a course in school.

The group discussions are a very good idea. They gave me a chance to work out problems with people who are on my level. This is more effective than watching someone do it on the blackboard.

Too much group work wasted class time. More of the problems should have been explained by the instructor.

What sense are we to make of such conflicting views? How are we to respond to student evaluations and recommendations when a practice that one student considers "outstanding" another deems a "waste of time"? Research on student development and learning styles sheds light on the first question, enabling us to recognize reasons for students' assessments and reactions. To that end, this chapter summarizes the findings from this research that are most pertinent to freshmen. The chapters on teaching in Part Two recognize the developmental and stylistic differences among freshmen, and many of our suggestions reflect a concern for responding to students' needs in ways that are inclusive rather than exclusive, supportive rather than frustrating.

Student Development

Among the many changes students undergo during the college years, one of the most significant is the change in their perceptions of learning. William Perry (1970, 1981), among the first to study the intellectual development of college students, found that students' assumptions and expectations about teaching and learning change while they are in college and that the changes follow a predictable pattern. Although he distinguished nine "positions" in the developmental sequence, they are usually categorized in four groups: dualism, multiplicity, relativism, and commitment in relativism.

A full discussion of the now extensive research on student development is beyond the scope of this book. Kurfiss (1988) provides a good overview of the developmental path, one that integrates Belenky, Clinchy, Goldberger, and Tarule's studies of women

(1986). Here we trace student development in broad outlines, giving closer scrutiny to those positions in which we find most freshmen and passing more swiftly through the later positions, those that freshmen have not yet reached. Like Kurfiss, we combine Perry's terminology with that proposed by Belenky and her colleagues.

Dualism/Received Knowledge. Students in these positions view knowledge as truth—as factual information, correct theories, right answers. They view professors as authorities who know these truths, and believe that teaching constitutes explaining them to students. Learning means taking notes on what the authorities say, committing them to memory, and feeding them back as answers on tests. Although Belenky and her coauthors heard differences in the ways women in these positions respond to instruction—they tend less than men to imagine they might become authorities and are more inclined to listen than to reveal what they know, even if they have an authoritative source—they nonetheless found the same belief in right answers and faith that authorities know them (Belenky, Clinchy, Goldberger, and Tarule, 1986, pp. 43–45).

Students in these positions expect to receive important information and right answers, and they become anxious or impatient if they sense they are missing either. A freshman chemistry student, for example, criticized the instructor for "leaving things out when he covers a chapter. . . . I think the instructor should go over topics a little more carefully . . . writing concepts and theories on the blackboard so we can copy down the concepts. There are not enough notes." A freshman in English suggested: "I think more time should be spent on each story so that I can get a clearer picture about what is the most important aspect in the story." Students in positions of dualism and received knowledge are uncomfortable if we skip sections of the text, which is, of course, another authoritative source. They can handle abstractions and discussions, but in the end they want "a clear picture" of the "most important aspect of a story" and "enough notes."

Assignments that ask students to think independently, to state their own opinions, or to draw their own conclusions are a second source of uneasiness. Students assume that right answers exist and that authorities know them, and they wonder why we do not reveal them. They may conclude it is because we do not do our jobs very well. A student in a philosophy course commented that the course was confusing "because you're answering questions with questions and you never get a complete picture." In an English course, a freshman expressed a widely shared feeling: "I'm not really sure how my essay answers can be improved to give her what she wants."

Students' comments reveal that our challenges to them to *think* are interpreted very differently than we intend. To them, thinking appears to be an academic game in which we "answer questions with questions" or ask them to guess "the meaning of a poem." Whatever thinking is, it is not learning, and they tolerate the diversion only so long. The sentiment was expressed most clearly by a freshman in chemistry: "The teacher is good in his field. He encourages us to think. But he doesn't define things. Thinking is fine, but learning is what I'm here for."

Class activities or assignments that ask students to learn from their peers are a third source of recurring criticism. Instructors know the right answers; students do not; therefore, little, if anything, can be learned from other students. Class discussions are "a waste of time" that would be better spent listening to the instructor explain things. Asking students to critique one another's papers sometimes provokes similar responses. One student complains: "I think [the instructor] should grade our assignments. I don't think students know what he wants, at least I didn't."

Because dualists depend on authorities as sources of knowledge, few things are more unsettling to them than uncertainty or disagreement among authorities. One freshman, commenting on a team-taught course, describes the mixed feelings that disagreement among professors often elicits:

> I'd never seen two professors disagree with each other. Both of these guys seemed really smart, but they disagreed all the time. I mean, I don't think they were playing devil's advocate. They *really* disagreed. It was interesting to see how they looked at things. But at times that really drove you crazy! You couldn't figure out what you were supposed to assume. . . . Lots of

times I never did figure out who was right. And they
wouldn't tell you. They left you hanging. That both-
ered me.

Disagreements between professors can "drive you crazy" but this
student remained sane—as many in these positions do—by assuming one of the professors "was right." Being "left hanging" did not
disturb the student's faith in right answers. That remained intact.

Such faith in authorities and in right answers gradually
erodes, however. Many freshman courses emphasize multiple perspectives and diverse interpretations. Again and again, freshmen are
asked what they think; they are praised for offering ideas that their
professors haven't provided. They discover more and more disagreements in texts and among professors. Eventually, they conclude that
in some areas, at least, no one knows the answers.

Multiplicity/Subjective Knowledge. Once students realize
that in some areas or on some issues no one yet has definitive
answers, they revise their assumptions about teaching and learning.
Knowledge no longer consists of right and wrong answers; it becomes a matter of opinion. Faculty, therefore, are not authorities
who know the answers; they are people with opinions or theories.
And when it comes to opinion, everyone, including the student, has
a right to have one.

Initially these new assumptions provoke students into claiming equal status with faculty. One opinion is as good as another,
and teachers "have no right to call [the student] wrong" (Perry,
1970, p. 97). Convinced that all positions are equally valid, students
in early multiplicity see little need to justify or support their conclusions. Because they do not yet appreciate the difference between
a gut reaction and an informed opinion, they wonder how and why
we criticize their work. Many conclude that it is because we disagree
with their positions. A freshman in an English course writes: "The
professor . . . has to be more open to other views of stories besides
her own. Not everyone gets exactly the same thing out of every story.
The other person's view is not wrong." Another criticizes an art
history professor for similar reasons: "Art is interpreted in different
ways, and there should be no wrong answer. There is no way

anyone should get below a *B* on any of the essays." Summarizing such views, Kurfiss (1988, p. 54) writes: "Students at this level recognize complexity but have not yet learned how to navigate its waters. They perceive no basis other than intuition, feeling, or 'common sense' on which to judge the merits of . . . opinions."

As they encounter more and more faculty who demand support for their opinions, students begin to temper their claims. Students in late multiplicity still see knowledge as opinion or theory, but they realize they must support opinions or provide evidence for theories—at least in academic settings. They see, too, that faculty know the rules for finding support or evidence and now assume that teaching means helping students learn those rules. Grading continues to be a major worry and topic for criticism, but the focus shifts. They criticize their professors not for being opinionated but for failing to make evaluation criteria clear, as this freshman does: "The essays are graded hard and the grading is not really explained thoroughly enough. I don't really know what to write and not to write, how to support my interpretation."

Belenky and her coauthors (1986) observed several differences between women and men in these positions, differences that seldom surface in our day-to-day conversations with students, but that lead them to pursue different paths. They saw men—at least as Perry portrayed them—responding to the freedom from authority with vigor, proclaiming their rights to their own opinions, and later justifying them with reason and evidence. They heard some women's tentative "It's just my opinion" contrast with the men's assertive "I have a right to my opinion." From women they also heard a tendency to rely more on their own experiences than on objective evidence, to express concern that their views might sever their connections with others, and to be silent while they listened to discussions going on around them. Because thinking skills develop through practice and feedback, the tendency to keep their thoughts to themselves may prevent some freshman women from profiting from classroom activities unless they are specifically drawn in.

As students in multiplicity gain skill in supporting their opinions, the transition to relativism occurs. In the process, students learn to consider counterarguments and alternative conclusions. They begin to weigh evidence and to distinguish strong from weak support. They recognize that what they initially viewed as "academic" rules for argumentation, analysis, or problem solving lead in fact to more informed and more persuasive conclusions. With the development of these skills come new insights about what it means to know and to learn.

In contrast to Perry's studies (1970), in which most students eventually adopted the perspectives of relativism, Kurfiss notes that "subsequent studies have found fewer than half of college seniors subscribing to this epistemological perspective" (1988, p. 55), and she believes that the majority of college students view teaching and learning from positions of multiplicity and subjective knowledge. Although we frequently hear freshmen express assumptions and views characteristic of dualism and multiplicity, we think that the step into relativism takes us beyond the developmental positions of most freshmen. Our discussion of subsequent positions will, therefore, be brief.

Relativism/Procedural Knowledge. Students in these positions recognize that knowledge is contextual. What one "knows" about something or concludes in a situation is colored by one's perspective, assumptions, and methods of inquiry, which makes most questions and problems more complex. Recognizing the need to consider many factors, to look at them from different perspectives, to use systematic methods of analysis, and to provide evidence, these students consider us resources who can help them learn disciplinary methods of analysis. Learning becomes the use of those methods to understand complexities.

Belenky, Clinchy, Goldberger, and Tarule (1986) heard two different voices from women who were in positions of relativism and procedural knowledge. The louder voice for most women emphasized traditionally academic procedures for knowing—stepping back, looking at things objectively, trying to understand by remaining impartial—"separate knowing." In some women, they heard a different voice, however, one that emphasized "imagining themselves into" (p. 121) situations and that placed greater value on insights gained through personal experiences. For these women, empathy and personal experience—"connected knowing"—represented not only alternative procedures for understanding, but also the primary procedures for learning important things. These researchers suggest that integrating these two voices is a major developmental task for some women who are in these positions, and quite possibly for some men as well.

Students in positions of relativism and procedural knowledge often find that the more they analyze complexities, the less able they are to make decisions or draw conclusions because doing so seems to neglect some important factor or insight; they prefer exposing the complexities. Assignments that ask them to take a position or commit to some action are especially challenging.

Because we ask students to take positions or recommend actions, they do so, secure in knowing that they can change their minds and that the decisions they make will have no dire consequences. The academic environment thus allows them to test different choices and commitments tentatively until they find those they can commit to more permanently.

Commitment in Relativism/Constructed Knowledge. To recognize that choices and commitments must eventually be made casts learning in a somewhat different light. Students seek understanding of complexities and diverse perspectives not just as academic pursuits but also in order to create a personal world view, one from which they will make choices and commitments. For many women and some men, that world view must somehow integrate the more objective, distant, and rational procedures of academic study with the more empathic and experiential approaches they tend to use in other domains of life.

But these concerns are well beyond the developmental positions of almost all freshmen. Several general observations and recommendations are more pertinent to them. First, given their developmental perspectives, freshmen are likely to find many of our methods puzzling and troubling. Earlier we identified several targets for their criticisms—our refusal to give clear answers where none exist, assignments that require independent thought, disagreement among authorities, discussion activities, insistence on support for opinions. Criticize though they may, freshmen need these challenges to stimulate the transformations in their views of learning.

In later chapters we suggest ways to help freshmen cope with the anxieties these activities may raise and learn from them.

Second, as Perry has recently noted, the developmental scheme is useful to us "less as a way of classifying students than as a way of hearing 'where students are speaking from' so that communication can be more fruitful" (1989, p. 1). If, for example, when we hear student criticisms of group discussions or recommendations that we lecture more, we recognize a desire for right answers or a dependence on authority, then we might look for ways to reduce their anxieties but not necessarily to follow their advice.

Finally, several gender differences identified by Belenky and her coauthors have serious implications for the freshman class. Noting that many women enter college less confident in themselves as thinkers than men, they write, "Our interviews have convinced us that every woman, regardless of age, social class, ethnicity, and academic achievement, needs to know that she is capable of intelligent thought, and she needs to know it right away. Perhaps men learn this lesson before going to college, or perhaps they can wait until they have proved themselves to hear it; we do not know. We do know that many of the women we interviewed had not yet learned it" (1986, p. 193). At the very least, we can be watchful to see that Hall and Sandler's findings (1982) that men speak more during class and receive more praise for their contributions do not characterize our classrooms.

Learning Styles

Some time ago, we attended a conference in which Peter Briggs-Myers introduced a discussion of learning styles by inviting members of his audience to try a simple experiment: to write our names first with one hand and then with the other. In doing so, we learned two lessons. One, we all could write with both hands. Two, writing with the hand we do not normally use felt awkward, required concentration, and took longer (Perotti and others, 1987).

The analogy between right- or left-handedness and learning styles may be oversimple, but it highlights some very important considerations. The term *learning styles* loosely refers to preferences for some kinds of learning activities over others. We will examine some dimensions of those preferences below, but we stress at the outset that we are discussing *how* people learn, not *what* they learn. Just as we can write our names with both our hands, so too are students with different learning styles capable of learning the knowledge and skills we teach. Our learning styles affect our responses to different learning activities, however. Some activities seem natural and come easily; others feel awkward, require concentration, and take longer—like writing with the hand we do not normally use.

Understanding learning styles—the differences among people in the attitudes, values, and approaches they bring to learning—provides a basis for developing the class activities and assignments needed to teach the diverse students in freshman courses and to understand more fully the needs of all freshmen. Our discussion samples only three research perspectives; Claxton and Murrell (1987) provide a more extensive survey of the field.

Witkin's Field Independence. Cognitive styles—our characteristic and preferred ways of perceiving, interpreting, organizing, and thinking about information—have occupied researchers for more than five decades. Their findings indicate that people differ on several dimensions of cognitive functioning. One of the most widely studied areas in cognitive style is that of field independence, initially identified by Herman A. Witkin in the late 1940s.

Although several different tests of field independence exist, all measure the extent to which people are "able to deal with a part of a field separately from the field as a whole, or the extent to which [they are] able to disembed items from organized context" (Witkin, 1976, pp. 41–42). In the *Embedded Figures Test,* for example, subjects must be able to identify a simple geometric figure embedded in a more complex geometric pattern. Those who quickly recognize the simple figure, presumably because they are relatively uninfluenced by the surrounding field, are called "field independent." Those who have difficulty locating the figure in the allotted time, presumably because they are heavily influenced by the surrounding field, are usually referred to as "field dependent." Concurring with those who prefer more neutral terminology, we use the term "field sensitive" to designate this orientation (see Claxton and Murrell, 1987, for discussion of this issue).

People are not either wholly field independent or field sensitive; test scores of this dimension are distributed along a continuum. The labels designate the extremes and "like the designations, 'tall' and 'short,' are relative" (Witkin, Oltman, Raskin, and Karp, 1971, p. 4). Tendencies toward field independence or field sensitivity, however, appear related to a variety of other learning characteristics. Chickering (1976), Claxton and Murrell (1987), Fincher (1985), Messick and Associates (1976), Witkin (1976), and Witkin, Oltman, Raskin, and Karp (1971) discuss these characteristics more fully, and our summary draws primarily on these sources.

Students who are more field independent tend to approach learning tasks analytically. They identify parts of a whole or individual aspects of a situation, consider them independent of context, and impose their own organization on them. When they listen to lectures, for example, they extract information, organize it, and record notes in outline format even when instructors do not provide an organizational framework (Frank, 1984). Accustomed to considering information separate from its context, these students have little problem with tasks that require pulling some element out of context and using it in a next context or relating it to some other element.

Tasks that require attention to context, particularly to human or social contexts, require more concentration from field independent students. They tend to focus less on people than on things or abstractions. They are comfortable working alone and often prefer to do so. Field independent students are more likely to major in mathematics and physical sciences than are their field sensitive peers, and men tend to be more field independent than women.

Field sensitive students approach learning tasks more globally. They see ideas, issues, and problems in context and tend not to consider individual aspects separate from their contexts. Because everything seems interrelated, breaking problems into parts, isolating ideas, or restructuring problem situations are not natural acts for field sensitive students and require their concentration. Frank (1984) found that when students took notes from lectures in which no organizational framework was provided, all recorded about the same amount of information in their notes, but field sensitive students were less likely than field independent students to use an outline format and did not perform as well on a follow-up test. The differences in their test scores vanished when the lecturer provided an outline.

Field sensitive students are more attuned to the human or social aspects of the environment than their field independent peers. Field sensitive students, for example, show better memory for information that has social content and for people's faces. In situations in which they are unsure of their opinions or expertise, they are more likely to consult authorities or peers, to consider their views, and to change their minds. They want others around when they are learning and prefer courses that emphasize student discussion, small groups, and collaborative learning. Field sensitive students are more likely to select majors in which interpersonal relationships are important—the social sciences, education, the humanities, and areas in business such as personnel or sales. Women tend to be more field sensitive then men, probably because their socialization focuses their attention on human interactions.

In short, at one polarized end of the continuum, students can't see the forest for the trees; at the other, they can't see the trees for the forest. What these distinctions mean for us who teach freshmen is that what comes easily to field sensitive students requires field independent students to concentrate more, and vice versa. Often the issue is not whether students can learn but how they learn. Knowing that, we can vary our assignments so that neither style is consistently disadvantaged and build in appropriate support when we know that an assignment or activity requires behaviors to which one style is unaccustomed.

We might offer field independent students, for example, occasions to work alone and opportunities to pursue studying in their own ways, but we may need to give more explicit cues or directions when tasks demand attention to social issues or interpersonal skills and allow them more time when considering context is important. We can provide opportunities for group work and collaborative learning to field sensitive students, outlines or study questions to help them organize information from lectures and readings, and more time when problems or tasks require breaking things into parts or taking something out of context.

Kolb's Learning Style Inventory. Kolb's identification of learning styles is grounded in an experiential model of learning, which he calls a learning cycle (Kolb, 1984, 1985). The learning cycle includes four phases, each requiring different processes to acquire information and learn skills.

1. *Concrete experience,* which occurs when we involve ourselves fully in a new activity in order to encounter it firsthand.
2. *Reflective observation,* which occurs as we look back on the experience, recognize significant aspects, events, or reactions, and think about their meanings from different perspectives.
3. *Abstract conceptualization,* which occurs when we compare our observations to conceptual or theoretical material we are studying and seek to develop generalizable explanations or hypotheses for what we have experienced.
4. *Active experimentation,* which occurs when we test our generalizations in different situations and problems, thereby extending and elaborating their meaning until we are ready to consider greater complexity or new ideas.

Cycling through these four phases, we come full circle to concrete experience and begin the cycle again.

Drawing on an extensive experiential learning research and theory base, Kolb (1981, 1984) maintains that learning will be more meaningful and retained longer if we work through all four phases of the learning cycle. Stice (1987) reports that retention increased from 20 percent when only abstract conceptualization was emphasized to 90 percent when all four phases were incorporated (p. 293). Svinicki and Dixon (1987) list several instructional activities that support the different learning processes in the Kolb model. Logs, journals, discussion, brainstorming, and questioning are ways to support reflective observation. Lecture, papers, building models, and creating analogies are among the activities that support abstract conceptualization. Simulations, case studies, laboratory work and fieldwork, projects, and homework support active experimentation;

and concrete experience is gained by laboratories, observations, simulations and games, fieldwork, trigger films, readings, problem sets, examples, and reading of primary texts (p. 142). They also illustrate how such activities might be sequenced in several disciplines to include all phases (p. 143). In Chapters Seven and Eight, we also suggest a variety of activities and assignments that could be sequenced to follow Kolb's learning cycle.

Learning styles come into play in Kolb's model because each of us is more comfortable and more skilled in some phases of the learning cycle than in others. As Kolb (1981) points out, two dimensions figure prominently in this model of learning, each requiring "abilities that are polar opposites" (p. 238). On one dimension, concrete experience and abstract thinking represent the opposites; on the other, reflection and action. Because most of us lean toward one end of each pole, we feel more at home in some phases of the learning cycle than in others. Some students easily immerse themselves in direct experiences, understand abstractions better when they consider them in terms of their own experiences, but may have to work at thinking beyond their experiences. To others, direct experience feels awkward, often because it involves social interactions; they are more comfortable thinking about things in the abstract and sometimes need reminders that theories must fit reality. In terms of the active-reflective dimension, some students prefer doing things, experimenting, and participating; they may need prompting to stop and think about what they are doing. Others are accustomed to observing, listening, and thinking about things; they may need prodding to test their ideas in action.

Although Kolb identifies four different learning styles based on the four possible combinations of "polar opposites," we do not review them here. If we take the learning cycle as a model for planning instruction, we think it is enough to know that students will feel more accustomed to some phases of the learning cycle while other phases will require more concentration and support.

The Myers-Briggs Type Indicator. The most complex assessment of learning styles considered here, the Myers-Briggs Type Indicator (MBTI) measures preferences on four bipolar dimensions and identifies sixteen personality types, each with different preferences for learning. To describe all sixteen types or even all four dimensions of the MBTI exceeds our purpose. We focus instead on two dimensions of the MBTI that we find illuminating and helpful in working with freshmen: extraversion–introversion and sensing–intuition.

The extraversion–introversion scale measures preference for the "outer world of people and things" or the "inner world of ideas" (Briggs and Briggs-Myers, 1983). Extraverts "rely on activity . . . , think best when talking, learn well in groups, and may have difficulty sitting in front of a book for a long period of time" (Jensen, 1987, p. 183). Introverts "need quiet time for concentration and study, for they think best when alone. . . . They are more comfortable than extraverts with teacher-centered or lecture-based instruction and long stretches of solitary study, but, unless they anticipate questions beforehand, they may perform poorly during in-class discussions" (Jensen, 1987, pp. 183–184).

The sensing-intuition scale indicates preference for perceiving the world through the realities of experience or for intuiting meanings and possibilities. As Jensen describes them, "sensing" students "tend to focus on the concrete aspects of the here-and-now; they attempt to master first the facts and details of the learning environment. . . . Sensing types also like to put into use what they have learned; they are, in general, practical and realistic. . . . They like teachers who give clear directions that are concise and to the point" (1987, p. 184). He observes in contrast that intuitive students "tend to master first the theories and concepts. . . . Intuitive types are less likely to be patient with routine or overly structured mechanical approaches to learning. They desire and seek the opportunity to let their imaginative instincts work, and thus tend to prefer open-ended assignments . . . their greatest weakness is a reluctance to observe details and learn facts" (p. 184).

In the summer of 1988, about half of the incoming freshmen on our campus—over one-thousand students—completed the MBTI. On the extraversion–introversion scale, extraverts (83 percent) far exceeded introverts (17 percent); students were more evenly distributed between sensing (48 percent) and intuition (52 percent). The discovery that a great majority of our freshmen were extraverts was important to our faculty. Our traditional practices of lecturing and assigning homework to be done in solitude are better suited to introverts—a small minority of our students. It became clear that we needed more discussion, more collaborative learning assignments, and less lecturing in order to accommodate the majority of our freshmen.

The even distribution among our freshmen on the sensing-intuition scale was also important. Many of our teaching practices—the syllabus created for flexibility, lectures on theory and concepts, assignments asking students "to think about this issue for next time," essays instructing them to "explain the significance of . . . " or "discuss your reactions to . . . "—are better suited to intuitive students than to their sensing peers. Our sensing freshmen, nearly half our enrollment, learn more naturally when we supply more structure and direction, emphasize practical applications, and pay more attention to concrete situations.

Most of us tend to ignore such differences in learning styles among our students. "I've not been inclined," a colleague told us, "to use discussions even in my smaller classes. I stop to answer questions, of course, and sometimes a discussion results. But I never really got much out of discussions—the kind where you sat in a circle and the professor didn't say much—when I was a student." We are likely to teach as we were taught, adopting the methods we preferred, eschewing those we hated, forgetting that our classmates reacted very differently to the courses we were taking. Most of them did not go on to major in our areas or pursue graduate study in our specializations. The majority were less successful academically; many dropped out or flunked out. What worked for us did not work for them.

Nowhere in the undergraduate curriculum will we find so many students who differ from us and from one another in so many ways as in freshman courses. If we are to succeed in teaching to such diversity, we must look beyond our own experiences and reactions, try to understand how our students learn, and find methods and practices that suit their learning styles rather than our own habits and behavior. The goal of employing any model is to understand the differences among students, to develop teaching strategies that build on the strengths of individual students, and to help students expand their repertoire of learning strategies.

We need not be experts in learning style models to meet these objectives. As Fuhrmann and Grasha remind us (1983, pp.132-133), we can learn a great deal about basic differences among students simply by observing them and noting their behaviors: "Which students seem to appreciate a clearly detailed outline and lecture? Which respond enthusiastically to a group work setting? Which like to read and think on their own? Which demonstrate the concentration necessary to work through a lengthy laboratory procedure? Which plan their study activities most thoroughly? Which like the freedom of a creative assignment? Which learn best from films? Which seem to need active involvement? Which are motivated more by grades than by accomplishment? Which are turned on to the same topics you are? Which relish a heated discussion of issues? Which prefer the generation of alternatives rather than the specification of one right solution?" (pp. 132-133).

Informal processes such as asking freshmen to write a brief paper on "how I learn best" or to describe and analyze their most rewarding learning experience can be applied early in a class and used to modify the course design, if desired. Understanding some of the better known models and even using one of the simple instruments can further help to make sense of the differences we observe and add a new dimension to freshman instruction. For teaching to be effective, learning must take place, and that means understanding as much as we can about freshmen as learners—about the typical and not-so-typical beginning college student, understanding not only what they do or do not know, but also how they come to know it.

PART TWO

Teaching Freshmen

In Part One we discussed the high school environment, diversity among first-year students, the transitions and obstacles to learning that adapting to college life presents, and the learning styles and developmental positions freshmen bring to the college classroom—matters that make teaching freshmen different from other college students. Recognizing that context, we move into the freshman classroom in Part Two.

We begin in Chapter Four with a general description of what learning is, what we mean when we talk about knowing, understanding, and thinking. Freshmen benefit from a good beginning, and Chapter Five suggests techniques to allay concerns and to set the stage from the first day. Both the disadvantages of lectures and some proven approaches to make them more conducive to student learning are the subjects of Chapter Six, "Presenting and Explaining." Chapters Seven and Eight each deal in different ways with involving freshmen in learning, Chapter Seven focusing on classroom practices and Chapter Eight on out-of-class assignments. Chapter Nine looks at methods of evaluating freshman performance and some strategies for making evaluations fairer and more accurate. Chapter Ten addresses the difficult questions faculty have about grading—questions that range from what should count to what one should do about cheating.

4

Knowing, Understanding, and Thinking: The Goals of Freshman Instruction

Effective instruction demands consistency among course goals, instructional activities, and evaluation procedures. Because it makes no sense to talk about teaching practices without a clear vision of the goals to which those practices are aimed, let us begin by considering what we hope freshmen will learn in our courses.

When we are asked to identify the most important goals for instruction, "getting students to think" is high on everyone's list, and "knowing and understanding the subject matter" is not far behind. What we have in mind when we use these phrases is not so clear, however. Definitions are not shared, and important distinctions are often blurred. Stating the goals for instruction in the form of behavioral objectives, as educational psychologists for years urged us to do, too often emphasized the trivial because it was observable and neglected the important goals because they did not lend themselves to direct observation. In any case, behavioral objectives were no better at differentiating differences in instructional goals than are the words *knowing, understanding,* or *thinking* and have been pretty much banished from college campuses.

We are left, however, with language for talking about course goals that is inadequate for communicating with one another and for planning instruction. Thus, when we want to know what students are expected to learn in a course, we look at the *questions* faculty ask as well as the goals they articulate. We take a similar approach here. What follows are some working definitions of *knowing, understanding,* and *thinking,* definitions created largely by the questions faculty ask during class, in assignments, and on exams. Along the way, we preview some of the implications that different forms of learning have for teaching practices.

Knowing: Memorizing

If students are to think and to organize their thoughts, they need something to think about and to think with. Much of what goes on in freshman courses has the instructor presenting and explaining course content in the interest of providing food for thought or tools for thinking. If students are to have the information available for thinking and solving problems, they must commit it to memory and be able to recall it when needed.

The information freshmen are asked to memorize sometimes includes names, dates, definitions of terms, even a fact or two. We ask: "What is Avogadro's number?" "When was the Renaissance?" "What is the current rate of unemployment?" More often in college courses, students are asked to remember complex ideas and relationships—definitions of concepts, characteristics of styles or periods, key points in an argument, theoretical constructs, principles, laws, procedures, conventions, trends, findings. Such ideas and relationships provide the conceptual framework for combining and organizing course material that otherwise would exist as isolated pieces of information. Although these organizing ideas and relationships come in different forms, we shall refer to them generally as concepts. When faculty check to see whether students know important concepts, they ask questions such as the following:

So far, we have examined four different approaches to
critical reading: historical analysis, character analysis,
thematic analysis, and analysis of narrative point of
view. Describe each of these approaches, noting the

questions each asks and the conventions each uses for seeking evidence.

In *Habits of the Heart,* Robert Bellah suggests that American society has been shaped by four major cultural strands: the Biblical strand, Republicanism, Utilitarian Individualism, and Expressive Individualism. According to Bellah, what characterizes each of these cultural strands?

State in your own words the Law of Conservation of Mass, the Law of Constant Composition, and the Law of Multiple Proportions.

What are the distinguishing characteristics of each of the following artistic movements: Neo-Classicism, Romanticism; Impressionism; Post-Impressionism.

Summarize how Utilitarians and Retributionists justify punishment.

In most courses, students memorize basic information. In some courses, that is all they do. Following a major study of college testing practices, Milton (1982) concluded that undergraduates are tested almost entirely for their grasp of factual information rather than for their ability to understand, apply, or evaluate. Faculty argue that tests do not tell the whole story, but we have observed too many classes in which not much more can be said. Although the national obsession with cultural literacy encourages faculty to give free reign to impulses to ask students to memorize, we counsel restraint, largely for pragmatic reasons. If students are to remember the information they memorize beyond the next exam, then at least two conditions must be met. Both require time and attention.

First, practice is an important condition for all types of learning, including memorization. In fact, a primary consideration in selecting teaching methods or developing assignments is whether the activities under consideration provide practice for the goals to be achieved. Practice that facilitates memorization and retention takes many forms—reciting, paraphrasing, summarizing, taking notes in one's own words, talking to oneself, explaining to someone else, quizzing oneself. In general, the idea is to get students to *verbalize* the information to be remembered.

Establishing connections between the information to be memorized and the knowledge students already possess is the second, and perhaps the most important, condition for remembering. Such connections are made by appealing to students' interests and values, by elaborating or extending things students already know, by interpreting or reinterpreting experiences they have had, by linking those ideas that are abstract, distant, or unfamiliar with that which students regard as concrete, immediate, and familiar. Forging such links goes by many names—comprehending, understanding, making material meaningful—and leads us to other categories of learning. When memorization is disconnected from these other forms of learning, as it often is in introductory courses, the information memorized is soon forgotten.

Understanding: The Ability to Recognize Examples

We all know students who can rattle off definitions of concepts, recite principles and rules, and summarize entire theories. They can even do so in their own words. However, if we show these same students a particular example, they cannot name the concept exemplified. If we conduct a demonstration, they cannot recognize the laws or principles that are operating. If we present an analysis or interpretation, they cannot identify the theoretical perspective taken. Faculty are rightly concerned when this happens. It indicates that students are memorizing without understanding, and it foreshadows forgetting.

When students understand, they can see the relationships between specific instances and more general ideas. If we ask them to think of examples that illustrate concepts or principles, they can do so. Conversely, when we pose specific situations or examples, students can explain how they relate to the broader ideas. Whereas questions that get at "knowing" ask students to define concepts, state generalizations, or describe characteristics, as in our earlier five examples, the questions below require students to recognize those general ideas in specific situations. These questions measure understanding.

> Attached you will find an essay on Hawthorne's "Rappaccini's Daughter." Which approach to critical reading has the writer taken? How do you know?

> The U.S. Army sponsors an advertisement that claims that the Army is the place to "be all that you can be." Which of Bellah's four major cultural strands is most reflected in the Army's slogan?

> Which of the following chemical equations conform to the Law of Conservation of Mass? [Samples provided]

> The slide we are viewing is a reproduction of a painting we have not discussed. Do you think this is an Impressionist painting? Why or why not?

> A student is dismissed from the University for cheating on a quiz. The student admits cheating on the quiz but argues that dismissal is an extreme measure for a relatively minor offense. With which philosophical theory is the student's argument most consistent? Explain why you think so.

Understanding does not come cheap. It develops gradually as students encounter new examples and illustrations. Students begin with a sketchy outline of the ideas. As each new example or situation is met, students see different ways in which key properties and relationships are embodied or excluded, and they elaborate or revise the outlines they have in mind. In the process, what might have been learned as a meaningless sequence of words or phrases becomes connected, integrated, and elaborated.

Much is known about how concepts are learned and about the instructional activities that promote understanding. (For more comprehensive discussion, see Ericksen, 1984; Norman, 1982; Park,

1984; Tennyson and Park, 1980.) Here, we note two essential ingredients. First, examples and illustrations are critical because they provide the keys to meaning. We will have more to say about the selection and discussion of examples in Chapter Six. Meanwhile, suffice it to say that teaching for understanding moves back and forth between general ideas and specific examples.

Second, students need to practice recognizing or supplying examples and explaining how they represent the general ideas. Unfortunately, practice that leads to understanding is too often neglected. We typically introduce concepts, explain them by way of examples, perhaps even contrast them with nonexamples, and then move on to the next concept. We get a lot of practice while students watch and cheer us on. A far better use of time would see faculty posing examples and *students* explaining how the examples relate to the concepts under study.

Thinking: Applying What One Has Learned

It is one thing to be able to define a concept or to summarize a school of thought, another thing to recognize how these ideas look in specific situations, and yet another to use what one has learned to solve problems, explain causes and effects, draw conclusions, make recommendations, critique arguments, and a host of other things we ask students to do. These tasks require transforming, combining, creating something beyond what currently exists. Students must, of course, be able to recall ideas previously studied and recognize how they relate to the situation or problem at hand, but the job is not done until they can fashion something new of the ideas they bring to bear and the information given by the task.

In his review of research on thinking and problem solving, Frederiksen (1984) distinguishes between "well-structured" and "ill-structured" problems and tasks. The terms are useful in marking the ends of a continuum along which challenges to think fall.

Thinking about Well-Structured Issues and Problems. Like questions that lead to understanding, questions that stimulate thinking present specific situations, problems, examples, data, and the like. Unlike the questions that asked students to recognize concepts or ideas embedded in the situations, the questions below demand that students create something beyond what is given in the situation.

The editors of the campus literary journal have decided to devote an entire issue to critical analyses of Hawthorne's "Rappaccini's Daughter." They hope to include several articles, each reflecting a different approach to critical reading. You have been asked to write the "thematic analysis" article. As a first step, outline the major points you intend to make and note the passages you will cite.

Recently, *USA Today* reported the results of a survey in which "baby-boomers" were asked what was most important to them. Forty-two percent said "feeling good about themselves"; 26 percent said "job or career"; 20 percent said "religion"; 8 percent said "family"; 4 percent were undecided. Using these data, attack or defend Bellah's assertion that Expressive Individualism is the dominant cultural strand in our society.

Natural gas consists largely of methane. (A methane molecule contains one carbon atom and four hydrogen atoms.) When we light a Bunsen burner, the methane combines with oxygen in the air to form two products—liquid water and gaseous carbon dioxide. Write a balanced equation (that is, one that conforms to the Law of Conservation of Mass) for this reaction. [Adapted from Masterton, Slowinski, and Stanitski, 1983, p. 66.]

Posted around the room are reproductions of twenty paintings. You have been asked to organize an exhibit that captures the spirit of Impressionism, but space limitations permit you to include only five paintings.

Decide which five paintings you would select for the exhibit and explain why you would choose those five.

Consider the following observations. Criminals are deprived of their liberties when they are imprisoned. Carriers of infectious diseases are deprived of their liberties when they are quarantined. Would a Utilitarian view these practices as justifiable or unjustifiable and on what grounds? How would a Retributionist respond to the same questions?

Questions that stimulate thinking range from easy to difficult, depending in part on the amount of structure provided in the problem situation and the complexity of the information that must be brought to bear. Compared to questions we will see later, these are fairly structured. They do not contain much extraneous information. They explicity state or strongly imply what is to be applied. Finally, although the conceptual information that students are asked to apply is complex, it is easier to work with one approach, theory, assertion, or style than it is to work with several. As we increase the complexity of the information given in the question and reduce the structure and directions about how to proceed, the questions become more and more challenging.

Thinking About Ill-Structured Issues and Problems. In life outside college classrooms, issues and problems do not come in neatly wrapped packages complete with directions about how to solve or resolve them. In real life, challenges to think are far less structured. More information is available than one is likely to need, and key ideas or relationships are often embedded in a morass of conflicting or irrelevant detail. One is not told how to approach a task or which ideas might illuminate the situation. Thinking through an issue or solving a problem often requires performing a series of steps or combining information studied at different times. There is usually more than one acceptable conclusion and more than one way to reach it. Although the questions below are not identical to those one might encounter outside campus boundaries, they come closer to real-world challenges.

The editors of the campus literary journal have decided to publish a volume on Hawthorne's short stories. They want to include one article on "Young Goodman Brown," and they've invited you to write the analysis. Note that the editors have not specified which approach to critical analysis you should use. They are leaving it to you to decide which approach or combination of approaches will provide the most illuminating and insightful analysis of the story. As a first step, outline the major points you will make in the article and note the passages you will cite.

Benzene is reacted with nitric acid. Two products are formed, one of which is water. The other product is an oily liquid that has a molecular mass of 213. Propose a laboratory procedure for determining the composition of this unknown and for writing a balanced equation for the reaction of benzene with nitric acid [adapted from Masterton, Slowinski, and Stanitski, 1983, p. 84].

[A description of the purpose and method of the annual CIRP survey of freshmen and a four-page summary of one year's data are attached to this assignment.] Using these data as your evidence, write a paper in which you challenge or support Bellah's analysis of American society. Note that you need not use all the information reported in the survey, nor do you have to address all the assertions Bellah makes. Part of the challenge is to judge which of Bellah's assertions are worthy of attention in this context and which data are most relevant to those assertions.

When students confront ill-structured problems, they must do two things simultaneously. For one, they have to restructure the problem by pulling key elements out of the context in which they are presented, seeing relationships that are not immediately obvious, and deciding which features of the situation merit attention.

At the same time, they must sort through all they have learned and select that which is relevant and useful in the situation at hand.

How do we teach the structuring and restructuring, the weighing and choosing, the selecting and rejecting skills required for complex thinking and problem solving? Less is known about this form of learning than we might like. After their reviews of pertinent research, Gagné (1980) and McKeachie, Pintrich, Lin, and Smith (1986) agree that people learn these skills through problem-solving experience over time and in a variety of situations.

Meanwhile, faculty want to know what, if anything, to do to get students to think. While we cannot be as confident in talking about teaching that promotes the development of thinking skills as we were in discussing knowing and understanding, the following suggestions reflect current hypotheses about the factors that appear to make a difference.

First, there is little evidence that generic courses or programs are successful in teaching thinking skills that transfer across subject-matter domains. Thinking—critically, creatively, and other-wise—is intimately connected with the subject matter about which one is thinking (Kurfiss, 1988; McKeachie, Pintrich, Lin, and Smith, 1986). If we expect students to "think" in our courses, then we must give attention to both content and thinking skills.

Second, it makes sense to sequence instruction so that students begin thinking about limited and structured issues or problems and gradually move to more complex and unstructured tasks. In some freshman courses, the first challenge to think comes in the form of a project or paper assignment that more closely resembles questions in the "ill-structured" category than in the "well-structured" one. In other courses, students never get beyond the well-structured problems. Neither practice encourages the development of thinking skills. Few students can handle complex, unstructured tasks their first time out, but neither will they learn to handle them if they never encounter them.

Third, explicit emphasis on problem-solving techniques and procedures appears to help students develop thinking skills (McKeachie, Pintrich, Lin, and Smith, 1986). When freshmen confront even a highly structured problem, they do not always distinguish what is given in the question from what is being asked. After reading a problem, many cannot state what the question is, which may explain why faculty often receive answers to questions other than those they asked. Thus, highlighting problem-solving techniques and procedures might include addressing questions such as the following: What is given in the question? What are you being asked to do? What concepts or ideas are you asked to bring to bear? What steps will you need to take?

The instructional task becomes more complicated as we move toward ill-structured problems. We know that students often "read the problem and throw a formula at it" or "read the assignment and reach for the first idea that crosses their minds." If the formula does not work or the idea does not go anywhere, students give up.

Studies comparing experts and novices offer some ideas about how to help students tackle ill-structured problems. Experts, for example, report that as they read problems, they jot down key ideas and information, note relationships, list assumptions, outline issues, write themselves questions, draw diagrams and pictures, break complex problems into simpler steps (Frederiksen, 1984; Kurfiss, 1988). Such activities make sense as strategies for restructuring and understanding complex situations. We might explicitly tell students to use them.

Once the problem is understood students must sort through what they know and decide what is relevent in the situation at hand. A mental survey of what one knows may seem an obvious step, but students often give up if an idea does not leap immediately to mind. Teaching students some strategies for conducting these mental surveys may help. Such strategies might include: free-association techniques in which students take a few minutes to jot down everything that comes to mind when they first encounter a question; brainstorming ideas about a question or issue before trying to answer it; taking a tentative position and then "arguing the opposite" before committing oneself; imagining how several different theorists or experts might answer before developing one's own answer. Although further research is needed to determine the effectiveness of particular strategies and techniques, current reviews advocate that we explicitly teach strategies for thinking and problem solving along with the subject matter content (Kurfiss, 1988; McKeachie, Pintrich, Lin, and Smith, 1986).

Fourth, plan instruction so that students receive lots of guidance on early attempts to apply and less and less guidance on subsequent attempts. Students often need step-by-step prompts, hints, and feedback when they first encounter problems or situations that ask them to think. In fact, we recommend that initial practice exercises be done in small groups *in* class where instructors are available for such guidance. This is not the time to use the sink-or-swim approach. Many students find it too frustrating, give up prematurely, and drown in their sense of failure. On the other hand, students *do* need to learn to cope with problems or situations on their own. They will not if we continue to lead them through analyses or solutions or critiques. Gradually, we need to withdraw prompts, hints, and step-by-step questions.

Fifth, ask students to verbalize what they are doing and why they are doing it. The most recent research finds that verbalizing the reason for taking a step before the step is taken results in improved performance and that verbalization is most helpful during the initial stages of learning (McKeachie, Pintrich, Lin, and Smith, 1986).

Sixth, let students in on the fact that thinking involves some trial and error, often pursues a random course, and usually requires hard work. More often than not, students see us discuss final versions of solutions or analyses—as if the solutions or analyses emerged in polished forms; as if key ideas, questions, and relationships were self-evident; as if we never felt confused, got stuck, pursued blind alleys, or had to start over from scratch. Little wonder that students conclude they either "get it or they don't" and give up prematurely when an answer does not spring immediately to mind.

Finally, provide practice and plenty of it. If there is any hope that students can learn to think through issues and problems—well-structured, ill-structured, and everything between—that hope lies in practice. Unfortunately, many of us underestimate the amount of practice students need. We forget what it is like to be a novice in our fields—how it felt to encounter a problem the first or second or umpteenth time. We worry about covering content, fall prey to temptations to shortcut practice and hope for the best, and wind up feeling frustrated and disappointed when our hopes are dashed. If we are serious about getting students to think, it does not pay to cut corners on practice.

Learning How to Learn

We complain, often at great length, that freshmen do not know how to study. According to instructors, freshmen cannot read for comprehension, listen for the key ideas in a lecture, or learn from discussions. They do not know how to take notes, how to use them once they have them, how to approach or think through problems, or how to prepare for exams. Given all the things we allege students do not know how to do, it is somewhat ironic that our most frequent advice to freshmen is that they study more and learn to manage their time better. No doubt, many students could profit from following that advice, but it will not suffice.

We have assumed that freshmen will come to our classes knowing how to study. When we discover that many do not, we blame high school teachers for not preparing students and we resent the fact that we must teach study skills on top of everything else. Both development and cognitive research are making it increasingly clear that neither our assumptions nor our responses are tenable. The developmental findings summarized in Chapter Three tells us that students' views of knowledge and learning undergo transformations during the college years. With those transformations come changes in students' readiness and willingness to engage in different strategies for studying. Research on cognition indicates that capabilities for learning how to learn accumulate as students acquire more information about a subject, develop useful schemes for organizing their knowledge, and gain confidence in their abilities to use it in thinking and problem solving (Ericksen, 1984; Kurfiss, 1988; McKeachie, Pintrich, Lin, and Smith, 1986).

Adding it all up, it appears less and less that learning how to learn is a prerequisite that students should have mastered before admission to college, one that high schools failed to teach. Learning how to learn looks instead more like a penultimate goal for higher education, one that can be pursued only as students acquire knowledge, understanding, and the ability to think in a subject area.

What might we do beyond telling students to study more and to budget their time? First, teach students strategies for making material meaningful. Telling students that they should aim for understanding, not just memorizing, is not enough. Asking students to paraphrase information in their own words or to think of examples from their own experiences are steps in the right direction, but even this is not enough. Freshmen will engage in such activities when they are asked to do so, but they do not know what they are doing beyond following directions or answering questions. If we want them to see such activities as *strategies* for learning, we must ask them to verbalize what they are doing and why.

Second, teach students strategies for organizing information and connecting it to what they already know. Again, some specific techniques help students become active organizers of information. Outlining and summarizing served most of us pretty well. To that repertoire, we can add concept mapping, diagramming, clustering, and several other techniques discussed in later chapters. We can do more than use these as teaching methods; we can teach them as learning strategies.

Third, teach students how to make the most of opportunities to practice thinking and problem solving. We have already mentioned one strategy—verbalizing the steps one takes in thinking through a problem or issue. Later chapters introduce others.

We return to this form of learning in Chapter Thirteen. Between now and then, we have more to say about meaning, about the organization of information in memory, and about practice. As we talk about teaching methods and techniques, keep in mind that many of those same methods and techniques can be explicitly taught as learning strategies.

Students' Definitions of Learning

Our taxonomy of instructional goals was derived by looking at the questions faculty ask in freshman courses and classifying them in categories defined primarily by cognitive psychologists. In Chapter Three, drawing largely on research in developmental psychology, we saw that students' views of knowledge and learning change during the college years, and we traced those transformations from positions of dualism or received knowledge to positions of commitment or constructed knowledge. What happens when students in these various positions confront the challenges we have discussed?

Students who define learning as accumulating facts and right answers, as students in positions of dualism or received knowledge do, are likely to understand challenges to memorize. They may have doubts about *what* they are asked to memorize ("Why do we need to know all these different theories? Why not just learn the one that's right?"), but memorizing factual or authoritative information fits well with their views of knowledge and learning. But what sense do these students make of the other forms of learning we have discussed? They talk about understanding and thinking, but they complain: "The examples on the test were not discussed in class." "How are we supposed to know what Bellah would say about this? It wasn't in the book." "I don't think it's fair to ask us to write essays on stories we haven't discussed." In short, students in early developmental positions take understanding and thinking to mean remembering the thoughts of others.

In contrast, we would expect students in positions of multiplicity or subjective knowledge to welcome questions that ask them to explain, interpret, analyze, critique, or otherwise think through the issues and problems we pose. They, too, appear to transform our questions into something other than we intend. We expect *informed* opinions—recognition of the contributions of others, evidence, documentation. But these students say: "Who cares what Bellah would say? This is what I think." Students in positions of multiplicity or subjective knowledge may welcome questions that we have classified as understanding and thinking, but their responses are likely to neglect the role of factual information or authoritative opinion.

Not until students reach positions of relativism or procedural knowledge are they likely to understand fully the goals we set in our courses or the assignments we give. Most freshmen, remember, are in earlier developmental positions. Teaching and testing for understanding and thinking may seem a waste of time. Some faculty respond by emphasizing memorization and saving other forms of learning for more advanced courses. Two serious problems arise from this approach. First, when memorization is disconnected from other forms of learning, the forgetting curve is steep. Second, students transform their views of learning when they encounter challenges to those views. Postponing those challenges postpones the transformations and retards development. Sooner or later, faculty and students will confront these developmental issues. We advocate sooner rather than later.

At the same time, if freshmen are to meet the challenges, they will need support. So far, we have talked about what freshmen bring to college and what they encounter when they arrive. Now we begin to talk about what faculty can do to make those encounters productive. We start with preparing a syllabus and meeting the first class.

5

Preparing a Syllabus
and Meeting
the First Class

For freshmen, the first class is a Major Event, one they have been anticipating for weeks, even months. At last, they are to find out how college differs from high school, and of course they want to know how much work there will be. The prospects are exhilarating, but they create a good deal of anxiety as well. Will I be able to do the work? Are professors people? What will mine be like? What if I do something really dopey and humiliate myself in front of everyone? Am I the only one who feels in over my head?

Challenges are exciting when one feels some measure of confidence and support. As we saw in Part One, freshmen are more likely to feel doubtful of their abilities, isolated, and alone. A clear, informative syllabus and a carefully planned first class meeting can reduce their insecurities and get them off to a good start.

Preparing a Syllabus

When we ask students at the end of their freshman year to tell us what we might have done to help them, one of the three most frequent responses is "Provide a better syllabus." Instructors, convinced that students do not read the syllabus, find this one of the more startling things freshmen say. When anxieties run high, however, most people find structure and direction reassuring. A good syllabus—one that lets students know where the course will take them, how they are going to get there, and who is responsible for what along the way—provides such structure.

Course syllabi come in a variety of styles and sizes, and much can be learned from reviewing and comparing those prepared by colleagues. Good ones tend to be longer rather than shorter, and because the best may run several pages, we cannot reproduce them here. Speaking generally, however, a good syllabus includes the following information.

Names, Numbers, and Required Texts. Freshmen have a knack for finding themselves in the wrong place at the wrong time, and they forget names and numbers. It is easy enough to list at the start of the syllabus the course number and title, when and where it meets, the instructor's name, office location and phone number, and office hours. When it comes to introducing the texts, consider how much rides on whether students read them. It seems worth the trouble to include a few words about why required texts were chosen, how they will relate to class activities, and what students might expect to get from reading them.

Introduction to the Subject Matter. We may assume that because students have registered for a course, they know what they will be studying. Yet the content covered in many freshman courses is not obvious from titles such as General Chemistry or Introduction to Literature or Principles of Economics, and catalogue descriptions provide little elaboration. Students may read a catalogue description, register for a course, read the syllabus, and even sit through the first class without knowing what they will be studying. Students take it for granted that they will find out soon enough, but their complacency about this is not a good sign and should not be encouraged.

"What is this course about?" often leads to "Why would or should anyone want to learn this?" Freshmen take many of their courses in order to meet curricular requirements, and they bring about as much enthusiasm to the task as we might expect from people doing something that someone else has decided will be good for them. Yet, there is no getting around the relationship between motivation and learning, so we may as well address motivational issues at the outset.

The reasons freshmen give for coming to college and the objectives they claim are important do not provide much to go on. Few of us can claim direct links between our courses and better jobs or higher salaries, and we are not convinced we should even if we could. It is also true, however, that students are just as interested in what is happening in their lives right now as they are in "the good life" they envision down the road. If we can find even one or two connections between our subject matter and the questions or issues or dilemmas freshmen encounter, motivation would be strengthened. At the very least, we might mention why we find the subject matter interesting or important or otherwise worth studying. Enthusiasm may not be so contagious as some would have us believe, but it is more motivating than lack of it.

Statements of Course Goals. Because students are more likely to accomplish course goals if they know what the goals are, a syllabus should, if it does nothing else, inform students where all the reading and studying are leading. When all is said and done, what will students have gained? Knowledge, of course. But most courses aim for more—understanding, thinking, reasoning, problem solving, using one's knowledge somehow. We find it difficult enough to talk to one another about such goals. How are we to explain them to a group of students, many of whom assume "thinking" is whatever opinions one happens to hold or memorizing the thoughts of others? Not easily.

We have had some success in clarifying course goals and expanding students' definitions of learning by using an approach similar to that taken in Chapter Four. On the syllabus, faculty list course goals in the language in which they are typically stated, but clarify what would otherwise be vague and ambiguous statements by providing samples of questions that might appear on tests or assignments. The technique has much to recommend it, not the least of which is it gets students' attention by addressing one of the questions most on their minds—"What will the tests be like?"

Description of Evaluation Procedures. We may not like talking about how we evaluate learning and we may deplore students' preoccupation with grades. Nonetheless, both research and experience tell us that students work for grades, and their expectations about tests, papers, and the like largely determine what they study and how they study it. We can resist or ignore these motivational realities, or we can put them to constructive use. We urge the latter. Early discussion of what students will encounter on tests, quizzes, and paper assignments can go a long way toward reshaping their study activities and patterns.

Freshmen also want to know and should be told how their final grades will be determined. What counts? How much does each component count? How will scores or marks be tallied and converted to a final grade? Before such questions can be answered for students, we have to answer them for ourselves, and that is never easy. What should count? What are the consequences of giving this more weight and that less? Should I grade on a curve or set standards at the outset? These are troublesome questions, and we return to them in Chapter Ten, but they need to be answered and the answers should appear in the syllabus.

Preview of Class Activities and Assignments. Much of the anxiety freshmen feel springs from the expectation that college will be different without knowing how it will be different, as we noted in Chapter Two. Information about how classes will run and what students will be asked to do as preparation for class settles nerves and clarifies responsibilities. Another and perhaps more important reason exists, however, for including such information in the syllabus. Learning to think demands active involvement in practicing whatever forms thinking takes in a course. To the extent that students have learned to be passive receivers and transcribers of knowledge—and that is the portrayal emerging from studies of the nation's high schools and colleges, as we observed in Chapter One—class activities and assignments that call for active involvement are not always greeted with enthusiasm. To many freshmen, these activities seem a waste of time that would be better spent writing down what the professor says.

By itself, the syllabus is not going to convert passive learners into active ones, but it can pave the way. Some professors describe a typical class and indicate how students will be expected to prepare for class. Others describe the kinds of activities they have planned for the course and indicate why students will be asked to participate in them. Either way, including this information in the syllabus tells students that we have given some thought to course activities and that there is some method to what may seem madness.

Course Outline. One sure way to undo freshmen is to deprive them of a course outline and schedule. We do not recommend it. Freshmen depend on the course outline for structure, direction, and security. Opinions differ as to how much detail should be included and how precise the schedule should be. Freshmen tend to prefer more rather than less, but they find deviations from the schedule unsettling. In most courses, a week-by-week schedule of topics provides the structure freshmen need while allowing some flexibility for responding to their needs and interests. The course outline should, however, indicate the exact dates on which exams will be given and on which papers or other major assignments will be due. We sometimes forget that students are taking several courses and that exams fall at similar periods. Students need this information at the outset if they are to manage their time and be able to meet four or five sets of requirements.

Course Policies (or as one colleague describes it, "the fine print"). The syllabus should indicate policies governing attendance, late assignments, make-up work, safety regulations, and whatever other rules we deem necessary for the course to run smoothly. A sentence or two explaining why such policies have been adopted makes them seem less harsh or arbitrary.

Style and Tone. We need to pay some attention to style when preparing a syllabus because how we talk about course content, goals, requirements, and so forth, communicates beyond the words we say about them. A poorly written syllabus full of misspellings and punctuation errors undermines the credibility of a teacher's insistence that sloppy thinking and careless work from students will be unacceptable. A syllabus that talks about what students *should* do, *must* do, and *will* do—and what will happen if they do not do it—sets a different tone than one that talks about what students *may* do or *might want to* do. We create and convey different moods through anecdote, metaphor, parenthetical comment, quotation, and even cartoon. Good syllabi make good reading, and we can see something of the person between the lines.

A good syllabus, in sum, is more than a list of topics to be covered and assignments to be completed. At its best, a syllabus introduces the subject matter, gives a rationale for learning what is to be taught, and motivates students to do their best work. It provides an organizational framework that indicates major topics, suggests the relationships among them, and previews the order in which they will be explored. It describes how class meetings will be conducted and what students will need to do by way of preparation. It spells out how student progress will be measured, notes dates when work is due or tests are scheduled, and indicates how final grades will be assigned. And it does all this in a manner reflecting the instructor's teaching style.

Important as the syllabus is, it is only a part of getting a course off to a good beginning. Actions speak louder than words, and students will take their cues about their courses and instructors from what happens or does not happen in the first class meeting.

Meeting the First Class

If we wanted to start a course off on the wrong foot, there are several ways to do it:

1. Arrive late and then spend several minutes signing drop/add permission slips.
2. Distribute the syllabus and dismiss class.
3. Jump into the subject matter without bothering to find out anything about students.
4. Allow students to sit through the entire period without meeting even one other person in the class.
5. Lecture the entire period but tell students they should come to the next class prepared to participate in discussion.

Freshmen may be distracted, but they can still put two and two together and come up with four. Such practices do not convey messages that class time is precious, that the instructor cares about students, that the class is a community, or that their participation is important.

How do we start off on the right foot? Students want information about the course—the content, the requirements, the evaluation procedures, and so on. These matters constitute the explicit agenda for the first class meeting. Equally important is a hidden, or at least unspoken, agenda as students try to determine what the professor is like, who the other students are, how instructor and students will behave, and what climate will prevail. A good syllabus addresses items on the explicit agenda, but the hidden agenda is experiential. It, too, merits attention. In addition to distributing the syllabus, then, our agenda for the first class would include the following.

1. Find out something about students enrolled in the class. Information about their backgrounds, interests, activities, and aspirations can be helpful in planning classes. Requesting such information also suggests that the instructor is interested in students.
2. Help students meet and establish connections with other students in class. Feelings of isolation get in the way of learning.
3. Get students to talk. If they speak up on the first day, they will be more likely to participate in subsequent class meetings.
4. Include an activity that requires students to be actively involved—a problem to solve, a question to discuss, a paragraph to write. If they sit passively through the first class, they will do the same in the next.
5. Make an assignment for the second class. Some faculty are reluctant to give assignments until enrollments settle, but how are students to know what the course will be like without an assignment?

There are hundreds of ways to accomplish these tasks. We mention only a handful to sample the variety of opening-day activities and to stimulate the creation of other versions.

In small classes, we often begin by asking freshmen to introduce themselves and to say a few words about where they are from, what led them to select this college or university, what majors they are considering, why they registered for this course. Or we may ask students to talk in pairs for a few minutes, and then each student introduces his or her partner to the rest of the class. Either way, giving students a list of questions to answer helps them through the first awkward moments and encourages them to reveal more interesting things about themselves. Even the most intriguing introductions grow tedious after a while, however, so this technique is suited only to small classes.

One of the professors on our campus has developed an opening activity that is equally effective in small and in very large classes. He asks students to break into groups of three or four, to introduce themselves to others in the group, to agree on one question they would like the instructor to answer, and to write the group's question on a note card. After ten minutes, he collects the note cards, reads the questions, and answers each in turn. Freshmen become slightly more bold in groups, which is one of the advantages of this technique even in smaller classes, so a few questions go unanswered. Simply reading the questions seems to break the ice, however. "Answerable" questions range from "Where did you go to college?" to "Will we be talking about. . .?" to "If you were stranded on a deserted island, what would you most want to have with you?" (Answer: "The text for this course, because this is a good book, and speaking of that, your assignment for next time is. . .").

Another colleague, this one a scientist, uses learning styles as an entrée for introducing his course. After students complete Kolb's Learning Style Inventory and tally their scores, he outlines Kolb's version of the "learning cycle" and explains that high scores indicate the phases of the learning cycle where students are likely to feel most at home and will probably prefer. He then talks specifically about his course and where the various activities and assignments fall on the learning cycle—the small-group discussions, laboratory experiments and reports, team research projects, and even exams. Along the way, he asks students to look at their learning-style scores and to make some notes to themselves about which activities and assignments are likely to seem easy and enjoyable to them and which might feel more difficult and require more concentration, persistence, and support. Afterward, he asks students to form groups of four, to compare their learning-style scores, and to talk about whether those scores ring true. For most students, they do. Even when they do not, the activity nonetheless accomplishes most of the tasks on the experiential agenda.

The Professional and Organizational Development Network used a variation of a scavenger hunt to encourage people to meet their colleagues at the opening of a conference, and the activity is easily adapted for classroom use. Give each student a sheet of paper with these instructions:

> Find other students who have done the activities listed below and write their names on the lines provided. To make things a bit more challenging (and to make sure you meet more of your classmates), a student's name can appear only once on the sheet. The first student to fill in all the blanks or the student who has the most blanks filled after 15 minutes wins the scavenger hunt.

Possibilities include:

> Has studied another language.
> Grew up in another state.
> Has done volunteer work.
> Hopes to major in . . .
> Knows who wrote "Leaves of Grass."
> Can name all the state capitals.
> Has acted in or directed a play.
> Plays a musical instrument.
> Has already bought the text for this course.

Distributing several versions of the activity list in a class achieves the best results. To follow up, collect the sheets, make a summary list of all the students named for each activity, and distribute copies during the second class.

An activity we have used to open workshops with faculty, who have in turn used the activity with their students, originally appeared in the group dynamics literature as a strategy for creating group norms and for developing discussion skills. Group members are told that each of them will receive a card or cards containing a clue to a murder mystery. If they put all the clues together, they will be able to solve the mystery—that is, to determine the victim, the murderer, the weapon, the time of the murder, where it took place, and the motive. People can read or paraphrase their clues for the group, but they may not show their cards to other members, which guarantees that everyone will contribute at least once. After the group has solved the mystery, members are asked to discuss three questions: (1) What happened in your group that enabled you to solve the mystery so effectively? (2) What did your group do that sometimes got in the way of progress? (3) Based on what you said, what ground rules might we establish for discussion in this course? The activity is fun, it gets everyone talking, and a basic premise of group theory is that members are more likely to abide by the rules if they set them. (For instructions and clues for the murder mystery, see Stanford and Stanford, 1969, pp. 23–26, or Johnson and Johnson, 1975, pp. 121–122.)

Not everyone is comfortable spending class time in activities unrelated to the subject matter, and many of the most creative first-class activities are those that faculty tailor to fit their course content. An English professor, for example, developed a variation of the mystery exercise for an introductory course in poetry. Students form groups of six, and each is given a card containing one line of a six-line poem (Levertov's "Leaving Forever"). Students must first reassemble the poem (students may not show their cards to anyone, so they have to read the lines aloud) and then decide what the poem means to them. After fifteen minutes or so, most groups have completed the tasks and are ready to compare notes. In the discussion that follows, the instructor asks whether students found it easy or difficult to reassemble the poem, how they determined the order of the lines, and what meanings the poem conveyed. The exercise is a fruitful one, not only because it gets students to talk and offers a taste of what is to come, but also because it leads to a powerful punch line. At the end of class, the instructor can point out that students have successfully read a poem, talked about its poetic elements, and interpreted its meaning on their own.

A sociologist tells us that if we want some interesting glimpses of what and how students think about societies (or a variety of other topics for that matter), we should look at what they regard as important in history. During his first class meeting, he asks students to break into groups of three to five and to list the ten most important events—or, alternatively, the ten most important people—in history. After ten to fifteen minutes, he polls the groups and notes their responses on the board. Their lists are fairly predictable, but nonetheless interesting and especially so to students. The events or people named are almost always modern if not recent; rarely does a group list something or someone before 1500. They are disproportionately American, occasionally European, but never Asian or African. "Important" history is made in political or military arenas; literature, art, music, do not make the lists. The instructor uses these lists, not to scold students for what they do not know, but rather as an entrée to reflections on what Americans do know, how they have come to know it, what the limits of their world views might be, and why the study of sociology will ask them to think about other societies, other sources of information about society, and other times in history.

In the sciences, experiments and demonstrations are naturals for first-class activities. They are dramatic, they play to students' curiosities, and it is hard to resist becoming involved in figuring out why something happens. Freshmen in an introductory chemistry course, for example, spend part of the first class watching their instructor perform an experiment while they record data—changes in temperature, color, mass, or some other indicator of a chemical reaction. After the experiment has run, students meet in small groups to discuss their observations, to formulate hypotheses about the identity of the reactants and the nature of the reaction, and to propose additional experiments that would enable them to confirm or reject their hypotheses. Before class concludes, each group reports its hypotheses and proposals for further experiments. Students are asked to decide (or to think about for next time) which experiments they would run first and why.

In an introductory biology course for nonmajors, the instructor uses case-study discussions from time to time to show students that the subject matter really does have some relevance to nonscience majors. The cases are all based on actual events. The case for the first class—and also the last class—is drawn from a newspaper account of a rape trial in which the prosecuting attorney based his argument on positive identification by the victim and DNA fingerprinting. The defense attorney's argument turned on the high moral character of the accused, an ironclad alibi, and the fact that DNA fingerprinting is not universally accepted by the scientific community. After reading the case, students are asked to discuss two questions in small groups: (1) If, as jurors, you were permitted to ask three questions of the expert witness on DNA fingerprinting, what would they be? (2) If you were not permitted to ask questions, what is your jury's verdict? Before the end of class, the instructor polls the groups, posts their verdicts, and lists their questions. Students find it difficult to reach a verdict and their questions reflect little knowledge about DNA fingerprinting, but they leave class more eager to learn about DNA.

First-class activities vary enormously, and we encourage creativity. Our point is that whatever occurs, the first class sets the stage for the rest of the course. Once the instructor and students assume their roles and the action begins, the plot may thicken and the characters may develop, but it is too late to alter the script dramatically. A good syllabus is an important prop in the first class meeting because it communicates details about course requirements and policies that otherwise might take an entire class period to convey—a practice to be avoided because it assigns students to relatively passive roles and does not leave time for other actions and interaction. Equally important to information about the course are activities that ask students to assume active roles, that encourage them to interact with one another, that get them over the hurdle of making a first contribution in class, that sample the ways in which classes will be conducted—the experiential agenda.

6

Presenting and Explaining

To most college students and faculty, teaching is lecturing. That equation makes sense if the aim is to transmit information that students are to remember for exams. Research indicates that the lecture is about as effective as other teaching methods when recall of information is tested. The lecture turns out to be less effective than other methods, however, when instructional goals include retention of information beyond the end of the course, application of information, development of thinking skills, modification of attitudes, or motivation for further learning (McKeachie, Pintrich, Lin, and Smith, 1986). In other words, there is more to effective teaching than lecturing.

We have titled this chapter "Presenting and Explaining" in order to put the lecture in its proper place as a method for presenting information that students are to remember, for explaining by way of example, and for demonstrating how one might use the information to solve problems or think through a variety of situations. Presenting and explaining are rarely sufficient when the goals call for understanding or thinking, but a clear explanation or demonstration is often a good place to start instruction.

Before suggesting some things faculty might do to improve their presentations, we explore briefly how the mind works—or at least, how psychologists currently think the mind works. A passing acquaintance with the research on cognition sheds some light on what students are doing (or should be doing) while their instructors are presenting and explaining and sets the stage for the recommendations that follow. Our discussion will be brief, so we suggest consulting other sources for additional information (Ericksen, 1984; Fuhrmann and Grasha, 1983; Kurfiss, 1988; McKeachie, 1986; McKeachie, Pintrich, Lin, and Smith, 1986; Norman, 1982).

How We Process Information

We do not see things as they are or hear things as they are said, and it is not because we pay too little attention. Amazing as the human brain is, it is nonetheless limited in its capacity to apprehend the world as it is. We catch bits and pieces, work them over, and reconstruct what registers on our senses. To use the metaphor that currently dominates the study of cognition, we "process information" as we perceive it, and apparently we process it in stages.

When we first encounter information, we take it into "short-term memory," where it is stored while we try to make sense of it. Short-term memory is severely limited, however, in the amount of information it can hold—usually not more than seven plus or minus two pieces of information. And information cannot be stored there for very long; we have only a few seconds to make some sense of it before we lose it.

A simple experiment illustrates both the limits and the possibilities for short-term memory. Show the following sequence of thirteen letters to a few colleagues, let them look at it for a few seconds, and then ask them to recite the sequence of letters: SATIQGPAABCDF. Chances are good that they will not be able to repeat the sequence accurately. Then, repeat the experiment, but present the letters as follows: SAT IQ GPA ABCDF. Most faculty will exhibit perfect recall of the sequence, because the information is organized into chunks that are meaningful to them. By presenting the information in chunks, we reduce the load on short-term memory from thirteen pieces of information to four. Because the chunks already have meaning for most faculty, it takes only a few seconds to make sense of them. Thus, chunking material and making it meaningful are two ways to extend the limits of short-term memory.

If the information in short-term memory has meaning or can be made meaningful, it is transferred to "long-term memory." Long-term memory is a lot like the filing system many of us use.

We collect ideas and information, put them in a file, and affix a label indicating the file's contents. Barring flood, fire, or a compulsion to clean, those files and their contents are there forever. In theory, we should be able to pull out their contents whenever we need them, months and even years later. In practice, we do not label our files very well, and we rarely cross-reference their contents. More often than not, we cannot find information when we want it. The information in long-term memory often suffers the same fate. If it is "filed" in isolated bits, the chances of remembering it are about as good as finding an unlabeled ten-year-old set of notes in your file.

If the information in long-term memory is organized around meaningful concepts and if those concepts are connected, the chances of retrieving the information go way up. When we encounter a new problem or question, we recognize some cue that prompts us to recall one of those interconnected concepts. The concept we initially retrieve may not be the one we need, but one thought leads to another, and eventually we find the needed information. Thus, our abilities to think and to solve problems depend a great deal on whether the information and ideas in long-term memory are interconnected.

When presenting and explaining course content, then, we must be concerned about two issues. First, only meaningful information is transferred to long-term memory, so we need to be sure students are making sense of what we are presenting. A word of caution is in order here because we sometimes forget that meaning does not reside in the material. Those of us schooled in American education systems quickly make sense of SAT and GPA, but those sequences of letters may have little or no meaning to faculty in other educational systems.

Second, we need to be concerned—much more than many of us appear to be—about what students do with the information and ideas stored in long-term memory. Ideally, students continue to process the information. They extend, elaborate, and integrate new ideas by thinking of other examples, considering them in other contexts, and testing them against what they already know. Along the way, they reconsider previous experiences and prior learning, see new meaning in those events and ideas, and revise the ways they have interpreted or connected them. Students who engage in these activities, which cognitive psychologists call "deep processing," are more likely to be able to remember information in a variety of contexts and problems.

In reality, many students engage in what psychologists term "surface processing." Students set out to learn information exactly as it is presented. They memorize phrases and definitions verbatim. They consider only those examples and problems that the instructor happens to present. They do little to elaborate and extend the meaning of ideas or to relate them to what they already know. The information is stored in long-term memory, but it is inaccessible unless the prompts to retrieve it—the questions or problems or contexts—closely resemble those the instructor presented during discussion.

Research on memory and retention underscores the limits of presenting and explaining. In the end, students must become actively involved in elaborating the meaning of ideas and connecting them with other information stored in long-term memory. We cannot do these things for students, no matter how good our lectures are. We can, however, inhibit or encourage students to process information at these deeper levels.

Suggestions for Presenting and Explaining

Many of our suggestions for presenting and explaining boil down to two pieces of advice: Avoid practices that lead to surface processing; adopt practices that promote and support deep processing.

Abandon the Nonstop Fifty-Minute Lecture. This suggestion is probably the most important thing we could do to improve learning, but even well-intentioned faculty find it hard to give up the nonstop lecture. Our content is important, and we can cover a lot of it in class if we are not interrupted. Most acknowledge that it makes no sense to cover material if students do not understand it and will not remember it. Nonetheless, covering content is a powerful drive, and it often rules the day, usually at the expense of activities that would result in greater learning.

Compulsions to cover so much material in class are usually counterproductive, but they are especially destructive in freshman courses. They reinforce the passive listening, verbatim note-taking, and superficial information-processing strategies that many freshmen bring to college. Students need to learn course content, to be sure, but freshmen also need to be weaned away from their conviction that it cannot be important if it was not covered in class—and we need to give up our apparent belief that students cannot learn it unless we say it. Once students develop the deep-processing strategies noted earlier, they will be able to get more from reading and to process information faster during lectures. Meanwhile, we need to restrain our inclination to cover everything in class and to give up those nonstop lectures.

A more productive use of class time is to present for no longer than ten or fifteen minutes at a stretch and then provide time for students to work with the ideas before moving on. McKeachie (1986) reports research indicating that students remember about 70 percent of the information presented during the first ten minutes of a lecture, but only 20 percent of the material covered during the last ten minutes. Minds begin to wander after about ten minutes. Daydreams are sometimes the lures, but students often tune out because the information is coming too fast and they have no time to think. Most of us have caught ourselves not hearing what a speaker is saying because we were thinking about an idea presented earlier.

Ten minutes is usually enough time to introduce a concept or procedure and to provide an example or two. Then students need time to think about the ideas—to summarize the material in their own words, to come up with their own examples, to try using the ideas to solve a problem or analyze a situation. Once students have tried their hands at working with the material, we can come back to elaborate and extend or to move on to the next topic.

Define Objectives. After identifying two or three topics to be explained in class, we need to decide what students should then be able to do with the information. Will they merely need to remember definitions, procedures, factual information? Should they be able to recognize new examples or illustrations? Will they be asked to use the information somehow? A clear vision of what students should be able to do with information presented indicates what the presentation itself must include and points to the questions, problems, or tasks that should follow.

Plan an Introduction. A good introduction does two things: it captures students' attention, and it focuses it on the objectives— usually in that order. Generally, questions are more interesting than answers, the unexpected is more intriguing than the expected, the personal seems more important than the impersonal, and curiosity is a great motivator. The problem with many lectures is that they do not play to curiosities. They jump to conclusions, solutions, and resolutions before raising the issues, posing the problems, or draw- ing the tensions. Students have no time to become curious or to see how course material relates to things about which they are already curious. They would pay more attention if they did.

More interesting lectures open with a problem, question, quandary, or dilemma; if it is grounded in students' experiences, all the better. Or they start with something students take for granted and confront them with information or observations indicating things are not so obvious or certain as they initially appear. Or they present a list of incongruous facts or statistics and ask, "How can this be?" They start with an experiment or a film clip and ask, "What is going on here?" They remind students of a campus inci- dent or current event and promise that the day's material will shed some light on it.

The first order of business is to get students' attention; the second is to focus it on the objectives. Knowing what they will be expected to do with information presented in class influences how students listen to those presentations. Most freshmen assume that they will be asked to recall the information, so they go to great lengths to get it all down in their notes, and they memorize every definition, example, and detail presented. Many freshmen assume that is all there is to it. Thus, they do not attend to instructions on how to recognize or use the information in new contexts, nor do they engage in the thinking activities—the extending, elaborating, relating—that might prepare them to cope with new problems or situations. Telling students what the objectives are for each class— what they should know and what they will be asked to do with what they know—is a first step toward transforming the ways they listen to lectures and think about the ideas presented.

Highlight the Major Points. Key ideas may be obvious to those who have worked with the material for years, but they are not obvious to freshmen. At least once, every faculty member should try asking students at the end of class to jot down the main ideas discussed that day. The results are often shocking, but they are instructive. Freshmen have trouble distinguishing generalizations from examples, conclusions from evidence, trends from isolated events, the main idea from the details that surround it. If the examples, evidence, isolated events, and details are vivid and compelling, as they should be, students are even more likely to forget what is being exemplified. The ability to sort out these things comes with experience with the subject matter. Meanwhile, students lament after exams that they "studied the wrong things." Outlining key ideas on the board or on a transparency, reviewing them periodically, and summarizing them at the end of class are good strategies for highlighting major points. It also helps to label explicitly generalizations and examples, conclusions and evidence, and so forth.

Select Appropriate Examples. Much of what we learn, we learn by way of example, illustration, or demonstration. Indeed, some evidence suggests that what we retrieve from memory is not the definition of a concept or statement of a principle. Rather, we remember some prototype example and use it to reconstruct definitions and relationships (Norman, 1982; Park, 1984). Good teachers know the power of a telling example, and they go to great lengths to find one. Several considerations merit attention when selecting examples.

First, it is crucial that the examples and illustrations do, in fact, embody the key ideas students are to remember. Examples should clearly depict the characteristics that define concepts, demonstrations should clearly show how principles or laws look in action, and models for problem solving or reasoning should clearly indicate critical considerations and procedural steps. We cannot afford to settle for examples or illustrations or demonstrations that miss or muddy some critical point because students are using these examples to construct the prototypes they store in memory.

Second, explanations should begin with relatively clear-cut examples and should gradually introduce more complex and subtle illustrations. The first task is to show the key properties or relationships. If the early examples are too complicated, abstract, or unfamiliar, students get lost in the complexities and lose sight of the key ideas. On the other hand, if all the examples and problems are simple ones, students will not learn to handle more complex situations.

Third, examples, illustrations, and problems should be drawn from a variety of situations and settings. The hope is that if students see a few good examples or illustrations, they will be able to transfer their learning to new situations and problems. It is an optimistic hope because research shows that not much transfer of learning occurs even in the best instructional circumstances. It appears, however, that the ability to transfer improves if the examples and problems used during instruction sample the range of contexts in which students should eventually be able to use the information.

Fourth, most of us underestimate the number of examples and illustrations that students require. The concepts and relationships we teach are highly complex, abstract, and usually unfamiliar to students. Yet we assume students will understand them after seeing two or three examples. Eventually, when we give an assignment or exam, we discover how foolhardy our assumptions are. How many examples and illustrations does it take? Obviously, the answer depends on the material and will differ for individual students. One way to find out if students have seen enough is to pose one more example and ask them to explain how it illustrates a concept or how they would solve the problem. If they cannot do it, they need more illustrations and practice.

Finally, we should have available in our notes a few more good examples than we anticipate using. Having a sufficient number of good examples avoids the embarrassment of being unable to produce one on the spur of the moment if needed or of creating one that confuses or misleads rather than clarifies.

Discuss Examples. It is important to state explicitly how examples, illustrations, and demonstrations relate to the broader generalizations they are intended to exemplify. Students need help in recognizing how particular examples embody the characteristics of conceptual categories—what features of a painting make it an example of Impressionist art, what specifics exist in a novel that lead us to call it an initiation story, why we classify a chemical reaction as oxidation-reduction. In the absence of explicit cues, students may attend to other details in the example, mistakenly take them as the characteristics that define the concept, and totally miss the important points. Similarly, students often get so caught up in watching their instructors solve particular problems that they miss the problem-solving procedures and steps that the instructor intends to demonstrate. Presenting the example, illustration, or demonstration is an important step. Explaining how the particular relates to the general increases the likelihood that students will get the point.

Use Visual Aids. We process information better and faster through the eye than the ear (McKeachie, 1986). Playing to both senses increases attention and facilitates learning. Outlines, diagrams, flow charts, and concept maps highlight key ideas and show their relationships. Slides, videotapes, and films present examples far more vividly than do verbal descriptions alone. A single slide can provide visual focus for defining a concept; a series of four or five can trace a course of events. Videotape, videodisc, and film offer ways to bring life outside the classroom into it, to magnify the microscopic, to quicken or slow the pace of time. Students learn more from watching an experiment run than from hearing it described. Granted, searching for visual aids is time consuming, and there is often an initial expense, but most can be used semester after semester. It is usually worth the trouble.

Guide Note Taking. By and large, freshmen are not good note takers. They furiously try to get down every word that is said, often without a thought about any of it. They ask that relatively unimportant details be repeated, but if instructors ask about an important point just made, answers are nowhere to be found. If we chance to look at their notebooks, the errors and omissions are disturbing. The only thing more depressing than their lack of skill in taking notes is their belief in them. Some students measure learning by the number of pages filled in their notebooks. Because people do not generally abandon bad habits until they have better ones to replace them, telling students to stop taking verbatim notes will likely be ignored. We will have more success if we think in terms of "weaning" freshmen from verbatim note-taking habits. To that end, here are three suggestions.

First, provide a skeletal outline of the main points covered (point by point as you come to them or all at once at the outset) and allow time for students to get the outline in their notes. The outline will provide the basic structure freshmen need.

Second, pause from time to time and ask students to paraphrase what they have written in their notes in their own words, as if they were telling a friend—to rewrite definitions, to restate relationships, to retell an example. Freshmen often find this difficult to do, and they will need more time for it in the beginning. It is time well spent, however. Paraphrasing is a step toward making material meaningful, and developing this skill will increase understanding and retention.

Third, encourage students to elaborate their notes by completing thoughts such as: "Another example of this might be . . ." "The last time I saw a problem like this was . . ." "I remember talking about this issue with . . ." "This information might explain why . . ." Such prompts encourage students to forge connections between new material and what they already know, another step toward meaning, understanding, and retention.

Several of the writing-to-learn techniques discussed in the next chapter are also useful in helping students develop better note-taking strategies. Other suggestions appear in Chapter Thirteen (see also Carrier, 1983, and Kiewra, 1987). More generally, attention to how freshmen take notes is important not so much because students need to have good notes. If that were all, we could simply hand out copies of our notes. What matters is that note taking provides a tangible focus for efforts to engage students in processing information more deeply.

Check for Understanding. If the aim of presenting and explaining is better understanding, it makes sense to stop now and then to see if students are understanding. Pausing to ask "Are there any questions?" is better than nothing—but not much. In order for students to respond to this invitation, they must both recognize (and admit) that they have not fully understood and also be able to formulate a question quickly. Carefully planned and smoothly presented explanations tend to lull students into complacency. Not until later, when they review their notes or try an assignment, do they realize that they have missed or misunderstood something critical. Much time and energy are lost when faculty and students have to go back over material explained two days or two months earlier.

A more efficient and effective strategy is for the instructor to ask the questions and for students to try to answer them. "We have gone over several examples. Look at one more, and you tell me whether it illustrates this concept and why." "We have worked through several problems. Now you try one just to make sure you understand." When students try to answer questions on their own, they frequently discover that things are not so simple or so obvious as they thought and that they do not fully understand after all. At that point, they may be ready to respond to the invitation, "Are there any questions?"

Summarize. Sometimes a lecture tailored for a particular class of students is clearer and more understandable than a text, but only if we compensate for what is lost when students must listen to rather than read an explanation. When they read, students control the pace of ideas, stopping often to retrace their steps—to look more closely at an idea passed by too quickly, to reassure themselves that they read it right the first time. When they listen to a lecture, however, students do not control the pacing or retracing. They stop to think—at least the best ones do—but the presentation continues. Students miss a phrase here, a sentence there, sometimes a whole paragraph. They need to go over it again, but in a lecture they cannot scan a paragraph or turn back to a page. They can only hope that the instructor will repeat the information and review the important points. Frequent repetition and periodic summaries throughout a class meeting compensate for having no pages to turn back.

A summary at the end of class is also important. Although time seems to pass more quickly near the end of class, we cannot afford to run out of time before a conclusion for the class is reached. Too often, freshmen report that "the class was interesting but I didn't see the point" or "there was a lot of discussion, but we didn't really learn anything."

A strong conclusion does three things. It reviews the major ideas, those ideas that provide the conceptual framework for organizing illustrations, elaborations, details. Second, the conclusion reminds students what they should be able to do with the information now that they have heard it. Finally, a strong conclusion includes an assignment designed to give students practice in doing whatever it is they should be able to do.

Get Feedback. It makes sense to ask students for help in determining what is working and what merits some attention. Taking five minutes at the end of a class to ask students to summarize the ideas presented, to solve a sample problem, or to apply information to a new situation are good strategies for finding out what students understood and what they did not. We need not do it every class, but collecting such feedback from time to time is useful in tracking student learning.

Similarly, asking students to take five minutes to write their reactions to the day's class and doing so several times during the semester can help instructors know what they might do to strengthen instruction for a particular class of students. We conclude this chapter with a questionnaire (Exhibit 1) that our faculty have found useful in collecting feedback from students. Faculty like it because it focuses on a single class, it takes only five minutes to complete, it can be used several times during the semester, and it seems to elicit constructive feedback. The survey's questions reflect the issues raised in this chapter and summarize our suggestions for presenting and explaining.

Exhibit 1. Class Reaction Survey.

I would like to know your reactions to today's class. Please read each of the statements below and circle the letter corresponding to the response that best matches your reaction in today's class. Your choices are:

a. No improvement is needed. (Terrific! This works for me. Keep it up.)
b. Little improvement is needed. (Maybe a ragged edge or two, but don't lose any sleep over it.)
c. Improvement is needed. (Not awful, but this merits some attention.)
d. Considerable improvement is needed. (This is causing me problems. Please help.)

Today, the instructor

a b c d 1. Limited what was covered to a manageable amount of material
a b c d 2. Made it clear why the material might be important
a b c d 3. Told us what we would be expected to do with the material (memorize it, use it to solve problems, or whatever)
a b c d 4. Highlighted key ideas or questions
a b c d 5. Presented plenty of good examples to clarify difficult material
a b c d 6. Provided enough variety to keep us reasonably alert
a b c d 7. Found ways to let us know whether we were understanding the material
a b c d 8. Helped us summarize the main ideas we were supposed to take away from class
a b c d 9. Let us know how we might be tested on the material
a b c d 10. Provided exercises or an assignment so that we could practice using the material

11. What is your overall rating of today's class?
   A Excellent
   B Good
   C Satisfactory
   D Fair
   E Poor

12. What made you rate today's class as high as you did?

13. What kept you from rating today's class higher?

7

Encouraging
Student Involvement
in the Classroom

Although we have much yet to learn about how understanding and the ability to think develop, one thing is clear: practice is an essential ingredient. As Edgerton remarks, "Students learn *about* things by being told; they learn how to *do* things by doing them" (1987, p. 13). Based on an extensive review of theory and research in problem solving and creativity, Frederiksen (1984) concluded, "The theory and research reviewed shows that it is possible after much practice to perform remarkable feats of problem solving. Such skill is developed primarily through a great deal of practice and it is specific to a relatively narrow area of expertise, such as algebra, mechanics, or chess. There appears to be little if any transfer from one domain to another, being an expert in chess apparently does not transfer to *go,* and skill in solving physics problems does not transfer to politics or economics. However, a given individual may acquire such skill in a number of domains" (p. 391). More recent reviews (Kurfiss, 1988; McKeachie, Pintrich, Lin, and Smith, 1986) reach the same conclusions. Instruction for thinking and problem solving must take place within subject-matter domains and must engage students in practice.

In suggesting methods and techniques for getting students involved, we have in mind those factors that appear to promote the development of thinking skills: practice, student discussion, explicit attention to problem-solving steps and procedures, and verbalization of how one is thinking (McKeachie, Pintrich, Lin, and Smith, 1986). At the same time, we recognize the expectations and assumptions about teaching and learning that freshmen bring to their courses (see Chapter Three), and their particular needs prompt many of our suggestions about how to use these methods in freshman courses.

Small-Group Discussion Methods

When we think about class discussion, we usually envision an instructor posing questions and providing direction for an exchange of ideas involving all students in the class. The conventional seminar discussion is designed for small classes of twelve to fifteen students, not for freshman courses where enrollments are typically higher, and attempts to use it in these settings often spell disaster. We need not, however, abandon discussion in freshman courses. Small-group methods offer practical alternatives for engaging students in discussion no matter what the class size.

To use small-group discussions, the instructor divides the class into groups of three to five students. Each group is given a question or problem and asked to prepare a group response within a specified time. While students discuss the task, the instructor moves from group to group, monitoring students' progress, offering help when they need it, and noting areas of confusion for later review. When time is up, the instructor reconvenes the class and asks the groups (or a sample of them) to report their answers or conclusions. Depending on the nature of the task, group reports may stand as given, call for feedback or comment from the instructor, or stimulate further exploration and discussion.

Using small groups effectively is not quite so simple as that description implies, of course. The method requires careful planning, experimentation, and practice. We offer the following small-group activities as examples; they were contributed by faculty from diverse disciplines, and the tasks represent practice for a variety of learning outcomes. Additional suggestions are given at the end of the chapter.

Chemistry. Each group will receive a beaker containing NH_4Cl, a second beaker containing water, and a sponge. First, dissolve the NH_4Cl with water. Then place a few drops of water on the damp sponge and set the beaker on it. Record what happens. Then explain your observations using the thermodynamic and chemical reaction theories we've discussed.

Philosophy. Suppose that you are taking your nightly walk and come upon a burning house. The firemen believe there is a baby in one of the rooms upstairs but cannot get close enough because of the intense heat. You dash into the building and save the baby. Rescuing the baby clearly has a high utility, but would the act of continuing on your walk have been wrong? Why or why not? How does your response compare to what an Act Utilitarian would say?

Mathematics. Exercise 13 in the applied maximum and minimum problems tells you that "A parcel delivery service will only accept parcels such that the sum of the length and girth is at most 96 inches. (Girth is the perimeter of a cross section taken perpendicular to the longest dimension.) Find the maximum acceptable volume of (a) a rectangular parcel with square ends, (b) a cylindrical parcel" [Fraleigh, 1986, pp. 184–185]. Try working this problem in groups of three. As you work, ask one member of your group to write down each step you take and why you are taking it.

English. In order to explore how authors use different techniques for revealing and developing character, each of your groups will work on one of the following questions about Virginia Woolf's *Mrs. Dalloway*. (1) What impressions or insights do you have about Mrs. Dalloway based on what she reveals to the reader about herself? Support your comments by identifying

passages in which she expresses her thoughts and feelings directly to the reader. (2) What impressions or
insights do you have about Mrs. Dalloway based on
the way you see her in interactions with other characters? Find excerpts in which her interactions with
other characters provide insights into her character.
(3) What impressions or insights do you have about
Mrs. Dalloway based upon the imagery that the author associates with her? Identify passages in which
the author uses images to describe her or in which the
author has Mrs. Dalloway using imagery. After you've
completed your part of the analysis, we'll compare
notes and summarize what we know about Mrs. Dalloway so far.

Art History. The slide you are viewing is a reproduc-
tion of *The Scream* by Edvard Munch. In order to
practice your interpretive skills, work with other
members of your group to write an interpretive statement that includes an idea, feeling, or attitude conveyed in the painting. Then develop and support your
interpretive statement by summarizing how each of
the following contribute to the idea or feeling: (1) styl-
ization; (2) postures or facial expressions of figures; (3)
setting; (4) relationship of the figures to the environment; (5) relationship of the figures to each other; (6)
color; (7) line and shape.

Small-group methods have some advantages over the other
methods discussed in this chapter. First, they invite all students, not
just those few who are verbally assertive, to participate in discussions. Second, they allow students to collect their thoughts and talk
them over with peers before venturing a contribution to the whole
class, an advantage not only for shy students but also for the "ex-
travert" learning styles discussed in Chapter Three. Third, small-
group methods enable us to interact, if not with individual students,
at least with small groups of them. We may not be able to visit every
small group in every class meeting, but over time, we can talk to

most of the small groups. Because of these advantages, many faculty use small-group discussions in combination with other methods, either as a warm-up or a follow-up activity.

Case Study Methods

A case study tells a story, complete with characters and actions, tensions and conflicts, ambiguities and dilemmas, problems and questions. When used as a focus for discussion, case studies often bridge the gap between theory and practice or between the abstract and the concrete.

Case study discussions can vary enormously, and two dimensions of this variation are worth noting when using case methods with freshmen. First, the cases themselves can range in length and complexity. Some will be short—a paragraph or two presenting a fairly well-defined problem in its barest outlines. Other cases may be quite long, often several pages, telling complicated stories rich in detail, with all the ambiguity and confusion of "real life."

Second, case study discussions may differ in the amount of structure and guidance the instructor provides. At one extreme, faculty might pose a series of questions that lead students step by step through an analysis of the case. At the other, students may simply be asked to "analyze the case," and the opening question would be something like "What do you want to say about this case?" Students are on their own to identify the issues and structure the discussion, making this a useful strategy for providing practice in dealing with the kind of ill-structured situations that are described in Chapter Four.

Room exists for a full range of case study discussions in a college curriculum, but probably not in freshman courses. Students do not learn to handle real-life situations by being overwhelmed by detail, totally confused about what they are supposed to do, and completely at sea about where to start. Shorter cases with less detail and more structure and direction are appropriate for freshmen. A philosophy professor, for example, created the following case by extracting an ethical dilemma from a literary source.

In Victor Hugo's *Les Misérables,* the hero, Jean Valjean, is an ex-convict living illegally under an assumed name and wanted for a robbery he committed many years ago. Although if he is caught he will be returned to the galleys, probably for life, he is a good man who does not deserve to be punished. He has established himself in a town, becoming mayor and a public benefactor. One day, Jean learns that another man, a vagabond, has been arrested for a minor crime and identified as Jean Valjean. Jean is first tempted to remain quiet, reasoning to himself that because he had nothing to do with the false identification of the vagabond, he has no obligation to save him. Perhaps the man's false identification is "an act of Providence meant to save me," Jean thinks. Upon reflection, however, Jean judges such reasoning as "monstrous and hyprocritical." He then feels certain that it is his duty to reveal his identity, regardless of the disastrous personal consequences. His resolve is disturbed, however, as he reflects on the shattering and irreparable harm his return to the galleys will mean to so many people, especially to the orphaned child in his care. He now reproaches himself for being too selfish, for thinking of his own conscience and not of others' needs. The right thing to do, he now claims to himself, is to remain quiet, to continue to make money, and to use it to help others. The vagabond, he comforts himself, will not do so much good. In the end, Jean Valjean is unconvinced by his own arguments and tormented by the decision he must make. He goes to the trial and confesses his identity.

The question is, "Did Jean Valjean do the right thing?" Before you answer the question for yourselves, decide how a Utilitarian would answer it and explain how a Utilitarian would reach that conclusion. Then point out which features of the case the Utilitarian analysis ignores but which a Deontologist would think are critical. Finally, decide how you would answer the question and explain why.

In mathematics, case studies are more sophisticated versions of the "story problem," and they serve similar purposes. They provide opportunities for students to practice mathematical reasoning skills, not just computational skills, and they indicate the variety of contexts in which mathematical reasoning might be required.

> The manager of a high-volume discount store has just received a huge shipment of cheap VCRs. The manufacturer who shipped them sometimes tries to unload a batch of "factory seconds"; that is, 45 percent of the VCRs are defective in some way. A normal shipment contains only 22 percent defectives. The manufacturer will allow the discount store to return any shipment, no questions asked, so long as the discount store pays the relatively small shipping charge. Testing VCRs is pretty expensive, so the manager doesn't want to test every one, but she does want to take a small sample and test them. If less than 30 percent of them are defective, she will accept the shipment. Otherwise, she will pay the shipping charges and send them back.
>
> What is the smallest number of VCRs she can sample and be 99.75 percent certain not to accept a shipment of "factory seconds." As you work through this problem, talk about the steps you are taking and why you are taking them. After you've solved the problem, write out explicit instructions on how to solve the problem, including the reason for each step toward the solution.

Zeakes (1989) describes a use of case studies in biology that engages students first in the creation of case studies and then in discussion of cases prepared by classmates. The student-created cases not only provided practice exercises for class discussion, but students also had to solve additional cases as homework. Although the strategy was used in a course for sophomores, juniors, and seniors, it seems appropriate for freshmen courses as well. Dooley and Skinner (1977) offer a good review of the purposes case study methods may serve, and Christensen and Hansen (1987) provide a useful bibliography for those interested in case methods.

Role-Playing Methods

Like case studies, role-playing exercises pose a real life situation or problem. Role-playing methods differ, however, in that they place students in the situations and ask them to assume the roles of the characters in the story. One role-playing strategy has a few students participating in the role play while the rest of the class observes. This approach allows the instructor to focus everyone's attention on one way to deal with a situation at a time and provides a common ground for discussion afterward. Its major drawback is that most students are placed in observer roles, which easily become passive roles, while only a few students actually practice wrestling with an issue or conflict.

An alternative is to divide students into groups, to assign each student one of the roles, and to run concurrent role-playing exercises. On the positive side, this approach involves more students more actively in coping with the role-play situation and often elicits a richer variety of responses for discussion afterward. The followup discussions are a bit more difficult to orchestrate, however, because students are reflecting on somewhat different experiences.

Whichever approach we choose, we set the stage by presenting a situation—the setting, the characters, and some action that has led or might lead to a conflict, a problem, or a dilemma. Students are asked to assume the roles of the characters and to act out the rest of the drama—knowing what their characters would know, thinking as their characters would think, and acting and interacting as their characters would act and interact. After the role play, students discuss the issues, actions, feelings, or interactions depicted.

McKeachie (1986), for example, describes a role-playing activity designed to involve students in comparing and contrasting two theoretical views, in this case Skinner's and Freud's. The activity asks students to imagine that Skinner, Freud, and a student are talking about a newspaper report that a baseball player punched his manager. The student notes that the player has been in trouble for fighting before and asks what should be done about him, and thus the stage is set for the role play. Several of the examples of small-group and case-study exercises presented earlier lend themselves to similar role-playing situations. Instead of talking *about* how different theorists would respond to particular situations, students assume the roles of those theorists and talk to one another or to some neutral character.

Another approach to role playing asks all students to assume essentially the same role—a task force, a committee of advisers, members of a consulting firm, or some other collection of "experts"—and to interact with the instructor, who assumes the role of the "novice." An economics professor, for example, often breaks the class into small groups and asks the groups to imagine they are economic advisory committees to the governor. Drawing on newspaper reports of economic events or trends, the instructor creates scenarios in which the governor must make decisions or comment publicly on the reports, but first wants advice from the "economic advisory committees." The committees have ten or fifteen minutes to decide what they will advise, before the instructor, playing the role of governor, asks for their recommendations.

This type of role-playing exercise offers one way to resolve the problem of getting all students actively involved without having several role plays going on at the same time. To increase motivation, faculty sometimes set up several tasks forces or advisory committees, introduce the idea that they will be competing for attention or selection, and give them some time to plan their strategies before the scene is acted out. This approach also reduces the anxieties that some freshmen have about their acting abilities or about being put on the spot.

In another variation of role playing, students do not actually act out a scene or situation, but during discussion they assume the role of someone whose opinions differ from their own. Such role taking encourages students to take a closer look at and give more serious consideration to alternative points of view. An English professor, for example, told us that she struggled for years to get students to consider the possibility that Bertolt Brecht's Mother Courage might have been a good mother. Most freshmen thought not, which always put her in the position of arguing the other side, while they went to work to prove their original opinions, ignored evidence to the contrary, and paid little attention to the ambiguities or nuances in the play. Now she opens discussions with the same question, "Was Mother Courage a good mother?" After a show of hands, she asks students to pretend they hold the opposite view and to try to defend it with evidence from the text. The role-taking technique removes her from the discussion except as recorder; students look much more closely at the text, produce more compelling evidence for both possibilities, and reach stronger conclusions for having considered the alternatives.

The differences between talking *about* a situation and being *in* the situation, even when it is make-believe, are subtle but powerful. In taking the role of another, students acquire expertise that they otherwise might have little motivation to acquire, consider positions and points of view that they might otherwise dismiss quickly, recognize and acknowledge emotions that otherwise would be suppressed, and try out behavior that otherwise would feel too "out of character."

Writing to Learn

"Ask freshmen to write? Are you crazy?!" Accustomed to this response when we suggest writing as a learning activity, we stress at the outset that we are not talking about the writing assignments that strike terror in the hearts of faculty—the ones that elicit pages and pages of dreadful prose that must be carried home, marked up, and returned within the week. Traditionally, we assign papers or reports in order to assess what students *have* learned. Writing *to* learn is an altogether different enterprise.

Typically, writing-to-learn exercises are short; students write a few sentences, perhaps a paragraph. Although we might want to look at what students write in order to see what is on their minds, writing-to-learn exercises need not be graded. Students write to and for themselves in the interest of collecting their thoughts and getting them down on paper where they can be inspected, extended, connected, organized, and revised.

In Chapter Six, we talked about paraphrasing, summarizing, and sentence-completion exercises—three forms of writing-to-learn exercises—as strategies for taking notes. Such activities encourage students to make material meaningful by restating it in their own language, by organizing it into "chunks," and by relating it to questions, examples, problems, or issues that they already know but might not think to consider. Writing-to-learn exercises come in a variety of other forms as well.

Word-association exercises ask students to write down everything that comes to mind when they hear a particular word or phrase: "determinism," "poverty," "quadratic functions," "acceleration." Students are encouraged to jot down not only what they know about the topic, but also any questions, feelings, experiences, or events that come to mind. Such techniques encourage students to do some preliminary thinking about a topic, and they often surface information that can help us know how to connect new ideas to the knowledge, beliefs, attitudes, or experiences that students bring to learning tasks.

Concept mapping asks students to arrange key concepts and other ideas in some form of spatial diagram, to draw lines or arrows between ideas that are related, and to label the lines to indicate the nature of the relationships (for example, cause and effect; concept and example; conclusion and evidence; argument and counterargument). Some faculty begin by giving students a list of items to be mapped: "Draw a diagram that shows the relationships among the following ideas." Others begin with one focal concept, ask students to brainstorm ideas that are related and then to map the relationships among those ideas. Either way, concept mapping encourages students to see connections and relationships, which brings them another step closer to making it meaningful. Further, labeling the nature of the relationships helps students recognize the differences between general concepts and examples, between main ideas and details, between conclusions and evidence—distinctions that freshmen often gloss over.

Paraphrasing, summarizing, sentence completion, word association, and concept mapping encourage the deep processing of information that leads to retention and understanding, but writing-to-learn ought not be overlooked as a method for providing practice in thinking and problem solving. The examples of small-group discussion questions, case studies, and role-playing exercises presented earlier, as well as many past test questions, are easily transformed into writing-to-learn exercises. Connolly and Vilardi's *Writing to Learn Mathematics and Science* (1989) is another useful resource for faculty in those disciplines.

As a form of practice, writing-to-learn activities have some unique advantages. In small-group discussions, students who sit back and wait for others to do their thinking often go unnoticed. In a writing-to-learn exercise, an idle pencil is conspicuous and flags a student who needs our attention. Further, written responses are tangible. When students look at what they have written, they confront what they can and cannot do. Writing may not correct misconceptions or fill gaps in understanding, but it exposes them and thus provides impetus and direction for additional study.

Small-group discussion, case study, role playing, and writing to learn are not, of course, the only techniques for getting students involved during class, but they constitute a good beginning repertoire for faculty who teach freshmen and provide the means to incorporate the conditions for learning with which we opened this chapter. They are flexible methods that can be tailored to fit most disciplines, class sizes, and objectives. Taken together, they offer a varied menu, one likely to sustain interest and appeal to a variety of learning styles. In addition to sources already cited, Clark (1988), Frederick (1981, 1986), and Fuhrmann and Grasha (1983) offer other strategies and suggestions.

Some General Suggestions

Any teaching method, including those discussed here, is effective only insofar as it promotes achievement of objectives. Sometimes those who press for getting students involved sound as if it matters little what students are involved in, as long as they are involved. It does matter. We can and sometimes do involve students in things that have nothing whatsoever to do with what they are supposed to learn. If these methods are to promote achievement of course objectives, then they must pose challenges and provide practice geared to those objectives. Effective use of any of these methods begins with a clear notion of what the objectives are.

Some faculty can create activities for getting students involved on the spur of the moment as the need for them arises, but most of us are mere mortals who need to plan these activities in advance. Most of the examples of small-group, case-study, role-playing, and writing-to-learn activities presented in this chapter have two parts. They begin by posing a situation—a problem, a demonstration, a case, a scene and some characters, some form of specific example. Where do we find these situations and examples? Real life is a good source. In what settings do people actually use or discuss the subject matter? Who are those people and with whom do they interact? What questions or problems or dilemmas do they confront? We can sometimes draw upon our professional experience when we create problem situations; more often, popular media— newspapers, magazines, television, radio, film—will contain data, story lines, characters, conflicts, and dilemmas that we can easily transform into case studies, role-playing scenes, or problems for small groups to consider.

Creating the problem situation is only the first step in designing a practice activity. The key to whether these methods provide *appropriate* practice lies in the questions we ask about the situation. A case study, for example, can provide focus for practicing most of the types of learning outlined in Chapter Four simply by changing the question asked about the case. Sometimes, however, a perfectly good case study turns into a disaster because the questions invite students to practice applying concepts when they first need to practice recognizing those concepts, or the discussion falls flat because we intend to give practice in applying concepts but our questions require only simple recall of information. The same can be said for the other methods discussed here. Our questions direct students' thinking; we need to plan them carefully.

When introducing any of these activities to students, it is wise to take a few minutes to explain why students are being asked to participate. As we have mentioned several times, not all freshmen greet opportunities for active involvement with equal enthusiasm. Some consider such activities a complete waste of class time. They cannot imagine what can be learned from a small-group discussion when the instructor is not leading it. They see no point in writing if we are not going to read and grade what they write. Case studies and role-playing exercises are, after all, only "make-believe." These students believe we would make better use of class time if we lectured more, went over material in the text, worked more problems (especially those that will be on the test), and let them take more notes.

Such reactions are not particularly surprising to faculty who know something about student development. Anticipating resistance, however, does not reduce it or make it easier to deal with. Abandoning efforts to involve students is obviously not the answer. To do so would be to give up our best hope for promoting understanding or thinking, to reinforce passive learning, and to deprive freshmen of challenges that might lead to transformations in the ways they view knowledge and learning. We urge instead providing the support freshmen need.

Structure is one source of support for freshmen, and we can provide it with explicit and clear instructions about what exactly students are to do when they are "actively involved." In most of the examples presented earlier, the instructions not only call for an end product (an explanation or a recommendation or a solution), but they also outline what students should consider along the way (particular theories or issues or questions). Eventually, we hope students will learn to think through these situations without so many prompts. Initially, however, freshmen need them to guide their thinking.

A second source of support is personal contact with the instructor. As noted in Chapter One, freshmen put this high on their list, though enrollments in freshmen courses often make it difficult. We encourage the use of small-group discussions because they enable faculty to talk with students in more personal terms.

Allowing time to think is a third source of support. A major strength in the methods discussed in this chapter is their flexibility; they can be designed to take only a few minutes or to engage students for an entire period. It is frustrating, however, when the task requires considerably more time than is allotted. Students need time to read a case, prepare for a role play, and think about a question before they can discuss it or write about it. Sometimes, it makes sense to assign the case, the roles, or the problems as homework so that students can give them some thought outside class.

Several of these methods call for followup discussion. The time required for this varies depending on the task and on the variability in the responses, but a working rule of thumb is to allow at least as much time for followup as allowed for the activity itself.

Once discussion begins, structure again becomes an issue. Small-group reports, case studies, role plays, and writing-to-learn exercises usually elicit a variety of ideas and proposals, but student contributions do not always come in orderly fashion, and it is easy to lose track of them. We need some way to help students record and organize their thoughts. Some faculty list key questions or issues on the board and record students' ideas under appropriate headings. Others record student contributions in the order they are offered but stop from time to time to ask students to organize the ideas somehow. However we do it, both the recording and the organizing are important. Recording students' contributions acknowledges that they are taken seriously and gives freshmen, who like to take notes, something to write. Organizing those contributions gives them a way to "chunk" the ideas and store them in long-term memory.

Finally, we need to support the students' efforts by reviewing what they actually accomplished. It is useful to think about these reviews at two levels. At one level, a review answers the question, "What should students take from this discussion or activity?" Freshmen prefer taking the answer to a question or the resolution of an issue, but most will settle for realizing they have explored the dimensions of a problem or looked at the situation from several perspectives or clarified how to approach and think through a problem—so long as the dimensions, perspectives, and problem-solving steps are made clear and are recorded in their notes. When they are not, freshmen are likely to say, "Class was interesting, but we didn't really learn anything."

At a second level, a review addresses the question, "Why did we go to all that trouble to make these points when the instructor could have explained it and saved a lot of time?" Once the activity is introduced with an explanation of why students are asked to participate, reviewing the virtues of active involvement may seem redundant. Further, such reviews do not dissuade some freshmen from their beliefs that these activities are a waste of time. The distinction between learning *what* to think and learning *how* to think is, however, a subtle one for freshmen; it takes some time to get it. Until they do, reviewing what students gain by participating in these exercises at least reminds them that we have a clear purpose in mind to aid and support their learning.

Finally, getting students involved in class often depends on our success in getting them involved outside class. Many of these activities succeed only if students do their homework, the topic to which we now turn.

8

Fostering Active Learning
Outside the Classroom

"It's a waste of time," some faculty argue, "to talk about getting freshmen actively involved during class. It doesn't work because students won't do the reading, have nothing to contribute, and prefer being told what they need to know." Watching an activity we worked hours to create die because students are not prepared is demoralizing. Frustrated, we begin to wonder what freshmen do between classes and to suspect the truth is "Not much."

Yet, many freshmen say they have never worked harder in their lives and frequently feel overwhelmed by the work expected. One freshman recently wrote on a course evaluation, "It is not humanly possible to do all the work. Professors should realize that students have other courses, not just theirs. Also this professor should stop thinking we're smarter than we are and get a textbook that we can understand." Each semester, we see scores of comments expressing similar sentiments, enough to make reasonable professors wonder if they are, indeed, expecting too much. All things considered, including courses that *do* demand too much, we suspect most freshmen study more than they ever imagined they would but less than faculty can reasonably expect.

The backward look we took at high schools in Chapter One and the kind and amount of studying students do explain why college assignments must surely come as a shock. According to the 1989 national suvery of incoming freshmen, less than half said they spent six or more hours per week studying or doing homework during the previous year; only 10 percent reported that they frequently did extra reading or work for a course ("Fact File," 1990). Boyer (1987), citing a study by the National Assessment of Educational Progress, reports that high school seniors actually spend less time reading books than fourth-graders do.

Freshmen expect to study more in college, of course, but recalling the description of the freshman year in Chapter Two, we know our assignments face stiff competition for their attention. There are people to meet, things to try, relationships to negotiate and renegotiate, hours to be worked, and identities to be formed. Academic matters easily pale in comparison, especially in the short term. Perhaps we should not be shocked by reports that most freshmen study about two hours a night or about one hour outside class for each hour in class, not the two or three we advise (Brittingham, 1988; Moffatt, 1989). After all, that does add up to more than twice the number of hours most studied in high school. Yet few freshmen are capable of keeping pace with their courses if they spend only an hour preparing for class, and it seems reasonable to us that faculty expect more.

Studying more does little good, of course, unless students know how to study productively. Entering freshmen anticipate needing help in basic study skills, faculty quickly confirm these assessments, and where they exist Learning Assistance Centers are busy places—matters we address in Chapter Thirteen. We tend to expect miracles from these programs, however, and to forget that all students, even highly capable ones, need to practice generalizable skills in the discipline for transfer to occur. In the end, if we want students to study more on a more regular schedule and in more productive ways—we need to reconsider some of the assignments we give and create others more suited to those goals.

Assignments to Reconsider

We join the ranks of those critical of term papers and term projects. However well-intentioned these assignments are, it is difficult to dispute charges that they elicit lackluster work, invite plagiarism, underwrite those who peddle prepared term papers, distract students from more fruitful study, and sometimes require students to do something we ourselves cannot do—complete four or five major projects in one term (Eble, 1988; Farber, 1984; Meyers, 1986).

Term papers and projects seem especially ill suited for freshmen. They ask students who know little about a subject to identify topics of special interest prematurely and require in-depth study before students know what resources could or should be consulted. Attempts to provide the direction and guidance freshmen need turn into impossible tasks because we cannot supervise what are essentially independent study projects for twenty or thirty or more students. The most serious reservation about these assignments, however, is that they do nothing to encourage freshmen to study on a day-to-day basis.

Many daily assignments take the form of "read the following pages for next time." Next time comes, students cannot answer questions about the readings, and we conclude they have not read them. No doubt some freshmen ignore these assignments, but most say they at least try to keep up. Many are passive readers, however. They highlight their way through an assignment and assume they are done. They tend not to use strategies that lead to understanding—paraphrasing, summarizing, questioning the text, testing themselves—unless an assignment prompts them to do so. Simply telling students to read an assignment does not provide the inducement many freshmen require to become active readers.

If term papers and projects ask too much and reading assignments ask too little, what assignments are appropriate for freshmen? Because reading plays such an important role in most of our courses, we begin with assignments that help freshmen learn from reading. Arguing that reading comprehension is an act of creation akin to composition, Egan suggests that "the best way to teach students to read—and to teach them the content of their reading—is to have them write about it" (1989, p. 15). Research supports the practice of writing as an adjunct to reading (Andre, 1979; Applebee, 1984).

Writing to Learn from Reading

Students need not write much in order for writing to be a productive complement to reading and thinking. Cuddy (1985) describes an assignment in which students write only one original sentence. For example, when students read Washington Irving's "Rip Van Winkle," she poses the following question: "In Irving's story, is Rip or his wife responsible for the quality (or nature) of their marital relationship?" Students are asked to write one complete sentence answering the question and to list three quotations from the text to support the answer. While the questions invite differences of opinion, restricting support to direct quotations demands attention to the text, which some freshmen (especially those in positions of multiplicity) tend to ignore.

Several professors have adapted Cuddy's assignment. A philosopher, for example, uses this variation: "In one sentence identify the type of ethical reasoning Singer uses in his article, 'Famine, Affluence and Morality.' Quote three passages that you think clearly reveal this type of ethical reasoning." An art historian asks students to write one interpretive sentence about a painting and to list three features of the painting that contribute to that interpretation. In the social sciences, students are asked to state opinions and quote three statistics that support or contradict those opinions. The number is arbitrary, of course; the idea is to focus attention on evidence.

Microtheme assignments that ask students to write 200- or 300-word essays on some question also are popular among our faculty. Bean, Drenk, and Lee (1982) describe four different types of microthemes. The "summary-writing microtheme" asks students to give an accurate and balanced account of the main ideas in a reading. The "thesis-support microtheme," like Cuddy's one-sentence assignment, asks students to state a position and support it with evidence. The essay form implicitly demands, however, that students also state the relationship between the thesis and the evidence, a skill that many freshmen need to practice. The "data-provided microtheme" presents data and asks students to draw conclusions. A sociologist on our campus, for example, gives students the results of a survey and tells them, "Write a paragraph in which you discuss one survey 'finding' in light of your reading." Faculty in the sciences provide experimental observations and ask students to explain the results using concepts discussed in the reading. A fourth variety of microtheme presents a problem or dilemma and asks students to explain their solutions in nontechnical language. Bean, Drenk, and

Lee include one example that asks students to explain a physics problem writing in "Dear Abby" style. Many of the questions and tasks discussed in the last chapter lend themselves to this type of microtheme, either to prepare students for discussion or to follow up on one.

Martin's discussion of microthemes in a general-education biology course presents some novel variations on these assignments. One asks students to "describe the white cells of the blood using an analogy of military defenders" (1989, p. 118). Another asks them to "develop a campaign to convince teenagers that loud music permanently damages their hearing" and requires that they explain "how the ear converts soundwaves of rock music to nerve impulses" (p. 119). The examples, thirty-six in all, are rich in ideas for getting students to write about material in nontechnical language, to extend meaning by way of analogy or metaphor, and to expand the contexts in which students think about course material.

Taking a somewhat different tack, Daniel (1988) allows students to write "survival cards" in his mathematics class in order to motivate them to keep up with their reading. At the beginning of every class, each student may submit one 3×5 card containing notes from that day's assignment. He stamps the note cards and saves them until the class before the test when he returns them to students. Students cannot add cards to their decks, but they may add information to the stamped cards and bring them to exams.

Problem sets continue to be the mainstay in science and mathematics courses, but faculty in these disciplines are beginning to add writing-to-learn exercises in order to focus students' attention on problem-solving steps and procedures and to encourage the development of metacognition. One of our colleagues requires students to choose one problem from each assignment and to "write step-by-step instructions for solving this type of problem." Another asks students to "select a problem for which you are not absolutely certain your solution is correct. Write about your questions or doubts. What are you not sure about and why?" Connolly and Vilardi's *Writing to Learn Mathematics and Science* (1989) suggests dozens more for these disciplines.

Writing-to-learn assignments such as these prompt many freshmen into reading closely and thinking about their reading.

Assignments using computers offer alternatives, ones freshmen often find intriguing.

Computers

Mention the word *computer* or *technology*, and many tune out the conversation. We confess to similar impulses. Technology conjures images too mechanistic, insensitive, uncaring, and unrelenting for something so human as teaching or learning. The innovations in computer-based instruction are exciting, nonetheless. Using technology, some faculty provide instruction more vivid, more patient, more responsive, and more individualized than is possible with traditional methods. The number of faculty using computer-based activities on most campuses is small—less than 10 percent, according to one estimate (Johnston, 1989)—but we expect that to change rapidly as the hardware becomes more affordable and the software more widely viewed. Therein lie the problems for many of us: finding out what is currently available and keeping up with the pace of new developments.

Heermann's *Teaching and Learning with Computers* (1988) is one place to start; it outlines the ways computer technology is currently being used, reviews specific software programs, proposes criteria for judging their worth, envisions developments likely to occur during the next decade, and lists resources for keeping up with those developments. Neither as ambitious nor as well informed, our discussion merely samples a few possibilities for using computers in freshman courses.

The interactive capabilities of many computer-based instructional programs allow students to practice a variety of skills. Videodiscs present spoken interactions in language courses, motions of stars and planets compressed in time in astronomy courses, animations of processes such as protein synthesis in biology courses, or problems illustrating motion in physics (Johnston, 1989; Heermann, 1988). Along the way, the computer stops the presentation, asks questions to check understanding, and provides explanations to those who need them. Heermann (1988) predicts that during the 1990s expert systems technology, which can store both content knowledge and procedural knowledge, will see the development of programs even more interactive, more able to handle complex problems, and more sensitive to different learning cycles.

One we have seen first hand is CHEM-TUTOR, an intelligent tutoring system for first-semester general chemistry students, developed by J. L. Fasching and colleagues at the University of Rhode Island. CHEM-TUTOR "knows" both the content and the procedures that "experts" (faculty) use to solve the 1,200 problems it stores, ranging from simpler problems to those that require multiple concepts and steps. CHEM-TUTOR also "knows" how faculty tutor students—when they intervene to encourage students to continue or to question the path they are taking, what questions they ask, and what hints they offer—knowledge gleaned from faculty who have paid close attention to what freshmen do when they work chemistry problems and how faculty respond. CHEM-TUTOR quickly "learns" about students who use it—what problems they have tried, what successes and failures they have had, and what level of difficulty they are ready for. Putting it all together, CHEM-TUTOR can present problems at an appropriate level of difficulty, monitor a student's work, encourage students when they are pursuing one of several fruitful tracks, ask a question or provide a hint when they are headed down a blind alley—and can do it hundreds of times.

Computer simulations, a second type of program, model reality, invite students to experiment with changing various features of the models, and show them the effects of their changes. In one example reviewed by Heermann (1988), an acid rain module, students manipulate several variables related to the operation of a coal-burning power plant and see the effects on atmospheric concentrations of sulfur dioxide, the acidity of a nearby lake, and the operating cost of the coal plant. In the physical and social sciences, spreadsheets, statistical packages, and graphics programs allow students to run a variety of "what if" experiments, to manipulate data quickly, and to observe the results.

Computers can also be a useful tool for faculty wanting to increase or personalize their contacts with students or to increase the interactions among them. Winifred Brownell, a colleague on our campus who uses teleconferencing software "to add a channel of communication" in her courses, outlined several possibilities and advantages of teleconferencing for other faculty in a recent workshop. She uses the system to send announcements, schedule changes, and reminders to her classes, for example, and to communicate with individual students. Because students can also communicate with one another, the technology opens many possibilities for group work. She assigns students to small conference groups whose members regularly discuss assignments, work on group projects, study for tests, and provide support for one another. The ability to interact through the computer is especially valuable to students who find it difficult to meet with other students due to family obligations, work, or commuting and to students who feel reluctant to speak during class.

A full array of computer-based options has yet to reach many of our campuses, making it difficult to discover the possibilities for our courses. We can start, however, by finding out what does exist on campus and talking to colleagues who currently use technology in their courses. Professional meetings and conferences provide occasions to review current software; some include new developments in technology in their resource areas.

Other Assignments

Writing-to-learn and computer-based assignments, like anything else done routinely, eventually wear. We sample here a potpourri of assignments that introduce variety but still emphasize day-to-day preparation for class.

Focused surveys, interviews, or observations offer many possibilities for heightening interest and extending meaning. To introduce a topic, some faculty create short attitude or opinion surveys, distribute copies to students, and ask them to get two or three of their peers to complete the surveys before the next class. Those who have used this technique report that freshmen seem keenly interested in what other students think and pay rapt attention when survey responses are tabulated during class. If survey questions relate to the major topics and issues to be discussed, this assignment generates data we can use to hold attention, clarify issues, raise questions, and spark discussion.

A similar assignment asks students to interview one other

student not enrolled in the course about some issue or problem being discussed. Freshmen are more likely to get beyond generalities and platitudes if the issues or problems are initially cast in specific and concrete terms—case studies, dilemmas, news stories, letters to the editor, or a specific scenario. This technique also allows them all to begin with the same question: "What would you do in this situation, or how would you respond to this, and why?"

Asking students to conduct observations generates data of a different sort but serves similar purposes. One faculty member gives students an observation guide, asks them to observe some public meeting, and tells them to record examples of behaviors related to certain leadership styles. Students' observation notes provide illustrations when the class meets to discuss leadership styles. Meyers (1986) includes an assignment that asks students to observe a conversation and record interaction patterns.

Sometimes a simple experiment makes a point. A colleague in a communication course asked students to find a friend who was willing to try carrying on a conversation for ten minutes at a distance closer than that of normal conversation and then record how it felt. In a course in family studies, the professor devised an experiment to give freshmen a sense of what it was like to be a primary caretaker. After being given an egg, each student was told to "take care of it" and to return it in one piece at the next class. Those who did would receive an extra credit point. Students returned with a variety of stories to tell, and their experiences provided concrete referents for material in the readings.

The popular media are rich sources of examples and problems for many courses. A colleague teaching environmental geology told us he relies heavily on newspaper articles and editorials as a focus for homework assignments. One, for example, asks students to rebut an editorial claiming that the victims of a volcanic mud slide could not have known the dangers. Another asks them to identify important issues not addressed in a news article about a proposed coastal development. He points out that in any given semester more than 200 newspaper articles or editorials are printed about topics related to his course, and few resources are better in helping students see the relevance of course material.

Most of us want freshmen to visit the library and learn how

to use it, powerful temptations to assign term papers. Arguing that other assignments may be more effective in teaching the materials and methods of library research, Farber (1984) describes alternatives to the term paper developed collaboratively by faculty and librarians at Earlham College. One example from an introductory philosophy course focusing on sexual ethics asks students to find several articles on affirmative action, to annotate two that take different stances, and to relate them to their own ethical positions. Another in U.S. history asks students to examine primary materials on slave life or the abolition movement, to compare them with their text's treatment of the subjects, and to write their own brief accounts of the issues or events. Library assignments focused on topics and issues discussed in class both encourage freshmen to prepare for class and enable them to develop library research skills.

We conclude with a more general recommendation that faculty create study groups and encourage them to meet regularly. An early finding from Harvard's Assessment Seminars, a three-year project to assess undergraduate learning, is "that students working outside of class in small study groups of roughly four to six . . . do better academically and are more engaged than students working either alone or in large groups" (R.J. Light quoted in Marchese, 1990, p. 5). The formation of study groups also holds potential for addressing the challenges of diversity. Smith (1989) notes that cooperative groups, membership in several groups, and involvement in groups that have a functionally important task are important for reducing the isolation and alienation experienced by minority students. Course-based study groups allow us to provide all three.

Creating study groups is easy; we need only ask students to sign up for a group during the first class. Getting study groups to work may be more difficult. Because freshmen tend to require more direction and structure than other students, we probably need to define some tasks for the groups, at least initially. Most of the assignments suggested earlier are easily transformed into group assignments. Similarly, the activities and questions discussed in the last chapter might be given to students in advance so that students could prepare for them in study groups. As examination dates draw near, we might distribute exams given in previous terms to focus study-group conversation and provide practice. Because they are a powerful way to provide learning assistance, we offer additional suggestions for study groups in Chapter Thirteen.

General Suggestions

We set out to find assignments that would encourage freshmen to study more on a more regular schedule and in more productive ways. We found faculty using a wide variety: writing-to-learn assignments, computer-based activities, focused surveys, interviews and observations, assignments that use popular media, experiential activities, study groups. We conclude with some general observations and advice.

First, these assignments are less ambitious than the papers and projects found in many undergraduate courses. From time to time, we might ask freshmen to synthesize and integrate their learning in a four- or five-page paper, especially if a series of shorter assignments leads to it. But if we want freshmen to study regularly rather than intermittently, we need shorter and more frequent assignments.

Second, these assignments are more focused than the usual "think about this for next time." They explicitly ask students to summarize, solve problems, find an example, state a position, and so on. Focused tasks and explicit instructions provide the direction and structure many freshmen need.

Third, many of these assignments call for a tangible product—a list, an outline, a paragraph, a solution to a problem, a clipping from a newspaper, a completed survey, something that gives shape to thought. Producing or finding something tangible not only helps freshmen organize their thoughts but also tells them when they are or are not done studying. The assignment may have been read, but if the paragraph is not written or the newspaper example has not been found, more remains to be done.

Fourth, like the class activities described in the last chapter, these assignments involve students in activities that promote understanding and thinking. Assignments that ask students to explain in nontechnical language, to find examples in the media, to talk about survey questions with friends encourage freshmen to create meaning. Other assignments provide practice. Still others focus attention on problem-solving or analytical procedures and ask students to verbalize how they are thinking. When developing assignments, we can deliberately and systematically build these conditions into instruction.

Fifth, in order to accommodate the different learning styles freshmen bring to their courses, we need variety. No single assignment is suited to all the learning styles outlined in Chapter Three. If we systematically vary the types of assignments and provide choices whenever possible, we have a better chance of reaching all freshmen at least some of the time.

Finally, we recommend frequent, short assignments to help freshmen keep up with their work and study productivity, but we do not assume faculty must review all or even many of these assignments. We distinguish assignments *to learn* from those that assess what students *have learned*. Although many assignments in this chapter could serve the latter purpose if we so designated them, we view them as assignments *to* learn. We might use some as a focus for class discussion, scan others for signs of understanding or misconception, designate a few as practice tests or essays and give written feedback, but we see no reason to grade or even to review each and every assignment. In theory, that is.

In practice, freshmen generally do not subscribe to these views. Accustomed to receiving grades on homework, most expect us to collect assignments, mark them, and record them in our grade books. If we do not, they see little reason to do the work. We are not enthusiastic about counting toward the final grade the marks earned on assignments such as those in this chapter (we say more about this from a measurement perspective in Chapter Ten), in part because this practice inevitably reduces the number of assignments we give. At the same time, we think it important that students do these assignments. We confess we have not found a good solution to the problem, only compromises.

Some faculty quickly scan assignments and record who did them in their grade books. These records do not affect final grades, but they may prompt an invitation for an office visit or a comment reminding students that they are falling behind. Although this can be done fairly quickly and seems to help, the record keeping is no small task. An alternative is to collect a smaller sample of assignments each time. In one class, students whose names begin with A through E might submit their work for review; in another, names beginning with F through L, and so on. Selecting letter groups randomly and not announcing them until the day the assignment is due should prompt students to do more of the assignments. Freshmen know they are too easily distracted from their assignments; we doubt they will object to such procedures if we explain them.

Indeed, freshmen rarely object to and often welcome the most powerful technique we know for encouraging them to study regularly—the weekly quiz. Although we have reservations about this strategy (as motivators, quizzes rely on external motivation and rather miss the point; they must be created and then graded; they do not always help students know how to study) they nonetheless "work" in getting freshmen's attention. If all else fails, consider quizzes.

9

Evaluating Student Learning

If faculty were to look at the exams their colleagues give, they might develop more sympathy for student complaints about exams and mistrust of faculty who give them. Questions such as the following do not inspire confidence that we measure meaningful learning or that we measure it well.

In the film series, Carol Rogers responded to Gloria with
a. Tears
b. Anger
c. A dinner invitation
d. Acceptance and caring

Long-range goals are usually achieved
a. By people with determination
b. In the distant future
c. By setting short-term goals
d. All of the above

Comment on this quote by Flaubert: "The author in his work must be like God in the universe, present everywhere and visible nowhere."

135

Fill in blanks with the correct word(s). (20 points).
a.   The most important metaphysical idea in Tao-
     ism is (   ).
b.   Wei-wu-wei means (   ).
c.   The Way eternal has no (   ).
d.   A block of (   ) untooled, though
     small, may still excell [*sic*] the world.

Obvious, trivial, ambiguous, and indecipherable test questions are only the tip of the iceberg, however. Beneath the surface
of many evaluation policies and practices lie problems that threaten
the validity of the entire process. They are all the more serious
because, unlike the questions above, they often go undetected by
otherwise competent teachers.

For starters, we claim that understanding and thinking are
the most important goals in our courses, but the evidence reveals
most tests require simple recall of information (Milton, 1982; Milton, Pollio, and Eison, 1986). Even more disturbing, faculty from
seventeen different departments said nearly a third of their test questions required complex cognitive skills, but when independent
judges examined the tests, they found 90 percent of the questions
to be recall tasks (study reported in Milton, Pollio, and Eison, 1986).
How are we to improve our tests if we cannot even recognize their
limitations?

We often blame multiple-choice tests for this state of affairs,
but they are not the only culprits. Essay questions, paper assignments, and lab reports fare little better under close scrutiny. Consider, for example, the following essay assignment, which appears
to require fairly complex analytical skills:

An "initiation" story dramatizes a naive, childlike
character going through a difficult, painful, or bewil-
dering experience that initiates him or her into a view
of the world that the reader perceives as more realistic
or mature. Compare and contrast the initiation patterns in two of the following short stories: "Editha,"
"The Open Boat," "The Bride Comes to Yellow Sky,"
and "I Want to Know Why."

Suppose, however, students have just spent a week or two discussing the initiation patterns in each of these short stories, noting similarities and differences along the way. To write the essay, students need only remember what was said in class. Many essay questions masquerade as tests of complex thinking skills when, in fact, they can be answered on the basis of memorization. The problem, then, is not that we give too many multiple-choice tests and too few essay tests but rather that neither form tests the learning outcomes we claim are most important.

A second major problem in evaluation is that we do not do enough of it. We would not think of basing our scholarly conclusions on one observation in a laboratory or on one passage in a text, but we often reach conclusions about what students know or do not know about a topic on the basis of one test question or one paper assignment. Little wonder we lack confidence in our evaluations.

Meanwhile, the debate continues over the relative merits of essay and multiple-choice tests. On the one side are those who think essays are the best, if not the only, way to assess reasoning and problem-solving skills. Further, they argue, essays encourage students to study more deeply and allow instructors to examine the processes by which students arrive at answers (McKeachie, 1986; Milton, 1982; Milton, Pollio, and Eison, 1986). Critics point out that essay grading is time consuming and faculty who rely exclusively on essays usually base their evaluations on too small a sample of student work. Further, essay grading is unreliable, which makes evaluations based on essays even more questionable. They advocate at least some multiple-choice tests, which have the advantage when it comes to evaluating a variety of learning outcomes, obtaining a broader sample of student work, and grading reliably. (See Ebel, 1972; Hills, 1976; or any other measurement text for discussion of the unreliability of grading essays and their limitations in sampling student performance.)

While we should be aware of the strengths and limitations in these forms of testing, little is gained from an either–or debate. Most of us will need to use both types of tests if our evaluations are to be valid and reliable. Fortunately, the strengths of one form tend to compensate for limitations in the other. The more important tasks are to develop questions that test the full range of goals in a course, not just memorization, and to find ways to combine questions so that evaluations are based on an adequate sample of student performance.

Multiple-Choice Questions

Although multiple-choice questions are the most widely used and highly regarded form of "objective" test items, they are targets of searing criticism, mostly on grounds that they test only rote memorization. We could more easily dismiss such charges as nonsense if they did not contain an element of truth. In practice, too many multiple-choice tests require nothing more than recall of memorized information, much of it trivial and the rest of it disconnected from anything important. Multiple-choice questions are not to blame; the people who write them are.

At their best, multiple-choice questions can test, perhaps not the full range, but certainly a wide range of the learning outcomes described in Chapter Four. The questions below illustrate multiple-choice questions that test knowledge, understanding, and application of concepts.

Knowledge: Remembering important ideas.
Which of the following statements best paraphrases what Marx meant when he called religion "the opium of the people"?
a. Religion is used by political figures to mislead the masses.
b. Religion creates euphoria artificially instead of allowing circumstances to create it naturally.
c. People become addicted to religion and are incapable of shaking it off.
d. Religion deadens the pain of suffering and expresses the flaws of current circumstances.

Understanding: Recognizing ideas in specific contexts or forms.
A critic recently observed that a great gulf separates the lives of blacks portrayed in TV programs like

"The Cosby Show" and the realities that most blacks experience everyday. Marx would say this is an example of which of the following concepts?
a. Real individuals
b. Fantastic realization
c. Material force
d. Political emancipation

Thinking: Applying ideas in new situations.
Henry Clay, an American statesman, said: "All religions united with government are more or less inimical to liberty. All separated from government are compatible with liberty." Which of the following statements best represents how Marx would most likely respond to Clay's statement?
a. Marx would agree with Clay's sentiments. The lack of religious freedom in Germany was the chief defect that prevented human emancipation.
b. Marx would disagree with Clay's sentiments. Liberty is something that is not connected to religion or, for that matter, to government.
c. Marx would disagree with Clay's sentiments. The Christian state developed from humanity's search for liberty and religious freedom.
d. Marx would disagree with Clay's sentiments. Liberty is possible only when the need for religion disappears, not when religious freedom is granted.

These examples merit study not only because they challenge the claim that multiple-choice questions test only rote memorization, but also because they provide patterns for creating multiple-choice questions to test a range of objectives. Faculty are, of course, well acquainted with multiple-choice questions that ask students to remember information or ideas. It is worth noting, however, that the example in the "knowledge" category does not merely check attendance; it asks students to recall a key idea.

The second question illustrates one way to determine whether students see the relationship between a general idea and a specific example, one test of their understanding. The stem of the question presents an example and asks which concept or principle it illustrates; the choices present possible concepts or principles. Alternatively, the stem of the question might present a generalization and ask students to identify an example from possibilities given in the choices.

Questions testing students' abilities to use their knowledge in a variety of situations almost always present a problem or situation in the stem of the question and ask students to select the best solution or explanation or conclusion from four or five choices. These questions tend to be long and complex, because solutions, conclusions, and explanations do not usually come in single words or simple phrases. These questions are also more difficult to write; not only must we think of several plausible explanations or conclusions but we need to be sure one is better than the rest. Nonetheless, it can be done.

The major objection to multiple-choice tests—that they can test only memorization—is not defensible. Two additional objections merit attention. Many see a difference between recognizing an answer and being able to produce one from scratch, but it is not at all clear what this difference is or whether it is important. Ebel (1972) cites research indicating that when students were asked the same questions in multiple-choice and essay forms, correlations between scores for the same students on the two forms suggested that the two tests measured identical aspects of achievement. To critics who charge that a multiple-choice question "does the thinking for students," Ebel responds, "Most good objective test items require the examinee to develop, by creative, original thought, the basis for choice among the alternatives" and concludes that "producing an answer is not necessarily a more complex or difficult task, or one more indicative of achievement, than choosing the best of the available alternatives" (pp. 124–125).

A third criticism of multiple-choice tests—that students study differently for multiple-choice tests than they do for essay tests (McKeachie, Pintrich, Lin, and Smith, 1986; Milton, 1982)—is less easily reconciled. Student descriptions of their study activities indicate that when they prepare for multiple-choice tests, they seek to memorize factual information exactly as it was presented. Their reports on preparing for essay tests reveal more concern for understanding and contain more references to activities such as writing summaries, drawing diagrams, working problems, and asking themselves questions. Such findings are not particularly surprising. Too many multiple-choice tests require recall of facts and details, phrased exactly as they were presented. If we were to write questions that called for thinking, students might learn to study differently for them. We do not change assumptions and study habits by pronouncement or overnight, however, and the ways in which students prepare for multiple-choice tests merit our concern. McKeachie (1986) recommends, and we concur, that whenever possible, faculty include at least one essay question on exams.

Nonetheless, we seriously and unnecessarily limit our evaluation options when we deny the potential for using multiple-choice questions to test understanding and thinking. In many courses, multiple-choice tests provide the only practical way to obtain an adequate sample of student performance on the objectives. Further, multiple-choice tests take little time to score and the grading is highly reliable, two advantages not to be dismissed lightly in freshman courses where enrollments tend to be high. For those who use multiple-choice items, our most important piece of advice is to make sure the questions test a variety of learning outcomes. In addition, we offer the following recommendations.

1. Start writing multiple-choice questions during the first week of the course and try to write four or five questions each week. Good multiple-choice tests cannot be created a day or two before the exam. These questions are difficult to write, and an exam that includes multiple-choice items requires more questions than one that comprises essay questions alone. Writing a few questions each week makes the task more manageable.

2. Make the distracters (the wrong choices) plausible and attractive to the uninformed, but avoid trick questions. Some multiple-choice questions fail because the distracters are obviously incorrect, while others suffer because the distracters contain errors too subtle for students at a given level to detect. Creating good distracters is the most difficult task in writing multiple-choice questions. Some tactics may help. Think about the errors students make or the misconceptions they hold. Mention relevant concepts or ideas

in the distracter but misstate the relationships among them. Include assertions that are correct but irrelevant to the question. Ask questions that require conclusions and explanations. This is a particularly fruitful tactic for generating more distracters because correct conclusions can be combined with incorrect explanations.

3. Make all choices approximately the same length. Often in order to create a correct or a best answer, we must qualify or elaborate statements, making correct answers longer than the alternatives. Test-wise students can select the correct answer on the basis of its length.

4. Be careful about words such as *always, never, all, none,* or *only.* Few things in college courses can be stated in absolute terms, and test-wise students automatically eliminate choices that contain them.

5. Make all choices grammatically consistent with the stem of the question. Sometimes students select the correct answer simply on the basis of grammatical rules. Watch especially the use of singulars and plurals, subject and verb agreement, and the use of the articles *a* and *an.*

6. Avoid negative wording whenever possible. Negatives usually make questions unnecessarily complicated and confusing. When using negatives, underline them.

7. Avoid choices such as "all of the above," "none of the above," and combinations such as "both A and C" or "only A and C." From a measurement perspective, some of these choices are more acceptable than others but rules exist for determining which are acceptable and how they should be used. By and large, these alternatives are not worth the attention they require or the trouble they make. We are better off avoiding them, with one possible exception. Because students in some programs must eventually take professional certification tests that use such choices, faculty also use these choices on tests to help students develop their test-taking skills. The practice makes sense because such items do require special test-taking skills.

8. Rotate the position of the correct answer in a random manner. For some reason, we tend to place the correct answer in one of the two middle positions. Test-wise students are aware of this

tendency. If they do not know the answer, they can increase their chances of guessing correctly by selecting choice *b* or *c*.

9. Take advantage of test-item banks whenever possible, but be careful. Textbooks often have test-item banks for each chapter, but not all items are well constructed or designed to test anything beyond memorization.

10. Make life easier by learning enough about computers to let them score multiple-choice exams. Many campuses have facilities for scoring and analyzing multiple-choice tests relatively inexpensively. Students need no. 2 pencils and we must provide machine-readable answer sheets (a dime each sheet on our campus), but the scoring is quick and item analyses are available to provide useful statistics about questions that were answered correctly or incorrectly and distracters that were most seductive in a particular question. Also, computers can create different versions of tests by scrambling the order of questions and the order of choices, and they quickly score these different versions.

Essay Questions

Although we use the word *essay* throughout this section, most of what we say also applies to paper assignments, lab reports, and even the sorts of problems one finds on exams in the sciences and mathematics. Certainly, these evaluation techniques differ, but they have one important characteristic in common: they all require students to produce an answer rather than to select one. For that reason, they have similar advantages and uses, share similar problems, and require attention to similar issues if they are to be used appropriately.

Writing a good essay question is no simple task. We have been told often enough that we should write clear and unambiguous directions, that we should state our expectations explicitly, specifically, and completely. We have good reason to feel annoyed with those who give such advice, for it begs the question of how clear, explicit, specific, or complete we must be. Consider, for example, the following essay instructions, the first from an essay exam in an art course, the second from a paper assignment in sociology. Are the instructions clear and unambiguous?

The two works shown (slides), *Anxiety* by Edvard
Munch and *Sunday Afternoon on the Island of La
Grande Jatte* by Georges Seurat, represent similar subjects but express different feelings or ideas. Compare
and contrast what is expressed by each. Support and
develop your interpretations by discussing the artists'
representation of the subjects, the *visual elements,* and
the *titles of the paintings.*

In *Habits of the Heart,* Bellah says that the way most
Americans think about life has changed. Specifically,
Bellah claims that "the good things of life, those objects that make up 'the good life,' are still important,
but they now take second place to the subjective states
of well-being that make up a sense of self-worth"
(p. 134).
      Is Bellah right about the relative importance of
material success and the development of self-worth?
Or has he overstated the case? Your essay should state
your position on this issue, provide examples or other
evidence to support your position, consider at least
one alternative position, and defend your position
against that alternative. Before beginning your essay,
you should consult your syllabus to be sure you understand what I expect in an opinion paper.

These assignments are more specific than the typical "Compare and contrast these two paintings," or "Attack or defend Bellah's assertion." Nonetheless, written between the lines of these—
and most essay questions and paper assignments—are dozens of
conventions governing how people within a discipline approach
issues and problems, what questions they consider, what they regard
as support or evidence, and how they communicate with one
another. At best, freshmen are just beginning to learn those conventions, and then only if instructors make them explicit. More often,
students are trying to guess what the instructor wants.
      What saves the examples above, at least in practice, from
being too vague is not the assignments themselves but rather the

instruction that precedes them. The authors of both assignments lay the groundwork in the syllabus; they describe the types of essays students will be asked to write, highlighting key questions and labeling tasks. During instruction, they use those questions and labels to structure lectures and discussions, reminding students that these are the questions and tasks they will need to consider in writing their essays. By the time students see these essay assignments, they have spent many hours practicing similar tasks. Not all students write excellent essays, of course. Some say, "I couldn't see anything in colors or lines" or "I couldn't think of a plausible counterargument," but they do not say, "I didn't know what you wanted in this essay."

Suggesting that clarity in essay questions depends on clarity during instruction does not imply that we no longer need to worry about stating expectations specifically and completely in an assignment. On the contrary, most of us need to worry about defining and articulating our expectations much earlier and much more explicitly than we now do. Telling students that we will ask them to write interpretive essays or position papers or lab reports is not enough. We must be able to expose the pattern or structure in the types of essays we assign. Freshmen do not automatically know, for example, that we expect a position paper to provide support for a position and refutation of counterarguments. Indeed, many of the conventions for argumentation, interpretation, and analysis run counter to views held by students in positions of dualism and multiplicity, making it even less likely that freshmen will think of them on their own. Exposing the patterns is the first step. Showing students how thinking, discussing, and writing in a course follow essentially the same patterns is the second. Both tasks require clarity, specificity, and explication.

Our discussion of clear and unambiguous instructions for essays and papers has taken us back and forth between the assignments themselves and the instruction preceding them because we think the two are inseparable. We turn now to an issue that is primarily an evaluation issue—the reliability, or lack thereof, in grading. If we read an essay at two different times, the chances are good that we will give the essay a different grade each time. If two or more of us read the essay, our grades will likely differ, often dramatically so. We all like to think that we are exceptions, but study after study of well-meaning and conscientious professors find that essay grading is unreliable (see Ebel, 1972; Hills, 1976; McKeachie, 1986; White, 1985). Eliminating the problem is unlikely, but we can take steps to improve grading reliability.

First, using a scoring guide helps control the shifting of standards that inevitably take place as we read a collection of essays and papers. The two most common forms of scoring guides reflect the two approaches to grading most widely used in college courses: analytic and holistic.

Those who use analytic scoring guides identify important components of the essay and assign points to each component. As they read an essay, they award points up to the limit specified by the scoring guide and then total the points to determine the essay's grade. An analytic scoring guide for the paper assignments discussed earlier might read as follows (Exhibit 2):

Exhibit 2. Sample Analytic Scoring Guide.

Total points possible: 6 points

Statement of position: 1 point
   The essay clearly states the student's position. One
   does not have to read between the lines.
Support for the position: 2 points
   The essay cites examples or evidence in support of the
   position. The quality or persuasiveness of the evidence
   is worth one point. Originality (i.e., support is drawn
   from the student's own observations rather than borrowed from the lectures or the text) is worth one point.
Statement of an alternative position: 1 point
   The essay raises a reasonably significant objection,
   counterargument, or alternative to the position taken.
Refutation of the alternative: 2 points
   The essay provides examples or other evidence that
   render the alternative false or less persuasive.

Holistic grading methods assume that an essay is other than a sum of particular parts so we read the essay as a whole. Whereas the analytic scoring guide designated points for particular aspects of the essay, the holistic scoring guide (Exhibit 3) describes the characteristics of excellent, good, and not-so-good essays.

Exhibit 3. Sample Holistic Scoring Guide.

Highest possible score: 6

6: The essay clearly states a position, provides support for the position, raises a counterargument or objection, and refutes it. The evidence, both in support of the position and in refutation of counterpositions, is persuasive and original (that is, drawn from the student's own observations, not borrowed). The essay tackles a significant objection or counterargument, not a trivial one. The relationships between position, evidence, counterargument, and refutation are clear, and the essay does not contain extraneous or irrelevant information.

5: The essay states a position, supports it, raises an objection or counterargument, and refutes it. The essay may, however, contain one or more of the following ragged edges: evidence is not uniformly persuasive or original; the counterargument is not a very serious threat to the position; one has to read between the lines to see relationships between ideas and some ideas seem out of place or irrelevant.

4: The essay states a position and raises a counterargument, but neither is well developed. The objection or counterargument considered may lean toward the trivial. The essay may also seem disorganized. Nonetheless, the essay should receive a 4 in acknowledgment of the cognitive complexity of the task. It is more difficult to address arguments and counterarguments than it is simply to support one line of argument.

3: The essay states a position, provides strong and original evidence supporting the position, and is well organized. However, the essay does not address possible objections or counterarguments. Thus, even though the support seems stronger and the essay may be more well organized than the 4 essay, it should not receive more than a 3.

2: The essay states a position and provides some support, but it doesn't do it very well. Evidence is scanty, general, trivial, or not original. The essay achieves its length largely through repetition of ideas and inclusion of irrelevant information. The overall impression is that the essay has been dashed off at the last minute.

1: The essay does not state the student's position on the issue. Instead, it restates the position presented in the assignment and summarizes the evidence discussed in the text or in class. The essay may include an occasional "I agree with," but it provides nothing beyond what was said in class or in the readings. The essay receives a 1 rather than a 0 because there may be some merit to being able to summarize what the author of the text said.

Although analytic scoring is still the most widely used method for grading student essays, it has come under serious attack in recent years (White, 1985). In the realm of large-scale testing programs, holistic scoring has proved more economical and more reliable, but we need more research to determine the relative merits of both types of scoring for classroom use. Meanwhile, we recommend using some form of scoring guide to keep ourselves honest and to avoid shifting standards partway through a collection of papers. Other suggestions for improving the reliability of grading include the following.

1. Read a sample of essays or papers to see how they compare with expectations and standards. If many students are missing the same points or confusing the same issues, take another look at the question or assignment. If the problem lies in the question, the time to adjust criteria or standards is *before* grading begins, not partway through.

2. If exams include more than one essay question, read all responses to one question before moving on to the next. If we read one student's answers to several questions, our evaluation on any single question is likely to be influenced by the responses to other questions.

3. Grade essays and papers with the students' names hidden from view. This practice guards against being influenced by students' personalities or our knowledge of their previous work.

4. Whenever possible, arrange to have two or more people grade essays independently or grade them a second time, hiding the first score from view. Multiple, independent grading helps determine how reliable (or unreliable) grades are.

When two scores for the same essay differ, as they inevitably will, have a procedure for reconciling differences. Depending on the circumstances, it may make sense to give students the benefit of the doubt and take the higher score, to average the scores, or to ask multiple graders to discuss the essays until they reach consensus. This is time consuming, but there is no better way to improve the reliability of essay grading.

Multiple-choice and essay questions are not the only forms good testing takes, but they provide a good beginning repertoire for faculty who teach freshmen. The strengths in one tend to compensate for weaknesses in the other. Multiple-choice questions can test a variety of learning outcomes, they allow instructors to obtain a reasonable sample of student work, and they are quickly and reliably scored. They have drawbacks, of course: they are difficult and time consuming to write, and although many test banks are available, not all include questions that test anything beyond memorization.

As we move toward assessing students' abilities to handle more complex problems, it becomes increasingly difficult to use multiple-choice questions; we must rely on essays. However, it is a shame to waste essay questions on learning outcomes that could be tested in other ways, because grading essays takes longer and is less reliable and those who rely exclusively on essay questions may not obtain an adequate sample of student work. Finally, students who anticipate essay exams tend to process information more deeply than students who anticipate multiple-choice exams.

10

Grading

What should count toward the final grade? How many exams should I give? Should I grade on a curve or set standards at the outset? Half of my class is failing; what do I do now? What are my responsibilities when it comes to cheating?

Answers to the questions faculty ask about grading are not to be found in research, because grading schemes are largely shaped by assumptions, beliefs, purposes, and contexts. Faculty who believe, for example, that introductory courses should weed out students who show little promise for further study in a field use different grading policies from those who believe their courses teach content or skills important to all college graduates. Those who think a *C* is a perfectly respectable mark grade differently than those who think it not a very good one. Some place a premium on and give higher marks for getting things right the first time; others care little about how many tries it takes so long as the student eventually gets it right.

Although faculty tend to be more interested in getting their questions answered than in having their assumptions exposed, those assumptions and beliefs determine the answers. We do not hesitate to address questions about grading or equivocate with our answers; however, both our recommendations about grading and their rationale depend more on our assumptions and convictions about grading than on research.

One assumption is so fundamental that we cannot proceed without it. We take it as a basic premise that the primary function of grades is to communicate as accurately as possible the extent to which students have learned what the course was designed to teach. This is not self-evident, for some faculty use grades to serve other purposes: to motivate students, to provide feedback and improve learning, to reward hard work, to punish indifference, to rank achievements, to maintain academic standards. Grades often do serve these purposes, regardless of intentions, but they ought not distort the primary one: to provide accurate information about the extent to which a student has achieved course objectives. Keeping that in mind, we turn to the questions faculty frequently ask about grading.

Determining the Grade

What should count toward the final grade? There is little debate about whether tests, papers, quizzes, and lab reports should carry weight in the final grade. The question is "What *else* should count?" Our answer: "Not much." Anyone who has worked with freshmen can sympathize with the temptation to factor in attendance, class participation, and timely completion of homework. Freshmen are easily distracted from their studies and somewhat oblivious to the costs of not keeping up. Nonetheless, we advise against using these as factors in determining grades. Counting them is not likely to motivate students unless they count a lot, but the more they count, the less the grade can be used as an indication of what a student has learned. Furthermore, most faculty would agree that instruction should precede evaluation, but counting attendance, participation, or homework makes them one and the same. Finally, if we consider these factors in determining final grades, then we need daily attendance lists, systematic and reliable procedures for assessing student contributions during class, and records of homework submitted. Such is the stuff of which nightmares are made.

Nor do we recommend basing grades on the amount of effort or improvement students appear to make. If grades are to communicate the extent to which students achieved the course objectives, then how hard they tried or how much they improved merely confuses the message. Assessing effort and improvement also poses some difficult measurement problems. On what basis do we judge

effort? How do we detect improvement? Such assessments are usually impressionistic, haphazard, and unreliable. Even when faculty
use pre-tests and post-tests (and few faculty base their judgments
about improvement on anything so systematic), the differences observed for individual students are highly unreliable. Let effort and
improvement show in successful achievement of objectives.

    At the beginning of a course most faculty do not set out to
count extra credit toward the final grade, but the issue often comes
up during the semester. "I'm not doing very well on the exams, and
I really need a good grade in this course. Could I do something for
extra credit?" At least two reasons exist for denying such requests.
First, the extra-credit work usually takes the form of a paper or a
project, which would not be a bad idea if writing the paper or
completing the project required students to demonstrate their
achievement of important objectives. In practice, we rarely take time
to create such assignments, and students are left largely on their
own to select a topic and complete the work. Students may learn
something from such activities, but they do not necessarily learn the
content or skills most central in a course. Students would be better
off trying to correct whatever is causing them to do poorly on their
exams. Second, this practice is not equitable unless we publicly
announce that the options are available to all students.

    Some faculty do announce extra-credit options at the begin-
ning of a course, and we take a different view of extra credit in these
cases. A colleague in sociology, for example, gives extra-credit
points to students who enter the Max Weber Memorial Art Contest
and the Karl Marx Memorial Limerick Contest. To enter the first,
students must submit a drawing expressing one of Weber's key
ideas; in the second, they write a limerick about Marx's view of
society. Another colleague tells her art history class that they will
have opportunities from time to time during the semester to gain
extra points by participating in special class events. The events
include writing an interpretive essay in small groups, making a
collage that expresses the characteristics of some artistic movement,
and participating in the "test review game show" where teams of
students compete to answer practice test questions.

    Unlike the spur-of-the-moment responses to students who
request extra credit, these activities are designed to engage students

in thinking about important ideas in the course, and all students are invited to participate. Extra-credit options need not be so light-hearted as these, but there is something to be said for giving students a chance to play with ideas once in a while. In both cases, the number of extra points available is minimal, but they can affect grades in borderline cases. The extra-credit options thus offer an incidental bonus for instructors. It is easier to tell a student who has earned five or six extra-credit points and is still one point shy of a higher grade that the original cutoff lines will stand.

How many tests or papers should I assign, and how often should I evaluate student performance? Our answer to faculty who teach freshmen is "The more, the better." Grades based on several observations will generally be more reliable than grades based on fewer observations, but there are other reasons for testing frequently and beginning early in freshman courses. Frequent evaluations provide the structure many freshmen need to keep up with their work. Giving frequent quizzes is in fact more likely to get students to attend class and do their homework than is counting attendance and homework in the grading scheme. Early evaluations not only make course goals and standards understandable to students, but also enable them to determine whether their study activities are adequate before it is too late. We therefore advise giving shorter tests or written assignments and scheduling some form of evaluation every two or three weeks, at least during the first few months of the freshman year. Once freshmen have negotiated the transition from high school to college, there will be time enough to wean them from dependence on tests.

Should I grade on a curve or set standards at the outset? Before addressing this issue, let us agree on the procedures being considered and debated. Grading on a curve involves determining grades by comparing each student's performance to the performance of other students in the class. Although several variations on this approach exist, the most sensible one calculates the mean for a set of scores and uses the standard deviation to establish cutoff points for various grades. Scores at least two standard deviations above the mean might receive *A*'s, scores one standard deviation above the mean might receive *B*'s, scores within one standard deviation above and below the mean receive *C*'s, and so on. When we determine grades this way, an *A* means a student performed better than most students; an *F* means its recipient scored worse than most students. Grades based on a curve do not indicate how much or how little a student learned, however.

When we set standards at the outset, we determine grades by comparing each student's performance to that predetermined set of standards. Variations exist here, too, but we typically express the standards in terms of points. If 100 points are possible, we might announce that students who accumulate 90 to 100 points will receive an *A*, those who earn 80 to 89 points will receive a *B*, and so on. An *A* means the student met the standards for outstanding work; an *F* means the student did not meet minimum standards for passing. Grades determined in this way say nothing about whether the student did better or worse than other students in class.

Which grading approach should be used? We favor grading according to predetermined standards and making those standards explicit at the outset. Appropriate standards may be difficult to determine, and care should be taken to make sure they are reasonable, but grading according to standards holds more potential for communicating the extent to which students have achieved the course objectives. This seems especially likely in freshman courses where curve grading often leads faculty to give satisfactory grades to students who have at best a precarious grasp of the material and too often not a clue about what is going on. Freshmen are often all too willing to settle for this, but in the long run, it does no one any favors.

Furthermore, students are more likely to achieve high standards if they know what those standards are, if their attention is focused on meeting the standards rather than on competing with one another, if they participate fully in class activities, and if they are willing to help one another learn. Grading according to standards tends to promote these conditions for learning; grading on a curve tends to undermine them.

Finally, grading according to standards is more likely to point up problems and lead to improvements in teaching and testing practices. If several students do poorly on an exam, the low grades usually prompt some serious soul searching. Was instruction inadequate? Was the exam poorly constructed? Or did students simply not study enough? We can correct such problems, but only if we detect them. Grading on a curve too often hides ineffective teaching, poor testing, and inadequate learning. So long as we give a reasonable number of *A*'s and *B*'s and not too many *D*'s or *F*'s, no one makes a fuss.

Grading Problems

Half my students are failing. What do I do now? If ever there were a situation not to be in, this is it. The desire to avoid it probably accounts for why so many faculty continue to grade on a curve. When grades are assigned according to predetermined standards, and the first one or two tests produce many low scores, both students and faculty see the writing on the wall. Unless something changes dramatically, large numbers of students will receive *D*'s or *F*'s in the course. We do not view this as a mark of merit; the situation indicates something has gone terribly wrong in the course.

Students often pressure us to "scale the grades," by which they mean convert the predetermined grading scale into one with lower cutoff points for each grade. A typical scaling practice takes the highest score earned and regards it as the total number of points possible in a course. New cutoff points are then determined by calculating percentages of the highest score earned or by looking for gaps in the distribution. Measurement texts do not discuss such procedures—for good reason. Anchoring a grading scheme around one student's score—highest, lowest, or otherwise—is a questionable practice, and gaps in a distribution of scores are as likely to be produced by measurement error as by anything else. If original grading scales must be modified, we advise consulting someone with expertise in measurement for proper procedures for converting scores from one scale to another.

Even with that precaution, we are not in favor of scaling grades. Although the practice may placate students and spare us the angry complaints, it neglects the important issues. Why are so many students doing poorly? What can be done to increase their learning? We cannot afford to skirt these issues in freshman courses. Often the knowledge and skills we teach are essential for later courses or important as part of a general education. When we give passing grades and higher marks to students who miss a third or half of the questions on our tests, we lose the argument that we are testing fundamental, essential, or important learning. If that argument is to be lost, it should be lost before the test is given.

An obvious suggestion is to be more careful in setting standards and constructing tests. We can save ourselves a peck of trouble by consulting with colleagues about what we can reasonably expect freshmen to accomplish in one term and by asking others to review our tests before administering them. This is especially good advice for new faculty and for faculty who have been away from freshmen for a while.

Assuming we have reasonable standards and well-designed tests, high failure rates point to problems in instruction. Both we and our students tend to underestimate the amount of practice students require. We provide too few in-class exercises and homework assignments; students do not do the ones we assign. Such problems call for immediate attention and drastic action, and that is what we propose.

If many students do poorly on the first (or second or nth) exam, immediately schedule another exam on the same material a week or so later. Devote the intervening days to intensive review and practice: exercises in class, homework problems or questions to be answered in writing, practice quizzes, consultation with small groups during office hours, extra help sessions, and scheduled times when students may meet and study together. These activities require time, and we may have to revise the syllabus, but the alternatives—compromising reasonable standards or facing a potentially volatile political situation—are not pleasant to contemplate either. Reteaching and retesting hold promise that students will learn what they need to learn.

What are my responsibilities regarding cheating? When conversations turn to cheating, faculty tend to join one of two camps. In one are those who would avoid the topic altogether, claiming they do not have problems with cheating and intimating something is wrong with those who do. In the other camp are those who devote almost as much energy to catching cheaters as they do to teaching their classes. Neither camp is likely to promote or protect academic integrity.

We think it fair to say that most students would prefer not to cheat. We would have to bury our heads in the sand to say that most students do not cheat, however. Most surveys of college students find half to two-thirds of them admitting they have cheated ("Fact File," 1989; Haines, Diekhoff, LaBeff, and Clark, 1986; Scheers and Dayton, 1987). On the other hand, it is not a pretty sight to see students lined up outside a classroom, waiting to have their picture IDs checked under the watchful eye of a videotape camera or to look inside the room and see test police stationed every ten feet, ready to strip students of their tests if they make one wrong move. Nor do these measures inspire much confidence. In a contest between faculty trying to prevent cheating and students trying to engage in it, we would bet on the students.

What, then, are we to do about cheating? Our advice is, in a nutshell, talk with students about academic integrity and why we value it, reduce the pressures students feel in testing situations, take reasonable preventive measures, and pursue official action when cheating is discovered.

Given the importance of the issue, it is surprising how little many of us say about academic integrity. We do not define it except by negative example, we cannot articulate a case for it, and we are not willing to do much to protect it. We tell students that if they cheat, they will only be cheating themselves, but we are hard pressed to specify what exactly they are cheating themselves *of*. (For a comprehensive treatment of academic integrity issues, see Kibler, Nuss, Paterson, and Pavela, 1988.)

When students cheat, they usually have "reasons," and pressure to get good grades heads the list. Although we complain about the obsessive emphasis on grades, we often contribute to the pressures students feel when we could reduce them. Scheduling more opportunities for students to demonstrate their learning relieves some of the pressure. When we base a grade on only two or three exams or papers, stakes are high, failure is costly, and the pressure can be overwhelming to students.

We might also consider distributing test questions beforehand. Some give students the essay questions that will appear on the test; others give several questions from which a fewer number will be selected. One professor we know distributes the stems of multiple-choice questions but not the choices. Some faculty balk at this idea for fear of "giving away" too much, but tests of understanding and thinking are not compromised by distributing question stems such as:

> Which of the following statements best characterizes Freud's view of the relation between society and the individual?

> It is often said that humans are social animals. Suppose someone said this to Freud. Which of the following statements best represents his most likely response?

Although students eventually must select the answers from choices given, distributing the question stems encourages students to prepare for the exam in the same way they might prepare for an essay exam—by constructing answers. Thus, distributing multiple-choice question stems might reverse the finding that students process information more deeply for essay tests than for multiple-choice tests.

Another professor, convinced that tests are the only times we write essays without first bouncing ideas off someone else, allows ten minutes at the beginning of the second test period for students to discuss the essay question in small groups. As one might expect, the distribution of marks is higher on the second exam; most students write better essays. Contrary to what one might fear, "better" students do not appear to be disadvantaged. Their second essays are better than their first, and they are also better than those written by classmates.

Giving students opportunities to rewrite papers or to take a second or third exam not only reduces pressures but usually improves learning, often dramatically (Bloom, 1984; Cross, 1986; Fitzgerald, 1987). Still, many faculty are reluctant to give students more than one chance at a test or a paper. Some suspect that second chances reduce the pressures too much and that students do not really try the first time. Those who like the idea of a second chance compromise by taking the average of the first and second marks as the grade. Others fear they will be overwhelmed by work if they offer students these options; most are surprised when they are not. The sad fact is, many students would rather take a low mark, so long as it is passing, than rewrite a paper or take another exam. A colleague in physics was so frustrated by this that he adopted a version of group-based mastery learning in which students who score below 83 percent on each exam are required to take subsequent exams on the same material until they meet that standard (Letcher, 1989).

Testing more frequently, distributing questions beforehand, allowing discussion before writing of essays, permitting students to rewrite papers or retake exams—these practices make sense not only, and perhaps not even primarily, because they reduce the pressures students feel in testing situations. More fundamentally, they promote learning, which is the best deterrent to cheating in the long run.

We firmly believe, however, in taking reasonable preventive measures in the short run. We do not like to think students might cheat because "everyone cheats" or because they "can get away with it," yet students who admit to cheating say exactly that (Haines, Diekhoff, LaBeff, and Clark, 1986). We do not advocate practices that make classrooms feel more like maximum-security prisons than halls of learning, but we do recommend ordinary precautions.

1. Create new tests and essay assignments each semester. We have yet to devise a foolproof system for keeping past exams and papers out of the hands of students. Efforts to develop ever more elaborate security measures would be better spent writing new tests and assignments. Doing so allows us to return papers to students and to make previous exams available to all students for review and practice. Creating new tests need not be an overwhelming task if we write questions on a week-by-week schedule rather than the night before the exam.

2. Ask students to sit in alternate seats during tests. Many examination settings, if they do not beg students to cheat, certainly hold the temptation constantly before them. When students sit elbow to elbow, it takes some concentration to avoid the inadvertent glance at someone else's work and a substantial commitment to academic integrity to avoid the deliberate one. Taking the extra time to schedule rooms large enough to permit alternate seating is worth the trouble.

3. Create different forms of multiple-choice tests by scram-

bling the order of the questions and the order of the choices. Computers make it easy to create and to score multiple forms of exams.

4. Supplement evaluations completed outside class with in-class tests or essays. We gain some advantages when we ask students to complete exams, papers, lab reports, and other projects outside class. We can pose more complex questions when we are not constrained by what students can reasonably be expected to do in a classroom period, and we do not sentence ourselves to reading first-draft writing. Students need not race to beat the clock, and many work, think, and write better when they are not sandwiched between other students in often overcrowded classrooms. Unfortunately, take-home exams and other outside assignments share one major drawback: we can never quite be sure that students are submitting their own work. Tests and essays written in class ensure that students do their own work at least occasionally.

5. Arrange to proctor examinations. Although proctors rarely detect cheating, failure to proctor exams probably invites it. When we leave the room or refuse to line the walls with proctors, we assume that we communicate our trust in students. Apparently, students take these behaviors to mean we do not care about either them or the test, they believe that most other students are cheating, and they feel disadvantaged or foolish or both if they do not cheat themselves (Haines, Diekhoff, LaBeff, and Clark, 1986).

Suppose we discover that, despite our efforts to reduce pressures and take preventive measures, cheating has occurred. What then? Most institutions have policies governing what faculty may do. Typically, the options range from failing students on a particular assignment, to failing them for the course, to dismissal from the institution. By and large, faculty are reluctant to exercise any of these options. Some sympathize with the plight of students and are satisfied if students promise never to do it again; others prefer to avoid the legalistic procedures and confrontations often involved in taking formal action (Nuss, 1984; Jendrek, 1989).

Cases of cheating are never pleasant, but faculty reluctance in these matters is troublesome. Some professors show more sympathy for students who cheat than they do for students who do not understand, and it is easier to be dismissed from college for ignorance than for dishonesty. Surely, dishonesty is the more serious offense.

One would hope that if students learn nothing else in the course of their studies, they will come to value honesty and to eschew corruption. If, however, we are unwilling to put forward cases of academic dishonesty and to invoke sanctions, students get the message that academic integrity is not that important after all. We urge faculty to redirect their sympathies and to initiate formal action when they discover cheating has occurred.

PART THREE

Special Challenges
in Teaching Freshmen

As we indicated in Part One, freshmen have different needs from their more experienced classmates. The instructional strategies we recommend may seem difficult to achieve when freshmen are instructed in large or multiple-section courses. Most faculty find that the large class requires a different approach, and in Chapter Eleven we suggest ways to achieve instructional goals within the context of the large freshman class.

Freshmen have an acute need for expert advising and other personal attention from faculty, both to aid and support them in their transition to college and to involve them in learning. In Chapter Twelve, we discuss specific ways to provide that attention through improved advising, mentoring, and office hours.

We have also noted that even the most academically talented freshmen are often unprepared for the demands of a college curriculum. Virtually all freshmen need assistance in developing basic learning strategies and skills, topics we discuss in Chapter Thirteen.

Although we agree that teaching college freshmen is a demanding and often poorly rewarded enterprise, we do not believe it need be overwhelming. In Chapter Fourteen, we offer suggestions that can enhance mutual support, improve the teaching of freshmen, and garner the institutional support that faculty deserve.

11

Teaching Large Classes

Only the most courageous (or foolhardy) faculty member remains undaunted when standing before his or her first class of 100, 200, or even 500 students. Images of being Mark Hopkins on the end of a log with the student on the other fade from view. Instructional goals vanish; new questions arise: Untrained as I am as a professional actor, how can I be expected to hold their attention for fifteen long weeks? How can I ever test them? How are all these students to be controlled? How can I find the time even to write down all their names in a grade book?

The student in the back row of a large lecture hall to whom the instructor has become a dim, small figure is no more keen on the large class than her instructor. Admittedly, some few students willingly sign up for large classes, but typically for the wrong reasons: they believe they can hide in its anonymity or that the old tests on file at the frat house will serve them well.

Instructional goals may also be more difficult to achieve in the large class. When our goals involve the retention of information, the development of thinking skills, or changes in motivation or attitudes, studies have shown that large classes simply are not as effective as small ones (McKeachie, 1986). Why, then, are large classes so prevalent, particularly in universities? The rationale is simple. At some institutions large or even very large courses, with their low cost per student, "buy" a certain number of smaller classes and help to keep the overall student–faculty ratio at reasonable levels. Unfortunately, what is sold is often freshman instruction and what is bought is senior or graduate-student seminars.

165

Abolishing all large classes is an unlikely prospect, but large-class instruction could be more effective than it generally is. In fact, much of the research on class size is difficult to interpret because large-class instruction tends to proceed through lectures while small classes rely somewhat more on discussion methods. Because lectures are less effective in promoting understanding, thinking, or attitude changes, one begins to suspect that it is not so much the size of the class but rather the choice of teaching methods that accounts for differences in student learning.

Can faculty teaching large classes use instructional methods that promote understanding, thinking, and problem solving? The answer, of course, is yes. Most of the practices and methods discussed in previous chapters are suited to large classes as well as small ones. Indeed, many of the specific ideas and examples presented earlier were contributed by people who teach large classes. It is naive, however, to think that class size has no impact. If 10 percent of the students in a small class miss a class or do poorly on an assignment or seek extra help, we can give them the individual attention they request. The percentage might be the same, but it certainly feels different when twenty or fifty students come knocking on the door. It is hard to respond to that many individual students each week, every week. Enrollments do make a difference, and those who teach large classes have challenges not faced by colleagues teaching small classes.

Anonymity

Anonymity is the number-one problem of large classes, for it erodes motivation, commitment, and personal responsibility. Feeling that no one will notice or care, students cut class, wander in and out, neglect assignments, avoid seeking extra help, cheat on exams, and blame it all on being in a large class. Faculty, accustomed to smaller classes where they can call students by name or appeal to personal relationships, suddenly find they have no strategies for controlling student behavior.

Even though they might not learn the names of hundreds of students, much less establish personal relationships with them, some professors manage nevertheless to convey the message that they care about students and are concerned about their learning, and their course evaluations testify to this. When we ask them how they account for such student comments as "The professor really cares about students," they are initially puzzled—"How can I care about them? I don't even know who they are." Eventually, however, they suggest a hypothesis: "Maybe they think I care because . . . ." We present their hypotheses here in the form of recommendations.

Incorporate small-group discussions and problem-solving exercises during class. Such activities not only provide practice for students, but they also allow faculty to move among the groups, talking with students informally and more personally. Although such conversations are usually brief, faculty say they learn at least something about the students and feel more connected with them. If faculty feel more connected, probably so do the students.

Be more assertive in inviting students to visit during office hours. One faculty member requires each student to meet with him privately for at least fifteen minutes during the semester. Another tells students that she wants to see every student in her office at least once during the semester. They have the option of coming alone or with up to three classmates (the number of chairs in her office), but they should plan to spend at least thirty minutes in her office. Another brings an appointment sheet to class each week and encourages students who have not yet been to see her to sign up for an appointment.

Schedule extra sessions during the semester. We make this recommendation with some hesitation because we believe faculty who teach large classes are already overworked. As one colleague points out, he could quadruple his office hours and still have no hope of seeing more than a small fraction of his students during them. Instead, he offers a series of workshops during the first two weeks of the course on how to read the texts, how to learn from lectures, and how to prepare for exams. He schedules extra help sessions before each exam, which adds five or six extra sessions during the semester. These are not intimate gatherings; attendance, which is voluntary, usually runs 200 to 300 students. Nor is he sure that students who attend improve their performance on exams. They do, however, seem to have a good time, and he is convinced the extra sessions explain why students think he cares about them.

Much of the published advice about the importance of personal contact with students is not helpful to faculty who teach large classes. Now and then, however, we come across a useful idea. McKeachie (1986), for example, says he has tried announcing that he will meet any students who are free for coffee after class and periodically hands out invitations to ten students to join him for coffee in order to get acquainted. At other times, he distributes class observation forms to ten students at the beginning of class, inviting them to discuss their observations with him after class.

Johnson and Johnson (1987) suggest creating "base groups" to reduce student anonymity and its erosive effects. The purpose of a base group, a small group in which membership is stable, is to provide support for its members. At the beginning of each class, students meet in their base groups, tell one another about pleasant or stressful experiences since last they met, and report how much of the homework they completed. Each student gives a brief summary of the reading and his or her thoughts about it. Together, they summarize the main points and identify things they do not yet understand. Later, when faculty pause to give a discussion question or problem-solving exercise, base groups function like any other small group. During the last five minutes, students meet in their base groups once again to outline the major ideas of the lecture and to make sure everyone understands the assignment. Incidentally, having base groups ensures a productive use of time while papers are being returned or handouts distributed. The stable membership of base groups has potential for reducing isolation, creating a sense of responsibility to and for other students, and making support readily available. Faculty might give students one week to decide where they will sit for the rest of the term, and then form the base group.

Getting Students Involved

Faculty soon discover that the traditional class discussion, the tried-and-true method for getting students involved, does not work in large classes. On a good day, 10 students might volunteer contributions, but the remaining 90 or 190 or 490 students quickly settle into a passive state and eventually tune out altogether. Thinking that nothing can be worse than facing scores of vacant stares and bored expressions, faculty resort to the other teaching method they know best—the lecture.

Holmes (1985) writes of her early attempts to teach a large class: "After some desultory attempts at general discussions, question and answer sessions, and optional discussions for interested students, that [talking *at* students] is exactly what I settled into in 'Introduction to Art,' a class in art appreciation which I teach to two hundred students every semester. I clarified and refined my lectures. I distributed mimeographed sheets bearing artists' names and dates and the main points of each lecture. I showed slides of paintings and talked about them." The lectures, though they were well organized and always accompanied by visual aids, did not yield the desired response from students. She continues, "What I disliked about the large classes was the passivity and literalness of the students, their desire for precise answers to questions for which there are no precise answers, their tendency to busy themselves recording every word I uttered rather than really looking at the paintings, the poor quality of their interpretive essays, and the resentment that was inspired by exams. I came to believe that the speaker/listener dispenser/receiver structure of the lecture format . . . bred fear and hostility toward doing anything" (pp. 159–160). In the end, she turned to two methods that we find to be indispensable tools for instructors of large classes: small group discussions and writing-to-learn exercises. Holmes's essay includes examples of both.

The largest class on our campus is an introductory psychology course in which enrollments average over 500. When we asked the instructor to tell us how he tries to get students involved, he sent an outline listing 25 of the small-group discussion and writing exercises he uses. We include only a sample.

> [Small-group discussion following a vignette in which I act out how two very different people spent their time at the same party]: Develop two or three plausible explanations for what caused these differences. [Followup discussion codifies the answers to develop theories about the causes of human behavior

and illustrates that students already have complex theories about the causes of human behavior.]

[Preliminary out-of-class assignment]: Read the case study and write a short answer (one to three sentences) to this question: "What central aspects of Carol O'Brien's personality have remained constant over time?" Provide three supporting quotations from the case study. [Small-group discussion]: How are current students the same or different from the woman, Carol O'Brien, described in the case study?

[Small-group discussion]: If you were trying to select the ideal roommate, what kinds of things would you look for and what would be the best way to find out about each? [Followup discussion leads to lecture on prediction and personality assessment.]

[After identifying four major sources of information and illustrating each using examples from the "ideal roommate" task, a writing-to-learn exercise]: List one advantage and one disadvantage for each of these four sources of information about personality. [Followup discussion produces summary chart.]

Most of the small-group discussion, case-study, role-playing, writing-to-learn, and structured homework assignments discussed previously are suitable in large classes, but some things happen differently when we try to get large numbers of students involved. We pass on what our faculty tell us they wish they had known beforehand and learned the hard way.

1. Prepare explicit and clear instructions or questions for any small-group discussion, case study, role play, or writing-to-learn activity. Freshmen need structure and direction, and a large class is not the place to underestimate those needs. In a smaller class faculty might provide clarification or elaboration as questions arise, but the number of questions that can come up in a large class will quickly undo even the most patient professor.

2. Provide handouts with written instructions, directions, and questions for these activities. If instructions are only presented orally, expect that many students will miss them. Repeating the questions, often several times, is not only annoying but it wastes valuable time.

3. Do not try to visit every small group or to read every student's response to a writing-to-learn exercise. Instead, develop a procedure for sampling. These activities offer unique opportunities for instructor–student interactions, but the interactions often turn sour if faculty try to be in too many places at one time or read too many pages of freshman prose. Given a choice between distance from a sane professor and interaction with a crazy one, most students would opt for sanity.

4. Experiment with strategies for encouraging students to participate in these activities. Freshmen are not all that eager to become actively involved in learning, and their anonymity in large classes makes it easier to sit back and wait. Start with gentle encouragement: "You should try this because it will help you know how prepared you are." If that does not work, introduce subtle persuasion: visit with students or groups who appear idle and ask if they need some help. If all else fails, grades remain a strong motivator. Holmes admits she eventually resorted to using grades: "I collected all class exercises and used them to spot-check attendance. I instituted a new grading policy, awarding 'extra-credit' points for some group and individual exercises. All students or groups handing in an assignment received an attendance check, but one or two points were awarded only for adequate or superior answers to questions. Attendance was excellent, class morale high, and the interpretive essays on exams were much better. I believe that the single most important factor in the students' improvements from first to second semester was my decision to collect and grade in-class assignments" (1985, p. 162).

5. Do not panic or despair when you notice students not participating. Lack of involvement is easier to tolerate in lectures because it is not so visible to instructors. It is easier to live with in smaller classes because there are fewer students. In a small class, if 15 out of 20 students participate, we would call it a good class. If 50 students in a class of 200 sit idly, we panic. The percentages are

the same. If 25 percent of a class is uninvolved, there is cause for concern but no more so in a large class than in a small one.

Testing and Grading

Faculty who teach large classes rely more heavily on multiple-choice tests than their colleagues who teach small classes, and they should. If the questions test understanding and thinking, and not merely memorization, multiple-choice tests need no apology. The more difficult matter is persuading students that the tests will demand understanding and thinking. As we noted in Chapter Nine, this is always so, but in large classes especially, students are prepared to memorize and little else. Including sample test questions on the syllabus and distributing additional samples as the first test approaches alert students to the form the tests will take.

The typical student is not likely to pay enough attention to these examples or even to discern exactly how they are different from other test questions, however, so some faculty teach the differences between questions more actively. They describe the different types of questions, provide examples, and give students practice in classifying sample questions according to the type of thinking required. Other forms of testing are perhaps difficult but not impossible in large classes. Holmes (1988) includes one essay question on each of her exams, and she provides feedback to students in computer-assisted letters.

Assigning essays or papers in large classes can create a heavy burden, but some instructors do it and still lead relatively normal lives. Graduate or advanced undergraduate students are often provided to help with grading in large classes, but that, of course, necessitates carefully training them, preferably in the use of a scoring guide (see Chapter Nine). Faculty who do not have grading help, as is often the case in classes of 100 and sometimes even in larger sections, need not conclude that written assignments are out of the question.

One of our more ambitious colleagues, for example, requires all 300 of his students to write one essay during the semester, but not all on the same topic at the same time. At the beginning of the term, he assigns students to essay groups and announces the dates on which each group will be asked to submit their papers. Each group receives its assignment two weeks before the paper is due, and assignments are made on subsequent Mondays throughout the semester. Although he eventually reads and responds to 300 essays, the task is manageable because he reads no more than 45 in any given week.

Several faculty have turned to computers for help in responding to students' written work. They begin by remembering the marginal comments written in paper after paper during previous terms: "This evidence needs more development. An example here would help make your case." "What would someone who disagreed with you say? Is there another way to look at this?" "Your paper lacks coherence." They then type these comments in separate fields, creating a permanent bank of comments. When the essays or papers come in, they still have to read them, but they do not have to write the same comments over and over. Instead, using the merge capability of word processing programs, they produce a letter tailored to each essay.

In addition to saving time, faculty report that computer-assisted grading techniques provide two unanticipated improvements in their grading. First, they find that they can respond to students in much greater detail. One professor explained that whereas in the past he might have written in the margin, "You need stronger support for your position," he now chooses a response from several that address various ways a point might "need stronger support." One response might read:

> Your example is consistent with your position but it is not developed enough to be convincing. What you have done is similar to saying in a discussion about foreign policy, "Presidents are important. For example, look at Richard Nixon." This may be a good example, but unless one explains why Nixon illustrates the point, it is not convincing. The situation in your essay is like that.

Faculty say that the computerized letters to students also revealed problems in their grading that had been hidden in their marginal comments. In describing her first attempt to use this technique, Holmes (1988) confesses, "Having a bank of comments that were reasonable approximations of what I normally write on student essays was very revealing. I already knew, for example, that I tended to focus on what was wrong with the essays and gloss over the positive features with the blanket statement, 'You make some good points about the two paintings, but . . .' However, I did not realize how extreme my cataloging of problems was or how dismaying this was for students. In relation to my computer letters on the first essay, this was graphically illustrated when I saw that some students received two pages of single-spaced negative commentary on their essays" (p. 18). The discovery led her to add a variety of positive comments to her computer file and to make sure that every student received feedback on what they did well in their essays.

Finally, it is possible for instructors of large classes to provide some variety in their evaluation techniques. Holmes offers several options and tells students they may elect to do a limited number of them for extra credit points. Perhaps artists are more creative than most of us, but we think faculty in other disciplines might be able to adapt activities similar to these:

> On an 8½ × 11 sheet of paper or board, make a pencil or crayon drawing or a painting that incorporates significant aspects of Jessup's style of representing and organizing his subjects.

> Find a magazine advertisement influenced by a nineteenth- or twentieth-century artistic movement we have studied. Write a brief essay discussing what aspects or characteristic of the "fine arts" style the advertising designer has borrowed, what attitude or feeling the ad attempts to convey, and how effective it is in doing so.

> In pencil, pen, crayon, or paint, do a small-scale Cubist portrait of yourself and a small-scale Expressionist portrait of yourself. These should be small enough so

that you can present them side by side on a single 8½ × 11 board or sheet of paper.

Write a brief review (as if you were writing for a newspaper) of the current gallery show, "Made in USA." Inform your readers about the guiding idea of the show. Describe the range of objects and works of art (in terms of media, use, period, and so on) and describe a few in some detail. Comment about what you think is most and least interesting in the show.

Computerized test scoring and grading programs are indispensable tools in large classes for creating tests, scoring answers, and keeping records. Using computers, we can quickly and easily create different forms for multiple-choice tests; the computer scrambles both the order of test items and the order of choices within each item. We no longer need scoring keys. If students mark their answers on machine-readable answer sheets, the computer scores the tests and analyzes the items for level of difficulty and reliability. These programs quickly answer several questions: Which questions did most students miss? Which incorrect choices were selected most often? Which questions did students who earned high scores miss? Answers to these questions help detect unclear or misleading items.

Electronic grade books save many hours formerly spent entering and totaling test scores or grades. The computer automatically records scores from tests; we can manually enter scores from other assignments. At any time during the semester, the computer can recalculate total scores, percentages, averages, and a variety of other statistics. One colleague recalculates total scores for students before each class, brings a printout of the grade book to class (listing social security numbers, not names), and posts it for students to consult before or after class. Freshmen are often uncertain about how they are doing and appreciate the frequent feedback.

Working with Teaching Assistants

In many colleges and most universities, advanced undergraduates and graduate teaching assistants have taken on major responsibilities in freshman instruction. They assist faculty in grading, tutor individual students, lead the recitation or discussion sections of large courses, supervise laboratories, and perhaps lead a program of supplemental instruction (see Chapter Thirteen). Some graduate teaching assistants have full responsibility for teaching a course, particularly basic courses like freshman composition or college algebra. At some universities it is possible for a freshman to complete the freshman year without ever encountering a full-time regular member of the teaching faculty; at others, freshmen may be graded only by teaching assistants.

Our concern here is not so much that teaching assistants (and part-time faculty) have assumed a major portion of the responsibility for teaching freshman, though that does concern us, but rather with offering suggestions to those faculty who suddenly find that the assignment to teach a large class comes bundled with an inexperienced teaching assistant or two.

Training and supervising would-be college teachers is not a role to which we are accustomed, and it is a formidable task. Few graduate students have had any prior preparation for college teaching. They know little about the factors that affect learning and less about the skills required for effective teaching. Many will make their first attempt to present a lecture or lead a class discussion on the first day of class, and in the absence of any alternatives they approach the task by trying to imitate professors they liked. They forget, naturally enough, that they themselves are not very much like the vast majority of freshmen. As Ross reminds us, graduate students "are unusual in their achievements as undergraduates: they did well in most of their courses; they had well-defined and academic career goals; they wished to be like their professors in many ways. To a significant degree they need to be reminded of the students who sat next to them in introductory courses, those who went on to major in something else, those who got C's, and those who dropped out of college" (1986, p. 47).

Working with international teaching assistants poses an even more complex challenge. Unfamiliar with the philosophy and teaching practices of American higher education, they are surprised and even insulted when students interrupt lectures to ask questions, offer opinions, or challenge them. Although most passed a test of their ability to read and write in English for admission to graduate school, few are tested in spoken English. Rare is the new international student who understands American slang or is practiced in the quick interchanges, casual conversation, and small talk that American students expect from their instructors.

Although we depend on teaching assistants to help us solve the problems that come with large course enrollments, inexperienced graduate students cannot be expected to assume major instructional responsibilities without training, guidance, and support. Providing training and supervision for teaching assistants may not have been part of the bargain when we agreed to teach a large class, but necessity dictates. Our first suggestion is to follow the general maxim, "When faced with a difficult task, share it."

Working with colleagues rather than in isolation reduces duplication of effort and often makes the time spent more fruitful. On our campus, for example, faculty from the sciences, mathematics, engineering, and computer science work with the Instructional Development Program to sponsor a program for their teaching assistants that has three components. The program opens with a two-day orientation for new teaching assistants. Experienced teaching assistants from each department plan and conduct the informal meetings, tours, and social events scheduled during the orientation weekend. Their primary purpose is to introduce new students to the campus, to the surrounding area, and to other graduate students, but there is a strong emphasis on creating opportunities for international students to practice speaking and listening in informal conversations.

During the week before classes begin, new and returning teaching assistants meet with faculty in their departments during the mornings and attend five workshops on college teaching in the afternoons. In the department, teaching assistants meet faculty and other students, find out about their teaching responsibilities, review departmental policies and procedures, and begin to discuss the specific content they will be teaching. The afternoon workshops focus on aspects of teaching and learning that cut across departments—the characteristics of freshmen, meeting the first class, clarifying goals, presenting and explaining, and getting students involved. Faculty and experienced teaching assistants from each department attend all workshops and share responsibilities for conducting the sessions. Workshop activities include a variety of demonstrations, simulations, role-playing exercises, and discussions, but half of each session is devoted to microteaching. By the end of the week, every teaching assistant has practiced teaching at least five short lessons, has seen himself or herself on videotape, and has received feedback from peers and faculty.

Once the semester begins, each department offers a followup program that continues throughout the year. Although department activities vary considerably, most departments (1) videotape their teaching assistants and review the tapes with them, (2) collect student evaluations and discuss the results in individual consultations, and (3) hold regular meetings to discuss course content, teaching strategies, and the problems students are likely to have in understanding the material. The department-based programs are the heart of our efforts. Orientations and workshops, no matter how good they are, quickly fade to faint memories if that is all there is.

We are neither the first nor the only institution to offer training and supervision for our teaching assistants or support to faculty who must provide it. Nyquist, Abbott, and Wulff's *Teaching Assistant Training in the 1990s* (1989) describes programs on other campuses, discusses issues and problems, and lists a variety of resources available to faculty who work with teaching assistants.

None of the problems associated with teaching large classes is new, of course, but the increasing cost of higher education, concern about the quality of undergraduate education generally, increasing numbers of international teaching assistants, particularly in engineering, math, and the sciences, and recognition that a substantial number of today's professors will retire during the next decade have prompted most institutions to give the problems renewed attention. The training and supervision of teaching assistants is on the national agenda, and these issues may at last receive the attention they deserve. That freshmen will be the first to benefit fits well with our concerns.

12

Advising and Mentoring
as Teaching Opportunities

Several of higher education's recent critics have deplored faculty's distance from virtually every aspect of student's lives except formal instruction. To develop closer connections with our freshmen, we do not, however, have to go so far as to move into the dormitories. Advising, mentoring, and office hours provide opportunities for informal instruction and personal contact with students.

Advising

> The perfect adviser cares about the students' goals and makes the most tedious part of scheduling stress-free. Each student receives as much personal attention as the next.
>
> —Freshman

Since the curriculum, teaching, and learning are indisputably in the domain of faculty, it is rather odd that undergraduate advising, the student's link among the three, receives relatively little of our attention. Although at some institutions advising is increasingly removed from faculty altogether, the most recent survey of advising practices, conducted periodically by the American College Testing Program (ACT), reports that nationally most undergraduates are still advised by faculty (Habley, 1988, p. 69).

179

While more than three-quarters of all institutions continue to rely on faculty for academic advising, few couple that reliance with sufficient training, support, or reward. The 1988 ACT survey found that nearly 45 percent of all institutions provided no recognition or reward at all for faculty advisers. Faculty get some background information on advisees, but while only 58 percent receive high school transcripts (the more accurate predictor of college success), 75 percent get SAT/ACT test scores. They may also receive current grade reports (92 percent) and basic written materials, such as academic planning worksheets (84 percent), advising handbooks (65 percent), computerized student academic progress records (74 percent), and a directory of campus referral sources (65 percent) (Habley, 1988).

So armed, faculty are then left on their own. Only one institution in five reports a mandatory training program for advising; even then, a workshop of less than one day is the most common format (Habley, 1988). These data suggest that most colleges—and faculty themselves—still view academic advising as a casual service, with the adviser functioning as a living catalogue or human checklist, taking on a boring, routine task when the student hordes must be scheduled for classes. Computers can do such "advising," and probably should.

Virtually all the reports on higher education that surfaced during the latter half of the 1980s pointed to the urgent need to do something about academic advising. "Perhaps the most urgent reform on most campuses in improving general education involved academic advising," states the report of the Task Group on General Education; "to have programs and courses become coherent and significant to students requires adequate advising" (Association of American Colleges, 1988, p. 43). Similarly, Boyer (1987) found "advising to be one of the weakest links in the undergraduate experience" (p. 51), while also observing the crucial need for "advising and the academic priorities of the campus to be closely linked" (p. 57). The influential report *Involvement in Learning* (1984) recommends a strong advising system, particularly for first-year students, while reiterating the broader problem: "advisement is one of the weakest links in the education of college students" (National

Institute of Education, p. 31). Advising conceived only as an occasional service activity creates a loss for us as well as for students, for faculty distanced from student life find it harder, as Astin notes, "to identify with the typical student's problems" and to learn a great deal of value about the students' experience of the institution as a whole (1985, p. 165).

Too often all that we know of advising comes as a result of being victims of the "dump and run philosophy of advising" (Kramer and Gardner, 1977, p. 9). The chair dumps the task: "You'll be happy to know that you have been selected as the department's adviser to new freshmen for the next academic year. You will meet with them briefly as a group to talk about your department at orientation and then on a one-to-one basis to help them schedule courses. Call Sue Neverheardofbefore if you have any questions." One faculty member describes typical practice: "Of all the assignments a college teacher faces, none tends to be more casually discharged than advising students about their academic programs. At preregistration, as advisees roll in one after another, too many of us merely glance at their selections, toss off a general question or two, then sign, grateful for the absence of complication" (Cahn, 1985, p. 84). Unsatisfactory and unrewarding though it may be, what's in it for faculty to change this practice? What's in it for the freshman? If, as we suggest, advising is a teaching/learning activity, what, specifically, does that mean? How does that concept change advising?

Advising can and should be a major way connections are made between freshmen and their institution. As Astin has observed, academic advising is the best tool we have for helping students achieve a level of involvement. A large body of research suggests that the way to involve students in learning and in college life is to maximize the amount of personal contact between faculty members and students, and that most new freshmen need considerable help in making sense of the institution, in creating a coherent fit between their own vague goals, uncertain competencies, and diverse talents and the college's curricula, its academic opportunities, events, and special programs.

Advisers-as-teachers engage freshmen in serious academic planning with student growth as the goal and view the college years as a rich source of opportunities for personal and intellectual development. Advising in this sense is often called "developmental advising" and goes far beyond information giving, checklist style. One of the best ways to engage students and to learn from them is to serve as their academic adviser, but as an academic facilitator rather than a course scheduler, as one who listens much more than tells.

Advising and classroom teaching can support and inform one another. New objectives for advising often yield results beyond the obvious. When we meet regularly with freshmen and become acquainted with them outside of a "you perform, I grade" relationship, we frequently discover interesting and important things about our students, their goals and ambitions, their needs and learning styles, the ways college life fosters and impedes learning, all of which have important implications for the classroom and for any department's programs and courses. If we distance ourselves from the one-to-one relationship of advising, we miss these opportunities to understand more fully the students we teach.

On our campus close involvement in advising has led some faculty to new methods of classroom instruction and the development of innovative programs. A speech communications professor, for example, recognized a widespread need for a speech communications laboratory with workshops for undergraduates in assertiveness, listening skills, and other areas; a sociologist built the teaching of study skills into his basic course, with surprising results in student performance; a chemistry professor developed a "slow-boat" two-semester approach to the basic chemistry course, again with gratifying positive results. The relative difficulty and appropriate sequencing of courses, the skills taught in prerequisites and general education, opportunities for application, and other data about the curriculum can be learned by attending in a systematic way to what students say about these matters to their advisers. The awareness of students' complex needs that emerge from closely working with them as advisees can be a catalyst for significant changes within departments and within colleges.

Advising Skills and Tools. The same graduate training that emphasizes the development of research and scholarly skills and largely ignores those necessary for effective teaching, particularly of undergraduates, gives no attention at all to advising and mentoring. It is simply assumed that all faculty can teach and advise students with skill and confidence. Unfortunately, as Astin has remarked, generations of undergraduates can attest to how unfounded that assumption is. Advising well is difficult.

What gets in the way of good advising is that a clash often exists between the ways freshmen and faculty perceive higher education. As we saw in Part One, many new students view the college as a kind of intellectual supermarket where they can shop for the necessary credentials (and avoid those that may prove unpalatable) and consider their collegiate experiences as extended résumé building. College is not their first priority, and they have little long-term commitment to the subject matter or to learning for its own sake. Above all else, freshmen want their needs met, as they define them.

Faculty, on the other hand, often find the college a sanctuary for the pursuit of research in their subject matter, which is for them of highest priority. Not only is this clash in perceptions and purposes philosophical, as we noted in the first two chapters, it stems as well from the widening gap between a largely middle-class, middle-aged professoriate and an economically, socially, and ethnically diverse student body.

The most important skills for advising freshmen, therefore, are the ability to listen nonjudgmentally, with care and sensitivity, and to create an open, accepting climate so that students feel free to discuss their plans and dreams (see chap. 7 in Katz and Henry, 1988, and Crockett, 1985, for specific suggestions on interviewing students and ways to improve communication). Listening effectively, understanding student development and differences in learning styles, leading group discussion, teaching the process of making decisions, having respect for students from diverse backgrounds with diverse goals—these advising skills are as important to the classroom as to the advising office. Several recent works on advising contain concrete strategies helpful to faculty concerned with improving their advising (Crockett, 1985, and Winston, Miller, Ender, Grites, and Associates, 1984), and materials from the National Academic Advising Association (NACADA) are particularly useful.

Effective advising also requires familiarity with some basic resources and the same kind of time and attention we would devote to preparing a new course. Beyond the obvious need for a current catalogue and a referral list for various institutional support services, an advisers' handbook summarizing important policies and procedures is the most important advising tool. Advisers should also maintain an advising file for their advisees, a file containing background information (high school transcript, SAT or ACT scores, the results of placement tests, information questionnaire) and records of individual appointments. These records should contain the date, the subject (academic, career, personal, extracurricular, other) and brief comments, objectively stated. Worksheets and curriculum guides are useful tools, but they are no substitute for advising in its broader sense. Like "computer-assisted advising," "degree audits," or "academic progress reports"—all variations of the same computerized reassembling of an academic transcript to make it useful for advising and plotting progress toward fulfulling academic requirements—these tools are valuable insofar as they free faculty from the routine to do the serious work of advising.

Advising Tasks for the Freshman Year

Students' advising needs change over time. In general, freshmen need more direction, more structured interviews, and more frequent advising contacts than do more experienced students. Within the hierarchy of advising tasks described below, the most helpful things an adviser can do, as Kramer and Gardner remind us, are to try to understand the student's college experience, "to clarify what is being experienced, to illuminate more fully the problem and the ideas or feelings that surround it—and to do this in a manner that exhibits a high degree of respect for the advisee" (1977, p. 15).

Providing Information. Providing accurate information is of major importance, since seemingly trivial errors can be costly to students, particularly freshmen who rely heavily on the adviser's authority. Neglecting to inform a student of the timing of a key prerequisite in a tightly structured curriculum, for instance, can result in a delayed graduation date—an error of omission costly to students in extra tuition and lost income. If we do not provide accurate information we are unlikely to have an opportunity to do anything else, for students soon abandon an adviser who cannot give accurate answers to their questions.

The content for advising includes detailed information about courses and curricula, support services, special academic opportunities (even freshmen want to know about study abroad and internships), institutional policies and procedures (registration, deadlines for withdrawing from courses or from the college, how to take a leave of absence, what happens with incompletes, and the like). Even faculty who have been around for a while need to brush up on these basics and should receive (from department, college, or advising center) a well-indexed *Handbook for Advising* to make memorizing such information unnecessary.

Rather than plead ignorance about anything that is not strictly academic, we might add to our repertoire some basic information about major areas of student concern on their campus: how to register for parking, babysitting services, how to change roommates. Advisees will be surprised and grateful for the interest.

Making Referrals. All advisers refer students to other offices on campus when appropriate, though they vary considerably in determining when to make such referrals. Whether a student needs only a basic tip or two to improve study skills or a thorough evaluation by the Learning Assistance Center, whether a personal problem can be handled by a sympathetic adult or demands professional counseling, whether indecisiveness about a choice of major can be resolved with basic decision-making strategies or requires career counseling—these are all gray areas, judgment calls for the adviser.

Only experience and discussion with colleagues can aid in determining precisely where to draw the line. Some advisers rely on their own comfort level: when they begin feeling uncomfortable about the problem the student is addressing, they decide it is time to refer. Others always refer major personal problems, which we think wise. Drug involvement, eating disorders, sexual crises, and traumatic events are matters requiring expert psychological counseling. Advisers should alway refer students contemplating suicide, those whom they have been unable to help, or those with whom they cannot be objective. Referrals, particularly for psychological counseling, may seem difficult to make but a direct, matter-of-fact approach, indicating the reasons for your concern based on observations of the student's behavior, is usually effective. Members of the Counseling Center staff usually welcome the opportunity to help faculty deal with referrals.

Placing the Student. "Placing" means finding that critical balance between the needs and goals of the individual student and the demands of courses, programs, and the institution to create optimal conditions for academic success. When we say (or think) things like "I don't believe you should take more than twelve credits a semester," or "You may have some trouble meeting the department's requirements for four semesters of chemistry," or "The honors program is for you," we are mentally ranking a student's background, presumed ability, motivation, or available time, or all four against some notion of the norms for academic success in the college or department.

This is a legitimate and potentially very useful thing to do— the goal is, after all, to help the student experience initial success by recommending those courses appropriate to each student's background and level of skill—but it must be handled with tact and some humility, recognizing that individual freshmen consistently exceed our expectations or fail to meet them. Before judging, we must have confidence in the evidence on which we are basing our judgments.

Some institutions have offered placement tests for years, for instance, without really knowing whether they are valid predictive tools. And while it may be comforting to think that no student with a math SAT score below 400 or an ACT score of 15 could ever survive the rigors of our department, we should check the facts before conveying such opinions to students. On the other hand, we have all worked with students who persist in majoring in engineering or preparing for law school in the face of all evidence that such goals are entirely unsuitable for them and with others who refuse to consider challenging fields of study or an honors program that they seemingly could handle with ease. Helping students estimate the likelihood of success in their major and evaluating their progress throughout the year are among an adviser's most difficult tasks, particularly during the fragile freshman year. While it is good practice in advising to convey high expectations and to build confidence, we also must gently discourage students' belief in magical transformations.

Advising minority students requires particular sensitivity. Especially on predominately white campuses, black students and members of other minority groups are likely to feel considerable anxiety about close interaction with white faculty. While few faculty are so insensitive as to make overtly sexist or racist remarks ("Why on earth would a pretty girl like you want to be a petroleum engineer?" "Your people have tended to be more successful in the social sciences than in the hard sciences." "I know you won't have any trouble with calculus; everyone knows Asians are math whizzes"), many subtly convey lower expectations for women and members of minority groups. Even today many minority students and women arrive at college with less support from family and friends for their academic ambitions than white males enjoy; their self-esteem and their expectations for themselves tend to be lower. The interest of a faculty member in a good advising relationship, one who believes in their potential for success and supports their goals by helping them plan sensibly, can make a major difference to academic achievement.

Freshmen frequently have competing demands on their time. As noted in Chapter Two, not only do more students work at outside jobs for longer hours at many institutions, but more have family obligations as well. Some, like scholarship athletes, have a major time commitment to an extracurricular activity from the beginning; other students plunge into activities and find themselves drowning in their involvements by the second semester. Placing advisees therefore also includes assessing demands on their time. By plotting time for class, for study, for work, and for other obligations, students often find that they must reduce the number of courses they can handle in a given semester. Increasingly, students need—and take— five years to graduate from four-year programs.

Assisting with Course Selection and Conveying Information About the Major. New freshmen, often operating from a position of dualism or received knowledge as we noted in Chapter Three, want to be told what the "best" courses are and what the "right" major is and look to the adviser as the authority with all the right answers. Advisers want to give advice, not answers, and so we often tell students they must decide for themselves. This conflict of purposes may sour the student on the usefulness of advising early on.

Many advisers have found that one approach that works well with the student in a position of dualism is to be fairly directive for the first semester, perhaps by demonstrating the steps involved in choosing an elective from a small group of possibilities, discussing the ways each course might be valuable, not just in terms of its content but also its potential for developing various skills. The idea is to demonstrate for the student how one decides among competing possibilities while stressing that next time the student will be expected to handle this task with minimum assistance.

Dispelling prevalent myths about courses is another advising task. The particular myths vary from campus to campus, but the invariable selection of American history from a choice of history courses typifies one common type of myth. Freshmen believe that American history will be easier than other history courses because they have already studied it in high school—and junior high and grade school—but American history may prove as difficult as less familiar history courses, or even more so. Similarly, college accounting courses are rarely like high school accounting; introductory psychology does not necessarily help students figure themselves out, and geography is more than identifying rivers and drawing maps.

New freshmen seldom recognize that courses offer more than content, that along with information about a subject a course also provides practice in developing skills for lifelong learning: working cooperatively in groups, doing research (independent and library), speaking formally and informally in front of a group, writing, solving problems, applying general concepts to specific areas, and the like. Discussing such matters with advisees helps them understand the value in their instructors' varied teaching strategies and become more self-conscious about their own developing skills.

To many freshmen, the list of courses they must take represents a series of hurdles to be jumped, appealing though each course may seem; rarely do they understand on their own how the pattern of courses from one semester to the next forms a coherent whole (and if it does not, the department or institution has a problem to address). Specifically, students need help in understanding the reasons for the requirements in the major, for the general education program or the core curriculum, and the rationale for prerequisites.

Assisting in the Selection or Confirmation of the Choice of a Major. As noted in Chapter One, the body of data that highlights students' intense vocational interests tells only part of the story. Along with widespread anxiety about selecting a major (and hence a vocation), preferably the "right" major, a high percentage of students enter college openly or secretly undecided about that choice. Even those with a major have often chosen it tentatively, sometimes for the flimsiest of reasons. Because many students believe that preparation for a career is *the* purpose of higher education, lack of a major raises questions about their reasons for being in college at all. That means the connection of undecided students to the college may be very tenuous. Convincing students of the multiple purposes of higher education is often a more urgent matter than informing them about the major.

Some colleges exacerbate the problem by insisting that students enter with a major already selected or that they make their selection no later than the end of the freshman year. Whatever the case, advisers should expect that many advisees will change their major and need help and support in the process (estimates vary, but approximately one-third to one-half of all undergraduates make at least one change of major; see Gordon, 1984). Many faculty advisers who know only the career of being a faculty member understandably feel uncomfortable about having anything to do with career counseling. But we need not be a career counseler to give students information about the jobs or opportunities for graduate school available to graduates and, possibly, even to help freshman advisees make a connection with some recent alumni or with a senior or two. What most freshmen really need is guidance in learning a process for making decisions, which we can teach them. Articles and books dealing with career fields, particularly those that give a sense of what it is like to do the work on a day-to-day basis, also can provide freshmen with the information they lack.

Developing a Comprehensive Academic Plan. Freshmen are trying their best to prepare for a volatile future, but their crystal ball seldom includes any dimension of their lives other than the vocational. The most challenging, interesting level of advising occurs when the adviser serves as the coordinator of the student's entire academic career, as a facilitator who helps the student integrate academic experiences into a coherent whole and consider their preparation for their personal lives, civic responsibilities, and avocational interests as well as careers. Like Katz and Henry (1988, p. 160), "We envision advisors who point students to the partial, unfinished nature of their present interests, challenge them to explore actively areas outside of their present grasp, and convey to them some sense of the interrelation of the disciplines and the quest for knowledge that overrides and extends beyond any one discipline."

Ways to acquire or strengthen skills, to develop their values, to broaden their knowledge, and to apply what they have learned are all dimensions of the college experience that freshmen seldom consider. Many ways exist to work with freshmen toward these goals. For those comfortable with a structured approach we suggest a series of informal interviews based on questionnaires, to assist students in developing a comprehensive academic plan. This plan translates students' goals for personal as well as vocational development into the courses, activities, and experiences that foster their achievement. A vague goal of "understanding people different from me better" might translate into taking a course in Afro-American literature, doing volunteer work at a shelter for the homeless, or studying abroad. A desire to become more comfortable speaking in front of groups might be met through work at the campus radio station as well as through a course in speech.

The Advising Syllabus

The sample advising syllabus included in Exhibit 4 suggests how the goals for a freshman year advising program might be plotted into a schedule of activities. The approach is to handle the various advising tasks through group meetings, workshops, and individual appointments. We stress group advising as one of the most effective and least used methods of advising. It does not, as some fear, make advising impersonal, but rather supplements the one-to-one advising meeting with the strengths of a seminar, fostering connections among students sharing similar academic interests, prompting a deeper exploration of career and personal issues, and encouraging more probing questions of academic issues. It frees the adviser from the boring necessity of repeating material, allowing the individual meetings to be truly personal. Some colleges offer an orientation course, sometimes taught by the faculty adviser, with some of the objectives we suggest for group advising meetings.

The advising syllabus is a highly flexible tool that adjusts to the needs of advisees. The combination of group and individual meetings enables the adviser to discuss many more issues than possible on an individual basis and has the added value of giving students a small group of peers with whom to relate. A peer advising assistant, perhaps a sophomore, can be very helpful in the group meetings and in suggesting critical topics that need to be considered.

Mentoring

Given the significance that out-of-class contact with faculty has on students' satisfaction and persistence in college (Noel, Levitz, and Saluri, 1985), it is not surprising that many colleges have developed mentoring programs to create this contact deliberately. Usually such programs are directed at special populations of students, typically freshmen; mentoring programs for students undecided about a choice of major, for members of minority groups, for students on probation, for scholarship athletes, and others are widespread and often highly successful. Faculty participants are generally given a fairly clear idea of what is expected of them. Much of what has been said about advising also applies to those mentoring programs designed to support students through regular, frequent contact with a caring adult skilled in empathic listening and knowledgeable about institutional resources. Linking freshmen to faculty as research assistants is another mentoring project that has

Exhibit 4. Advising Syllabus for Freshman Advisees.

Professor Mary Doe
Department of Psychology
Room 3005, Harp Hall
Advising Hours: MWF 2–4 or by appointment
Office phone: 5563
Home phone: 555-4354

Preface
          This syllabus provides an overview of essential ad-
vising activities for your freshman year. Some of you will
seek advice more frequently; you are invited to make additional appointments. Others may believe they need no advice at all. Experience indicates that all students benefit
from meeting their peers and from participating in the advising activities recommended. Before any registration period, you must meet with me.
          The group meetings will give you a chance to meet
with other students interested in psychology or undecided
about their choice of a major. When I see your fall schedules, I will find a common meeting time for these group
sessions, and send you a brief reminder.
          Part of your task this year is to begin to develop a
comprehensive academic plan which we will spend some
time discussing in our individual meetings. [*In the syllabus, the adviser may wish to detail what the students may
or may not expect from the advising relationship, or that
issue may be a matter to be discussed at one of the early
group meetings.*]

Orientation
          Goals: General introduction to the university's ad-
vising system, basic information about the general education program and requirements for the major (and/or a
strategy for making progress though undecided), scheduling first semester courses.

1.   *Group meeting.* Topics: (1) Defining the boundaries of
     advising; what advisers do (and don't do). (2) Under-
     standing general education. (3) What placement tests
     reveal (and don't reveal). Complete Advising Question-
     naire for the individual meeting.
2.   *Individual meeting.* Scheduling courses for the fall se-
     mester. Discussion based on advising questionnaire,
     background information, and placement tests.

Exhibit 4. Advising Syllabus for Freshman Advisees, Cont'd.

Semester I
> *Goals:* Assist student in achieving academic success and in becoming involved in the institution. [*Because the first six weeks of college are the most crucial for student success, we urge that advisers meet frequently with students during that period.*]

> Week 1 or 2: Group meeting
>> Topics: (1) Becoming acquainted with other psychology majors and with other "undeclared" majors. Forming study groups. (2) Becoming involved at Helpful U.; working and going to school. Discussion of adjusting to college.
> Weeks 3 and 4: Individual meetings
> Week 5: Group meeting
>> Topics: (1) Career transferable skills; what they are, how to develop them; relationship to the study of the liberal arts. (2) Discussion of decidedness/ undecidedness.
> Weeks 6 and 7: Individual meetings
>> Mid-semester review and preregistration for spring
> Week 10: Optional workshop
>> Preparing for final exams without stress (led by guest from Learning Assistance/Counseling).
> Weeks 11, 12, 13, 14: Individual meetings as needed.

Semester II
> *Goals:* Selection/confirmation of a major; developing an understanding of the multiple purposes of higher education; achieving one's goals by using institutional resources; fuller development of Comprehensive Academic Plan. [*Part of the group may have been placed on probation as a result of the first semester; others may have demonstrated their aptitude for honors work. Advisers may wish to have additional small group meetings to discuss these issues specifically with the relevant students.*]

> Week 1: Individual meetings
>> Appointments as required to adjust spring semester schedule based on fall performance.
> Week 3: Group meeting
>> Careers in the field of psychology. Meeting some recent graduates.
> Week 5: Group meeting
>> Education for life. Goals for the nonworking hours of your life.

Exhibit 4. Advising Syllabus for Freshman Advisees, Cont'd.

Weeks 6 and 7: Individual meetings
    Mid-semester review and preregistration for
    spring.
Weeks 8, 9, 10: Individual meetings
    Developing the Comprehensive Academic Plan.
Week 11: Group meeting
    Discussion of summer plans; relevant jobs,
    summer school, and the like.
Weeks 12, 13, 14: Individual meetings as needed.

---

had some success (at the University of Utah, for example) and is worth emulating.

Other faculty are sought as mentors in less formal ways, and whether to cultivate such relationships depends, of course, on one's own wishes. Minority or women faculty may be inundated with students who seek them out, often for the vaguest of reasons. Offering to advise a club of, say, women engineers or otherwise meeting with students in groups may help overwhelmed faculty use their available time more efficiently. Having successful role models who are concerned about their college experiences is important to all students; it is absolutely essential to the success of disadvantaged students and those who may not have support from home and are unlikely to have other mentors.

Office Hours

Two members of our faculty, one the chair of a department and the other now serving as a departmental adviser, tell a story of their son, a freshman attending another college. When his first biology test was returned, he discovered that an error had been made in calculating his grade, an error that reduced his test score from a *B* to an *F*. His parents, logically enough, suggested that he go to see the professor during his office hours to get it straightened out. "I can't do that," their son protested. "He's the head of the department. He wouldn't have time for me." It took weeks of urging before their son, with the greatest reluctance, finally went to the professor. Fortunately, he was in.

Like the son in our story, students too shy to visit faculty on a one-to-one basis make office hours a less than useful adjunct to the classroom. Fear of "the professor" is far more common to freshmen than most faculty members themselves would dream. Many freshmen perceive faculty as great intellects, whose heads are filled with only the loftiest of ideas, folk far too busy with important matters to pay attention to the concerns of a lowly freshman. Some faculty, to be fair, cultivate such notions, giving the distinct impression that some major work has been fatally interrupted should a student actually dare to make use of office hours.

Other freshmen, perhaps recalling the high school experience discussed in Chapter One, seem convinced that the more the personal contact, the higher the grade, and make regular use of office hours, hovering about with vague questions on a weekly, if not daily, basis. This behavior understandably exasperates faculty who are uncertain about what to do with this student who is becoming a total pest.

Because freshmen have never experienced anything quite like office hours, it is helpful to spend some class time explaining their purpose or to include an explanation in the syllabus. Weimer (1989b, p. 8) relates this strategy of an acquaintance who gives students a handout that pays particular attention to office conferences.

> He begins by recounting the valuable experiences he had in meeting with professors, then offers a series of suggestions aimed "to help me do the best job possible helping you." His recommendations:
>
> - That students come to the office with specific questions, that they should write these down before they arrive.
> - That if they want to discuss readings they should bring the materials with them, with the appropriate passages or sections marked.
> - That if they are coming to discuss grades, they be prepared to argue *ideas,* not *points.*
>
> In the handout he states that he reserves the right to terminate any meeting with a student, if he feels the

student has not adequately prepared—although he says he's never done so. Does such a proactive stance scare students away? Not in this case. This faculty member generally sees 70% of his students in the office, most more than once.

Productive use of office hours doesn't just happen. We need to let students know how we expect them to use our office hours. Students will typically come for assistance when they are floundering academically, to clear up a matter (in the text or in a lecture) they find murky, to have a grade explained, or to discuss an impending project or paper. While exploring the reasons for a student's difficulty in a course and recommending courses of action are appropriate topics for office hours, we should be cautious about tutoring. Because extensive individualized tutoring can quickly become overwhelming, in Chapter Thirteen we suggest ways other than using office hours to offer academic assistance to freshmen.

Despite faculty clarity about the purposes of office hours, students come for reasons of their own. Often the ostensible reason is not the real reason. Be sensitive to the hidden agenda, an agenda of which even the student may not be fully aware. Some freshmen need to discuss a matter with an adult; others seek out faculty with whom they feel a sense of rapport to discuss a major problem. Others will go to an instructor in their department for advising when their adviser is or seems unsatisfactory. When students seek assistance on personal or advising matters during office hours, the faculty member's role changes to that of the adviser, a change that calls on those advising skills discussed earlier in this chapter.

More than other students, freshmen may need to be urged to visit during office hours. Students who can benefit from office hours the most are often the least likely to come, and you may need to make a particular effort to seek out older students and minority students and others who are unlikely to call attention to themselves. Like advising, office hours provide an opportunity for more than a perfunctory routine, but only if students can count on them. To counter the frequent student complaint that faculty are "never there," we need to treat office hours with the same degree of seriousness as class meetings and to make alternative arrangements for those students whose schedules do not neatly match the posted office hours.

Considering the convenience of students when scheduling office hours, being there, and being fully attentive to the student who comes may seem like matters too obvious to mention. As the editor of *The Teaching Professor* reminds us, however, "So often the behaviors we see in students—irresponsibility, inattention to details and lack of initiative—are a reflection of the kind of teaching behaviors they see in faculty. Those are hard words, yes, but the most important and enduring lessons we teach, we teach by example" (Weimer, 1989b, p. 8). And nowhere in our teaching is the example we provide more important than in our one-to-one relationships with students.

13

Developing Study
and Learning Skills

There is little doubt that most faculty take a dim view of the preparation freshmen have had for college work. In 1989, the *Chronicle
of Higher Education* reported that nearly "three-fourths of faculty
members think undergraduates at their institutions are seriously
underprepared in terms of basic skills," the findings of a nationwide
survey of nearly 5,500 professors conducted that year by the Carnegie Foundation for the Advancement of Teaching (Moony, 1989,
p. A13). Faculty sentiments are, ironically, echoed by freshmen. The
trends that emerge from the 1989 study of entering freshmen "suggest that the academic problems in our secondary schools are still
far from being resolved" (Astin, Korn, and Berz, 1989, p. 7). The
percentage of freshmen who say they will need remedial work in
math (26.5 percent) and in foreign languages (9.9 percent) "reached
record highs" while those who reported doing extra reading for
courses, studying with other students, or visiting an art gallery
reached "record lows" (p. 6).

The Basic Skills Problem

Dealing with such "admission mistakes," who somehow
mysteriously turn up at our colleges year after year, has led to an
extensive effort at remediation in higher education. As one would
expect, considerable difference exists by institutional type in the
number of remedial courses and services offered. But even among

the most selective institutions, few find assessment of academic skills unnecessary; instead, they share the widespread view that entering freshmen require assistance in the basic skills areas. Almost a third believe freshmen need assistance in basic writing and in basic mathematics, and 28 percent believe they need help in reading as well (Lederman, Ribaudo, and Ryzewic, 1985, pp. 11–12). Typically, institutions meet this need by offering (and frequently requiring) remedial courses in reading (82 percent), basic writing (91 percent), and basic mathematics (86 percent). Even ten years ago, the University of California at Berkeley, whose students come from the top 12.5 percent of high school graduates, required remedial writing of 50 percent of its freshmen, the same percentage as the Bronx Community College, which draws 75 percent of its students from the lower half of New York City's high school graduating classes (Maxwell, 1979, p. 230).

All the effort to remedy deficiencies is, apparently, insufficient to yield the desired results. Dropout and flunkout rates remain high, particularly for some minority groups. Fifty percent of minority student attrition occurs in the first year of college (Green, 1989, p. 40). Shunting certain students off into "developmental" or "remedial" courses neither totally removes their deficiencies nor addresses the needs of better prepared students who do not, strictly speaking, require remediation. At worst, relying on remedial or development programs alone to prepare underprepared students may create academic ghettos and convince some, particularly first-generation and minority students, that they are not "college material." Cumulative evidence suggests that retention of underprepared students is highest when basic skills are incorporated into regular courses to reinforce what has been taught in separate remedial courses (Green, 1989; Maxwell, 1979). That means, of course, attending to basic skills in freshman classes.

Instructional Controls for Success. Instructors of freshmen typically teach students who differ widely from one another in their ability and preparation, their habits and styles of learning, and their interests and motivations in pursuing college work. Like patting your head while rubbing your stomach, teaching freshmen requires doing two or more difficult things at once. As Snow and Peterson point out, "On the one hand, college teaching must somehow help individual students to meet the demands of college-level learning. On the other hand, and also in the meantime, teaching must be geared to meet each student where he or she is. The problem is one of fitting instructional methods to students' present aptitudes for learning while at the same time building students' aptitudes for further learning" (1980, pp. 1–2).

While the chapters in Part Two focus on teaching practices to enhance the learning of *all* freshmen, here we emphasize the development of specific basic skills and learning assistance. Paying attention to these areas offers students the most help; what they learn also lasts. Students who need learning assistance most are least likely to seek it outside the classroom. Only the most courageous (or the most desperate) freshmen are likely to admit to a learning problem, to acknowledge not being as able as their peers (Maxwell, 1979, p. 46).

In class, new students of all ability levels hestitate to ask for assistance or clarification for fear of being judged dumb by their peers. To work, much of the assistance for freshmen must therefore be deliberately addressed within the course by the instructor. As we have suggested throughout, that means creating different relationships in the classroom; it means relinquishing some of traditional faculty authority, professing less, listening more, and hearing better (Griffith and Connor, 1989).

The Critical Skills

What skills do freshmen most need help with? Levine said it well: "The skills of reading, writing, arithmetic, speaking, problem solving, 'crap detecting' (. . . identifying the drivel, exaggerations, and untruths that we hear and read each day). . . . These skills are critical for a generation raised on the media, weak in the three R's" (1980, p. 131). Assessment of entering freshmen tends to focus on the traditional three R's, which are also the subject matter for most remedial courses.

Reading. The popularity of speed-reading courses and programs attests to the terror with which many college freshmen face the long reading assignments often given by faculty and the lack of practice with reading mentioned in Chapter One. Difficulty in keeping up with reading assignments afflicts students at every level of ability and is one of the major adjustments new freshmen at all types of institutions report. Amann (1977) argued more than a decade ago that professors abuse books by assigning so many of them that students feel intimidated and ignorant and that needlessly long reading assignments result in superficial reading habits and may create an aversion to reading. Whether the value of a course hinges on the length of its reading list is questionable. On the other hand, resorting to texts that have been "dumbed down," written in monosyllabic words and in paragraphs of three sentences, does nothing to help students improve their reading skills. What helps is to select a reasonable number of texts for the course and to make sure that reading assignments clearly support course objectives. Reading is difficult for many students, and they are quick to catch on when the text is ignored in class and on tests. They then abandon it.

Freshmen need assistance in developing college reading skills, not in reading faster and comprehending less, so it is worth some class time to discuss the text and how to read it. One faculty member introduces each new text by having students take turns reading out loud, starting with the preface and the acknowledgments to get a feel for the author. After each paragraph or so, he asks questions that the reader and others can answer. While he acknowledges that this strategy may seem "silly" and "elementary," it does help to make the text a "friend and companion, not an adversary and enemy" (Lawrence, 1989, p. 3).

Discussing with freshman students the difference between the ways the reader of books and the viewer of television take in information and how and what they retain alerts them to the particular demands of the written word. Prepared study questions can help develop more sophisticated reading skills. After some practice with instructor-created study guides, students can develop their own, either individually or as a small group project. And it also does not take much to introduce students to the SQ3R method of reading the text (described later in this chapter), a skill we believe is quite valuable for freshmen.

Writing. Good writing requires constant practice (which most college freshmen have not had), adequate feedback, and skill in criticizing and editing one's own work. One of the deepest educational mysteries for many freshmen is what distinguishes good writing from bad, why a piece of writing receives a certain grade. To them, it is all subjective. As Maxwell notes, a "student who, in high school, receives an *A* for describing his feelings about an experience may later not understand when a college instructor grades the same kind of theme *F* because the assignment was to write an expository essay with a thesis statement" (1979, p. 228). Given the crushing instructional load of most high school teachers, we should not be surprised that few papers are assigned or that they seldom provide the feedback necessary for true improvement. Writing problems are further exacerbated by lack of reading.

Many of us have unrealistic expectations of what a single writing course, or even several, can accomplish. Because we believe that freshmen who have completed a basic composition course have mastered the intricacies of academic prose, we become annoyed at our English department colleagues when we discover otherwise. The truth is, whatever writing is taught in the freshman year must be constantly reinforced throughout the curriculum; if not, graduates will write little better than they did as entering freshmen, or even worse. Because writing is such a complex process, it takes a long time and considerable practice before a student can develop a mature style.

Students learn to write by writing, and the more opportunities a course provides for writing the better, even if some assignments remain ungraded. Requiring students to write a paragraph summary of the key points in a chapter, for example, is an assignment that can be rapidly checked, helps students read more carefully, and gives practice in writing. The writing-to-learn exercises discussed in Chapters Seven and Eight similarly develop writing skill.

In some courses keeping a journal is appropriate. The habit of recording responses or reactions to a topic on a daily basis fosters writing skills and makes a more personal connection with the subject matter. We once had an art history course that required a journal. Each week we received a new topic on which we were to record our observations and reactions each day. "This week," the professor would say, "you will look at light. Each day observe light—artificial, incandescent, and fluorescent, sunlight, morning light, noon light, evening light; light on living things and on objects; light indoors and out—and record your thoughts in the journal." Another week he would assign a similar intense examination of hands or faces or of lines or geometric shapes. We cannot now recall whether the journals were ever collected, and certainly they were never graded, but that exercise taught us something about art, a lot about seeing, and a surprising amount about writing. The journal can be a powerful teaching tool in many different subjects.

Quantitative Reasoning. Although our goals for development in the basic skills are all a little fuzzy—we want students to write "better," be "literate," to read "carefully" and "well," to comprehend what they read—we are least clear about the level of basic skill necessary in mathematics. Certainly the ability to discern useful data from snakes in the grass is somewhat dependent on a basic understanding of statistics, and adult life generally requires some facility with basic arithmetic, figuring percentages, and making occasional algebraic calculations, but beyond that little agreement exists. What people need to know mathematically is closely related to their major and eventually to their job. That said, students who lack basic mathematics skills not only close doors prematurely to many fields of study in college, but may also deny themselves future career flexibility. Current trends suggest we will all need more highly developed mathematical skills for the jobs of the future.

Many courses require unspecified skills that may create learning barriers. Science and social science courses, for example, often call for the ability to perform some mathematical manipulations. Pre-testing to determine students' skills and a supplemental class or two for those who need to fill in the gaps can remove barriers. Many courses also provide opportunities to keep students' math skills fresh and to help them understand elementary statistics, to extrapolate meaning from graphs and charts, and to review arithmetical computations. An introductory course in political science, for example, is a natural place to discuss the statistical basis for polls, how one determines the gross national product, how national mortality rates are determined, and so on.

Building Conceptual Frameworks

By the time we have studied our way through graduate school to become new faculty members, most of us have probably forgotten how ignorant we once were about our subject. We do not always remember that students do not share our frame of reference or have the conceptual framework necessary to learn and retain the course content. Without that framework, information from lectures can be an indigestible mass of facts that students cannot organize, learn, or retain. As a result, they revert to memorization and, when asked to discuss the issues, implications, or assumptions of the course, they cannot do so. Maxwell (1979) tells of engineering students taking their first economics course who may not understand that the formulas in economics are metaphors and cannot be solved like the formulas in engineering courses. And she describes a physical education major who responds to the English teacher's assignment to "write a theme on a controversial topic" by writing about a campus brouhaha over her swimming coach, not realizing that this would not be what her English teacher had in mind. A different reference base from their instructors is responsible for some learning difficulties, particularly of new freshmen.

What appear to be skill deficiencies may instead be inadequate knowledge of a brand-new subject or immaturity. Textbooks remain a muddle when students have not grasped the basic concepts, do not know the technical vocabulary, or have no basic framework on which to hinge the examples and references. Similarly, students cannot write skillful essays on topics about which they know little (Maxwell, 1979). The developmental position of dualism or received knowledge, discussed in Chapter Three, also may seem suspiciously similar to a deficiency in critical thinking skills, and it is not always easy to determine whether the student who thinks purely in terms of the concrete has low ability or simply lacks maturity. The instructor of freshmen needs to bet on the latter.

Learning Strategies

As we saw in Chapter One, most high school seniors recognize that they will face new demands in college, but they often lack any realistic strategies for accomplishing the improvement they desire, hoping instead for some sort of magical transformation. Few students, even highly capable ones, are sufficiently analytical about their approaches to studying and taking tests to know how to improve if something goes wrong, how to analyze their patterns of error, or even how to repeat their successes. Few are sophisticated about planning and managing their time. Some discussion of the process of learning and incorporating specific learning strategies into their courses will help freshmen develop workable strategies.

The typical course provides many opportunities for such instruction. While reviewing and answering questions during a break in a lecture, we can talk about self-review and some of the strategies for self-testing that are critical to monitoring one's own progress in a course. The announcement of a test is an obvious time to discuss the best ways to prepare to take tests, to test oneself, and to overcome test-taking anxiety; the assignment of a paper might be the time to discuss time-management skills. As Weinstein comments in offering these and other examples, the underlying principle "involves examining the curriculum for the types of learning that are required and reflecting upon the assumptions about learning strategies that form the basis for effective teaching strategies. This process is not very different from what a good teacher already does in preparing for class. The difference is that instead of focusing only on developing effective teaching strategies, the teacher is also focusing on the learning strategies implicit in teaching methods" (1982, pp. 91–93). Making these assumptions about learning strategies explicit and teaching students how to use them for their study is a method any instructor of freshmen can employ in the classroom. Repeated exposure to learning strategies in a variety of contexts can make a powerful difference in expanding and reinforcing the approaches students take to learning.

Study Methods. The following study methods have also proved useful over time to students at all ability levels. Our brief description is followed by a suggestion or two on how each might be applied in most freshman courses at an appropriate point.

1. *The Cornell lecture note system. Method:* Take class notes on two-thirds of your notebook paper and reserve the other one-

third for questions composed afterward on the content of the lecture. Write two to three sentences at the end of the lecture notes to summarize the lecture's key ideas. *Class use:* (1) Have students bring a piece of carbon paper to class and then take lecture notes on two-thirds of the notebook paper, making a carbon copy. End the lecture, have students write out their questions on the content, then go into small groups to exchange notes and discuss them and the questions. (2) End the lecture fifteen to twenty minutes before the class is over. Ask four to five students to write their summary sentences on the blackboard; ask other students to compare the summaries and the reasons for the similarities or differences.

2. *SQ3R. Method* for studying texts: *S* is for *survey*. Check headings and subheadings, scan graphs, maps, tables, read introductory and summary paragraphs. *Q* is for *question*. After surveying, answer these two questions: (1) What is the chapter about? (2) What are the key terms that I will have to understand once I have read the chapter? As you read, create other questions. *R* is for *read*. Read carefully, underlining or highlighting, and making notes in the margins (or on paper). *R* is for *recite*. Stop at appropriate intervals, and recite from memory the key ideas, restating major concepts in your own words. *R* is for *review*. Review the chapter at periodic intervals to refresh your memory and make the facts stick (Robinson, 1961). *Class use:* (1) Assign a chapter in the text to be studied by the SQ3R method. At the beginning of the next class, create small groups to discuss their responses to the two questions. Each group reports on their answer to the first question and their list of key terms and other questions the chapter raises. (2) Have a quiz-making contest. Break class into groups of four to five students. Ask each group to share the questions they came up with in reading the assigned chapter by the SQ3R method and to select the five questions that would be the fairest test of the key ideas in the chapter.

3. *Textbook annotation. Method:* Selectively underline key ideas, write brief statements summarizing key ideas in the textbook's margin, enumerate key ideas, and note with a question mark the parts of the text that are not understood. *Class use:* (1) Have students compare their selection of key ideas and their summary statements and discuss how one determines which is a "key idea" in a chapter. (2) Have a question box on the desk (a shoebox works fine) into

which students may anonymously slip any questions raised by their reading of the text. At beginning of each class, pull out questions, read, and allow class to respond.

4. *Concept cards for key terminology. Method:* From the survey and textbook annotation, select key vocabulary and place each term on an index card. On the back of the card write the definition of the term and provide several examples and applications. Concept cards are a valuable method for self-testing. *Class use:* (1) Collect students' concept cards, divide the class into teams, and use the cards for a "concept bee" as a test review. (2) Begin a class discussion by having students list on the board the concepts identified in the text assignment. Discuss any similarities and differences among the terms, such as which terms have different meanings in other contexts, which are fundamental to the field, which are closely related, and so on.

5. *Diagnosing error patterns. Method:* Ask these questions about a test or exam: (1) Why did I miss the question? Did I misread or misunderstand it? Or did I not know the information? Did I know the information but was unable to apply it? (2) If I didn't know it, where did it come from? Lecture notes? Assigned reading? Handouts? Films? Other? (3) If I misread the question, why? (4) What must I do differently next time? *Class use:* When a test is returned, after discussing the importance of this analysis, identify the source of the test questions for the students. Find out where most of the errors arose: lectures, reading, other?

Study Groups. Students frequently organize their own study groups, some highly successful, some short-lived. New freshmen, sometimes shy, often strangers to one another, need our help to begin the process and provide direction, at least for the first several weeks. During the first week or so of class, we can put groups together, describe their purpose in the course, and resolve such issues as finding a time and place to meet regularly. Specific out-of-class group assignments provide a sense of direction for the study group. Some might be designed to help students improve their learning strategies, such as to construct good test questions (five short-answer and two essay, perhaps) on a chapter of reading or a week's worth of lectures or class discussions, or to make a two-page study outline of a chapter of the text; others, to prepare a group project.

Even a small effort to encourage students to meet is beneficial. One idea for the first day of class comes from *The Teaching Professor*. The faculty member distributes 3 × 5 cards to each student and has them write their names, addresses, and phone numbers. The students then take a couple of minutes to exchange cards with two (or more) classmates. This strategy ensures that all students know several others to contact if they miss a class or have a question, and can be the basis for forming study partnerships or groups (Weimer, 1989a). Using a technique like this is particularly important in large freshman classes where students may not otherwise know anyone.

When they work well, study groups give their members assistance in the course from someone other than the instructor. Those who function as tutors or emerge as group leaders are likely to be helped as much as those they tutor—perhaps more—because they become more self-conscious about what they know and how they have come to know it. Study groups also foster cooperation and collaboration among students, but only if each student's work is graded according to specific standards. Grading "on the curve" or according to other relative standards creates competition that can undermine the cooperative spirit of study groups (see Chapter Ten and also Guskey, 1988). A partnership in which two students interact as teacher and learner in a one-to-one relationship is another effective way of structuring peer teaching (Whitman, 1988).

Some institutions have taken a more formal approach to study groups. At Appalachian State University, for example, students take a group tutoring course at the same time they take a content course. Studying for Biology and Studying for History are two such tutoring courses, taught by majors who attend class with the students and then meet with them twice a week to clarify content and assist in study skills for the course (Noel and Levitz, 1982).

Supplemental Instruction. Since its development at the University of Missouri, Kansas City, in the mid 1970s, supplemental instruction has been one of the most widely employed and successful models for improving learning, particularly in large lecture courses. Focusing on high-risk courses (that is, those with high failure rates) rather than high-risk students and emphasizing ways to increase student competency in reading, reasoning, and study skills, supplemental instruction is not only a good program model, but it also has specific features that can be adapted by the classroom teacher with or without assistance. It is a good idea, and it works.

Briefly, the original model of supplemental instruction enlists specialists (often advanced undergraduates) as leaders to attend course lectures where they take notes and complete reading assignments. The leaders then schedule and conduct three or four fifty-minute supplemental instruction sessions each week at times convenient for the majority of students in the course. Student attendance is voluntary. The leader's job is to serve as a model learner, demonstrating "proficiency in the subject while providing instruction in the reading, writing, and thinking skills necessary for content mastery," though the leader's role may vary somewhat according to the desires of the instructor and the nature of the discipline (Martin, Blanc, and DeBuhr, 1982, p. 76; also see Blanc, DeBuhr, and Martin, 1983). "Perhaps the most important aspect of SI," its developers comment, "is the leader's attention to reasoning and questioning skills. The leader makes a conscious effort to assess the quality of student questions and responses, and to identify those students whose present levels of thinking appear to limit their mastery of new concepts" (p. 76).

The content of the course thus becomes the vehicle for skills instruction by the trained leader. Here are some specific ways in which this is accomplished:

> Student lecture and reading notes are reviewed as the SI leader observes and models appropriate note-taking techniques. Reviews of reading assignments allow the leader to introduce effective reading styles and procedures. Vocabulary development, mnemonics, and other techniques which promote storage and retrieval of information are also integrated into the content review. Additional specific test-taking assistance—i.e., careful reading and interpretation of essay and objective test questions and the construction of sample

tests—are given pre-exam attention and periodic emphasis throughout the semester. Particular attention is given to helping students design effective study schedules and facilitating the formation of informal study groups. Finally, backup tutoring, either by the SI leader or through some other campus resource, is provided to students needing individual support [Martin, Blanc, and DeBuhr, p. 76].

Since supplemental instruction was initially described, several variations have been developed, including adding a credit-bearing Supportive Seminar based on this model to high-risk courses. Because it closely relates learning assistance to courses, most research concludes that the supplemental instruction model is more likely to provide long-term benefit to students by helping them plan, monitor, and evaluate their own learning (Simpson, 1986).

Unfortunately, supplemental instruction is not free, or even cheap. Those whose resources do not allow replication of the supplemental instruction model centered on a trained specialist can still, however, adapt its strongest feature. What really makes supplemental instruction work is the tight integration between the course and organized practice in developing essential academic skills, using course materials.

To illustrate the idea, here is the approach used by a colleague, C.B. Peters, who adds four supplemental instruction sessions to his introductory sociology course. "Supplemental instruction is not a fancy substitute for standard 'help sessions,' " he notes, and is "not designed merely to review lectures, to answer questions, and to clarify fuzzy thinking," but rather the sessions are "designed to provide instruction in academic skills . . . in a context tailor-made for a specific course" (1987, p. 186). For his sessions Peters focuses on skills in text reading, note taking, studying, and exam taking—the skills most important for success in his course. Because he believes that "the timing of the introduction and conduct of supplemental instruction sessions is crucial to their success" (p. 188), Peters schedules his set of sessions in the first two weeks of the semester. This timing, he finds, substantiates his claims that the course will require more than memory and encourages students to view the sessions as a normal part of the course rather than as a rescue operation.

Three general principles guide Peters's supplemental instruction sessions. The first and most important is to keep the session active. "Don't let your students just sit there and take notes on what you say, even if the skill you plan to cover is note-taking," he suggests. "What you hope they take away from the workshop is a set of new ways of doing things, not a list of things that would be good to do. If they are going to learn how to study, how to take examinations, how to take notes, how to read texts, they are going to have to engage in those activities. Lists of principles are fine . . . but . . . they must be derived from activity if they are to do the job" (p. 188).

The second principle is to make the workshop simulate actual conditions: "Don't give them a list of principles of text-reading; give them a list of principles that apply to the specific texts assigned in your course. Don't engage them in note-taking from a packaged lecture; engage them in note-taking from a video tape of a lecture you've just given in class" (pp. 188–189). Students need plenty of opportunity for practice. That is Peters's third principle: "Your workshops should give students plenty of opportunities to practice on real, live course material the skills they are developing. In your sessions, have them read and re-read the texts you've assigned. Help them to apply the principles to the material. Have them study for an examination. Give them the exam. Review it with them. Give them a chance to re-study. Give them a comparable exam, and so on. Whatever you do, give your students an opportunity to practice what you have been preaching" (p. 189).

Peters's low-cost version of supplemental instruction has some distinct advantages. It not only persuades students that this introductory course (and college) demands something different from them, but also makes it clear that the instructor recognizes his responsibility to provide the support they require to develop those different skills and approaches to learning.

Learning Centers

Ninety percent of colleges have some formal program or office for learning assistance, often centralized in a Learning Assistance Center. Tutoring, study skills and time-management workshops, individual analysis and counseling, remedial or development instruction in reading, writing, and less frequently, mathematics, are typical services. On some campuses, services are widely scattered, with the English Department perhaps supporting a writing lab, the Education Department, a reading center, and the Counseling Center handling individual assessment and workshops.

Students benefit most when learning assistance specialists and faculty collaborate. A good Learning Assistance Center not only offers help for students with learning problems that we may be ill-equipped to handle, but also welcomes our requests to work with individual classes. Learning specialists might lead a discussion, for example, on how to study a subject as part of the regular course. Some learning specialists also offer adjunct or supplementary skills courses (rather like the SI model discussed above) that parallel regular classes. By pre-testing in such supplementary courses, they can alert us to the knowledge and competencies that our students have—or lack—and keep us posted on other specific student needs.

Learning Center personnel can analyze texts for the level of reading required, work with instructors to develop and test study aids and other course materials, and diagnose students' reading levels or other basic skills (Maxwell, 1979). Working with faculty, personnel at the Student Learning Center at Berkeley, for example, have developed a self-paced math course and materials for a chemistry resources center, conducted minicourses in prestatistics, prechemistry, and problem solving, built computer-assisted instruction units in probability, organic chemistry concepts, and trigonometry, and written student guides for chemistry, biochemistry, physiology, and mathematics courses (Maxwell, 1979).

Learning Assistance for Special Populations

Some faculty still view the admission of students who are less than perfectly prepared for college-level work as an assault on academic standards. The cost of achieving equity appears to them to be the sacrifice of quality. We would argue that it is not. Not only does higher education have the obligation to provide the opportunity for a high-quality education to all our citizens, but we also can maintain quality while doing so. Academic quality is measured not by the capabilities of the students who are admitted but by the extent to which their learning is increased in college.

Most of the issues relating to teaching special populations of students are the same as those relating to all students. We know that gaining the active involvement of students, providing frequent feedback, understanding and allowing for different ways of learning, and holding out high expectations for achievement are proven ways to increase the learning of all students—minority and majority, young and older, able and disabled. Well-meaning instructors can do great harm when they lower expectations or inflate grades out of sympathy, pity, or false liberal sentiments. To inflate a grade is to offer a lie, undermining true achievement and leaving freshmen unprepared for subsequent courses.

Minority Students. In teaching any particular group of students, all of us need to closely examine our tacit assumptions. Black and Hispanic students, for example, come from every social class, from every educational background. To be a minority does not necessarily mean to be disadvantaged economically or educationally; it does not necessarily mean to be less well prepared for higher education than majority students are. The handbook *Minorities on Campus* (Green, 1989) reminds us of the research indicating that faculty form expectations about students "on the basis of prior achievement, physical attractiveness, sex, language, socioeconomic status, and race/ethnicity. Thus, instructors sometimes assume that minority students will be grouped at the lower end of the ability continuum and therefore they will have lower expectations of them" (p. 136). We may inadvertently communicate lower expectations by calling on minority students less frequently, interrupting them more often, giving them less time to respond to questions, or even by giving insincere praise. Such expectations may, of course, become self-fulfilling prophecies.

Whether minority freshmen are academically at risk or high achievers, they want faculty who truly believe students can learn. As Rendon notes, they want "faculty who will take the time to learn about minority culture and family; faculty who will include minor-

ity perspectives in the classroom; faculty who set high expectations
and help students reach them." (1989, p. 7). White faculty often
forget how difficult it is for many minority students to find a comfortable place on predominately white campuses. Some remain silent in class; others avoid seeking help no matter how desperately
they may need it. The recent report *Minorities on Campus* suggests
that in such situations we may need to initiate the contact: "Active
solicitation of their [faculty's] participation in a supportive manner
can make a crucial difference for minority students" (Green, 1989,
p. 138.)

Older Students. Older students are seldom underprepared because general reading and experience tend to give them a broad
knowledge base. But they often give scant value to what they know.
They view their time out of school only as a disadvantage and rarely
credit what they have learned working, raising children, or participating in the community. What is usually hardest for them is re-
capturing those skills first learned many years ago, particularly in
mathematics, languages, and sometimes writing. Courses in those
areas create considerable anxiety for many older students. Schooled
in a period of time when math beyond a minimal level was considered a subject for boys, not girls, women are often highly anxious
about their ability to succeed in math. Like all students, and perhaps even more so, the older freshman flourishes with an early
success, a success that proves returning to school is not a foolhardy
ambition.

Students with Learning Disabilities. Learning-disabled students fall within a wide range of intelligence, educators and psychologists say, and may have normal sight and hearing. With
varying degrees of severity, they suffer, however, from one or
another neurological handicap that affects their ability to process
and understand written, spoken, or visual information. Students
with a learning disability frequently encounter difficulty with foreign languages, mathematics, reading, and certain examination for-
mats regardless of subject area.

A specific learning disability may affect one or more areas of academic performance while leaving other areas relatively unaffected. Probably the best know and most common disability, dyslexia creates difficulty in learning and remembering printed words, letters, numbers, or symbols. Dyslexics may reverse letters, words, numbers, and symbols, or be unable to spell and sequence words well.

One percent of college freshmen reported having learning disabilities in 1988, the last time the question was asked on the annual survey, "The American Freshman: National Norms" (Astin, Green, Korn, and Maier, 1988). While some skepticism exists that millions of children do indeed have "minimal neurological dysfunction" as the source of their difficulty with learning (see Coles, 1987), the federal law is clear. Students with documented learning disabilities have the same legal entitlements as do students with physical disabilities. Federal regulations mandate "reasonable accommodations" for learning-disabled students just as they mandate curb cuts and ramped entrances to classroom buildings for the physically disabled.

For students with a verified diagnosis of their condition, "reasonable accommodation" is typically determined by the campus administrator responsible for providing services to students with disabilities, someone who in turn works with the students' faculty. Typical accommodations include granting additional time to complete exams, quizzes, or written assignments; permission to tape lectures or discussions; having exams or quizzes read or answered orally or having exam questions clarified; granting permission to use calculators during exams; and being examined in a separate room. Beyond the specific accommodations required, freshmen with a learning disability benefit from the same sort of instructional support needed by their peers: help in developing appropriate learning strategies and understanding the necessity for sufficient practice.

While each of us will no doubt encounter students with special learning needs from time to time, the typical freshman, the ordinary student, benefits from teaching practices known to have a close relationship to all students' academic success: clear goals, evaluation through frequent testing, self-paced learning, active involvement and small modules (Keimig, 1983, citing Cross, 1976). Incorporating basic skills and strategies for effective study into courses throughout the freshman year can be a powerful way as well for freshmen to build their academic strengths, to expand their academic capital rather than to reduce it through a worthless bargain.

14

Strengthening Commitments to Freshman Teaching

As we near the end, the voices of faculty with whom we work echo. Often, they reminisce about a time when their jobs were easier, when they knew less about their students, when research on teaching and learning was safely hidden in journals they did not read, when preparing for class was simply a matter of bringing their lecture notes up to date, and when the only pedagogical issue was whether they should teach to the middle or to the top of a class. That kind of teaching is indeed easier than the practices we propose.

Good teaching is far more complex, difficult, and demanding than is usually acknowledged by the public or within higher education. If we are to do more with freshmen than weed out the ill prepared or marginally motivated and give the rest something other than a once-over-lightly gloss of education, we must be concerned with freshman learning. That means understanding as much as we can about freshmen as learners—who they are, what experiences, expectations, and aspirations they bring, what challenges they face and adjustments they make during the first year, how they learn and what assistance they need.

But knowledge begs action, leading us to reassess everything from preparing the syllabus to determining final grades. Most of us find more we could be doing—should be doing—to challenge and support freshmen. That means devoting more time and attention to teaching; it means approaching the task with more imagination and creativity.

217

Most faculty members already work extraordinarily hard. We know that firsthand from working with hundreds of them over many years; Bowen and Schuster (1986) confirm that our colleagues are not unique. Conscious of the multiple demands on faculty, we acknowledge that the teaching practices we advocate take more time than reading notes from yellowing pages. They also yield far greater student learning and far greater satisfaction. To keep the task of changing teaching strategies manageable, however, we reiterate our suggestion: Focus on one thing at a time. A manageable goal for a semester, for example, might be to develop and test activities for getting students involved during class or to create some new assignments or to try out some new testing procedures. Over time, incremental changes make radical improvements and transform our teaching.

To improve teaching we also need the stimulus of ideas. The journal *College Teaching* and the newsletter *The Teaching Professor* are good sources of practical methods and advice. The Jossey-Bass series, *New Directions in Teaching and Learning,* is also excellent. Each volume in the series focuses on a single topic, such as teaching introductory courses and writing in the disciplines, and includes chapters written from a variety of perspectives. Some professional associations also publish journals on teaching their disciplines.

Ideas, even good ones, usually are not enough, however. To sustain the energy and commitment for teaching well, we must have support—the knowledge that our institutions esteem what we are doing and colleagues to cheer us on when we risk a new approach in class. But, as the classics scholar William Arrowsmith pointed out, "At present, the universities are as uncongenial to teaching as the Mojave Desert to a clutch of Druid priests. If you want to restore the Druid priesthood, you cannot do it by offering prizes for Druid-of-the-year. If you want Druids, you must grow forests. There is no other way of setting about it" (quoted in Smith, 1990, p. 219).

If they do not grow forests, some colleges and universities at least plant trees. About 50 percent nationwide have programs to help faculty improve instruction (Erickson, 1986). These programs go by many names—faculty development offices, instructional development programs, centers for teaching and learning—and offer a variety of workshops, seminars, and consultation services. Most are staffed by professionals in faculty development or by experienced faculty who have developed expertise in teaching beyond their own disciplines. Instructional development programs provide professional assistance and a forum for discussing teaching, trying out new ideas, and conducting classroom research under the guidance of an expert; they can be a source of continuous revitalization.

Where instructional development centers do not exist, faculty concerned about teaching freshmen may feel as lonely as Druid priests unless they can create their own support networks. Although we tend not to talk about teaching when we get together, colleagues are among the best sources of ideas and suggestions for teaching freshmen. Indeed, a major programmatic goal for many instructional development programs is to bring faculty together for conversations about teaching. Initiating conversations about teaching freshmen may be harder to accomplish without such programs, but because the stakes are high and the rewards can be great, it is worth a try. We suggest some ways to go about it.

One way to begin is to find a group of like-minded colleagues, preferably from several disciplines, who will agree to meet on a regular basis to share ideas about teaching freshmen. The conversation groups could include faculty teaching large classes or those teaching core courses or general education or anyone willing to come. The idea is to find some colleagues ready to set aside time on a regular basis to have a conversation about teaching.

Some faculty prefer a more structured or focused agenda, at least initially. Faculty at one liberal arts college, for example, created conversation groups to discuss books on college teaching. They chose Perry's *Forms of Intellectual and Ethical Development in the College Years* (1970) and Belenky, Clinchy, Goldberger, and Tarule's *Women's Ways of Knowing: The Development of Self, Voice, and Mind* (1986) and spent several meetings discussing the implications of each for their teaching. Because we are practiced in discussing what we read, books, journal articles, even newsletters on college teaching provide good entrées to conversations about teaching.

Another alternative is to create a semester-long seminar on teaching freshmen, one that has a reading list and an explicit schedule of topics. At the University of Rhode Island, for example, we offer a seminar on college teaching methods that meets every other week and focuses on one teaching method in each meeting. Faculty read about the method in preparation for the seminar meetings and discuss implications as well as the ways they use the method. In another seminar, we invite two faculty to each meeting to discuss how they have used a particular method such as small groups, writing-to-learn, or case studies. Seminar members then agree to try a variation of the method in their classes before the next meeting, when they report on their experiments. Many of the ideas in this book grew out of such discussions.

While colleagues are excellent sources of ideas and support, so are freshmen, and classroom research offers a strategy for consulting them. Cross introduced the idea of classroom research by calling for "a new breed of college teacher . . . a Classroom Researcher, . . . one who uses the classroom as a laboratory, collecting data and using a variety of research methodologies appropriate to the study of teaching and learning in his or her particular discipline" (1986, p. 10). Whereas traditional educational research searches for effective teaching and learning practices that are generalizable across classrooms, classroom research seeks answers to questions that faculty have about specific classes and specific learners. As Cross explains, "The procedure of the classroom researcher is to formulate the question, collect data, reflect on classroom practices, try a solution, and evaluate the results" (1987, pp. 13–14). Its purpose, Cross emphasizes, is "to provide continuous feedback on what students know and learn, so that teachers and students can relate to one another by making all those little connections that move teaching and learning closer together" (1988, p. 4).

Our faculty have found the approach useful and have conducted a variety of classroom research projects investigating a broad array of questions: "How does calling on students during class affect their motivation, preparation and evaluations of the class?" "Is there a relationship between students' learning styles and their reactions to the teaching methods I use?" "If I ask students to do a writing-to-learn exercise before we start discussion, will more students participate during discussion?'' Some of their projects are described in more detail in Kurfiss and others (1988).

Our approach to classroom research has been to encourage faculty to see how specific practices wear over time, but Cross and Angelo suggest a wide variety of shorter assessment projects. Their handbook, *Classroom Assessment Techniques* (1988), is filled with practical ideas to help us find answers to questions about students, what they are learning, how they are learning it, and how they react to instruction. Many of the techniques described in this handbook have particular value for freshman instruction. "Background Knowledge Probes" (p. 30), for example, provide data about students' knowledge of the topic and their skills in communicating what they know before instruction begins. "Student Goals Ranking" (p. 90) can help us know what our students hope to get from the course and make freshmen more self-aware as learners. "Punctuated Lectures" (p. 112) in which students "listen, stop, reflect, write, and give feedback" not only gives immediate feedback on how students are learning from a lecture or demonstration but also encourages them to become "self-monitoring listeners and, therefore, more aware learners" (p. 112).

The appeal to us of classroom research or assessment techniques is the simplicity of the approach, the opportunity to learn what we need to know quickly and with relatively modest effort. Although we find it rather complex and time consuming for most faculty members, we note another promising method for investigating the interactions between teaching and learning described by Katz and Henry in *Turning Professors into Teachers* (1988). Built on collegial observation of teaching and periodic interviews with students to provide feedback with the goal of making every "investigator" into "his or her own Perry or Piaget" (p. 22), Katz and Henry's approach yields rich data about students and their learning.

Although we have suggested several strategies to generate ideas for teaching freshmen and to create support networks, any discussion of support must eventually address rewards. We do not wish to add our voices to the seemingly endless squabble about the reward structure in higher education, but no book on teaching can ignore it altogether. Clark notes that "the greatest paradox of academic work in modern America is that most professors teach most of the time, and large proportions of them teach all the time, but teaching is not the activity most rewarded by the academic profession nor most valued by the system at large" (1987, p. 98). The message most frequently heard at many colleges as well as universities is that publication and research count more than teaching. They further faculty careers in ways that enhancing the learning of freshmen typically does not. If we are to meet the challenge of improving teaching and learning in the freshman classroom, this value system must change.

Discussions about changing the reward structure to redress the teaching/research balance are on the national agenda. The latest report of the Carnegie Foundation for the Advancement of Teaching, *Scholarship Reconsidered: Priorities of the Professoriate* (Boyer, 1990), proposes a broadened conception of scholarship, one that recognizes and honors the integrity of scholarly teaching. We expect it will provide focus for discussion of the reward system during the next few years and may stimulate some changes. Faculty, however, are not altogether innocent victims of a reward system that undervalues teaching. As Eble points out, "Such an obvious ill as 'publish or perish' is not imposed from the outside. Outsiders are not spawning the journals and writing the articles and voting on the promotions. A better reward system rests upon a responsible and enlightened faculty" (1988, p. 217).

In writing this book, we sought to expose the many and diverse needs of freshmen and to spell out what faculty must do in order to teach them well. We hope our discussion has enlightened not only faculty who teach freshmen but also those who write their annual reviews. Good teaching requires, among other things, time, attention, creativity, and imagination; good teaching in freshman courses requires them in greater measure.

Our nation depends on a highly educated work force; as a society we cannot afford to lose the talents and skills of large groups of young people. We share Levine's sense of urgency about succeeding in college: "Restoring the American dream is a national necessity, and today that dream has no more concrete manifestation than attendance at college" (1989b, p. 172). But we also recognize that, if all we do is bring freshmen to our campus and half or more do not survive the first year, we have enticed them with a lie and destroyed a dream. If we provide access to higher education but do not ensure that our students learn, then we have deceived not only them but society. The potential exists for the freshman year to transform undergraduates and undergraduate education. We believe that the challenges our freshmen present compel us to make teaching college freshmen an institutional priority. Our freshmen deserve no less.

References

Adelman, C. *Devaluation, Diffusion, and the College Connection: A Study of High School Transcripts, 1965–1981.* Report to the National Commission on Excellence in Education, March 1983.

Amann, C. A. "Teacher Spare Us the Unneeded Book." *The Chronicle of Higher Education,* Aug. 1, 1977, p. 32.

Andre, T. "Does Answering Higher-Level Questions While Reading Facilitate Productive Learning?" *Review of Educational Research,* 1979, *49* (2), 280–318.

Angell, R. C. *The Campus: A Study of Contemporary Undergraduate Life in the American University.* East Norwalk, Conn.: Appleton-Century-Crofts, 1928.

Applebee, A. N. "Writing and Reasoning." *Review of Educational Research,* 1984, *54* (4), 577–596.

Association of American Colleges, Task Group on General Education. *A New Vitality in General Education.* Washington, D.C.: Association of American Colleges, 1988.

Astin, A. W. *Achieving Educational Excellence: A Critical Assessment of Priorities and Practices in Higher Education.* San Francisco: Jossey-Bass, 1985.

Astin, A. W., and Green, K. C. *The American Freshman: Twenty Year Trends, 1966–1985.* Cooperative Institutional Research Program. Washington, D.C.: American Council on Education and University of California, Los Angeles: Higher Education Research Institute, 1987.

Astin, A. W., Green, K. C., Korn, W. S., and Maier, M. J. *The American Freshman: National Norms for Fall 1988.* Cooperative

Institutional Research Program. Washington, D.C.: American Council on Education and University of California, Los Angeles: Higher Education Research Institute, 1988.

Astin, A. W., Green, K. C., Korn, W. S., and Schalit, M. *The American Freshman: National Norms for Fall 1987.* Cooperative Institutional Research Program. Washington, D.C.: American Council on Education and University of California, Los Angeles: Higher Education Research Institute, 1987.

Astin, A. W., Korn, W. S., and Berz, E. R. *The American Freshman: National Norms for Fall 1989.* Cooperative Institutional Research Program. Washington, D.C.: American Council on Education and University of California, Los Angeles: Higher Education Research Institute, 1989.

Attinasi, L. C., Jr. "Getting In: Mexican Americans' Perceptions of University Attendance and the Implications for Freshman Year Persistence." *Journal of Higher Education,* 1989, *60* (3), 247–277.

Bachman, J. G., Johnston, L. D., and O'Malley, P. M. "Recent Findings From 'Monitoring the Future: A Continuing Study of the Lifestyles and Values of Youth.'" In F. M. Andrews (ed.), *Research on the Quality of Life.* Ann Arbor: Survey Research Center, Institute for Social Research, University of Michigan, 1986.

Bean, J. C., Drenk, D., and Lee, F. D. "Microtheme Strategies for Developing Cognitive Skills." In C. W. Griffin (ed.), *Teaching Writing in All Disciplines.* New Directions for Teaching and Learning, no. 12. San Francisco: Jossey-Bass, 1982.

Belenky, M. F., Clinchy, B. M., Goldberger, N. R., and Tarule, J. M. *Women's Ways of Knowing: The Development of Self, Voice, and Mind.* New York: Basic Books, 1986.

Blanc, R. A., DeBuhr, L. E., and Martin, D. C. "Breaking the Attrition Cycle." *Journal of Higher Education,* 1983, *54* (1), 80–89.

Bloom, B. S. "The 2-Sigma Problem: The Search for Methods of Group Instruction as Effective as One-to-One Tutoring." *Educational Researcher,* 1984, *13* (6), 4–16.

Bowen, H. R. and Schuster, J. H. *American Professors: A National Resource Imperiled.* New York: Oxford University Press, 1986.

Boyer, E. L. *College: The Undergraduate Experience in America.*

Report of the Carnegie Foundation for the Advancement of Teaching. New York: Harper & Row, 1987.

Boyer, E. L. *Scholarship Reconsidered: Priorities of the Professoriate.* A Special Report of the Carnegie Foundation for the Advancement of Teaching. Princeton, N.J.: Princeton University Press, 1990.

Briggs, K. C., and Briggs-Myers, I. *Myers-Briggs Type Indicator: Test Booklet: Abbreviated Version.* Palo Alto, Calif.: Consulting Psychologists Press, 1983.

Brittingham, B. "Undergraduate Students' Use of Time: A Classroom Investigation." In J. Kurfiss and others (eds.), *To Improve the Academy: Resources for Student, Faculty, & Institutional Development.* Professional and Organizational Development Network. Stillwater, Okla.: New Forums Press, 1988.

Cahn, V. L. "The Undervalued Task of Advising Students." In D.S. Crockett, *Advising Skills, Techniques, and Resources.* Iowa City, Iowa: American College Testing Program, 1985.

Carrier, V. "Notetaking Research: Implications for Classroom." *Journal of Instructional Development,* 1983, *6* (3), 19–26.

Chickering, A. W. "Commentary: The Double Bind of Field Dependence/Independence in Program Alternatives for Educational Development." In S. Messick and Associates (eds.), *Individuality in Learning.* San Francisco: Jossey-Bass, 1976.

Christensen, C. F., and Hansen, A. J. *Teaching and the Case Method.* Boston: Harvard Business School Publishing Division, 1987.

Clark, B. *The Academic Life: Small Worlds, Different Worlds.* Princeton, N.J.: Carnegie Foundation for the Advancement of Teaching, 1987.

Clark, J. H. "Designing Discussions as Group Inquiry." *College Teaching,* 1988, *36* (4), 140–143.

Claxton, C. S., and Murrell, P. H. *Learning Styles: Implications for Improving Educational Practices.* ASHE-ERIC Higher Education Report No. 4. Washington, D.C.: Association for the Study of Higher Education, 1987.

Coles, G. *The Learning Mystique.* New York: Pantheon Books, 1987.

The College Board. *College Bound Seniors National Report: 1988 Profile of SAT and Achievement Test Takers.* New York: College Entrance Examination Board, 1988.

Connolly, P., and Vilardi, T. (eds.). *Writing to Learn Mathematics and Science.* New York: Teachers College Press, 1989.

Corak, K. *Attraction and Retention of Students at the University of Montana.* ERIC Report No. 256264. Missoula: University of Montana Office of Advising and Retention, 1984.

Crockett, D. S., (ed.). *Advising Skills, Techniques, and Resources.* Iowa City, Iowa: American College Testing Program, 1985.

Cross, K. P. *Accent on Learning: Improving Instruction and Reshaping the Curriculum.* San Francisco: Jossey-Bass, 1976.

Cross, K. P. "Taking Teaching Seriously." Paper presented at the Annual Meeting of the American Association for Higher Education, Washington, D.C., March 1986. Printed as "A Proposal to Improve Teaching." *American Association for Higher Education Bulletin,* 1986, *39* (1), 9–14.

Cross, K. P. "The Need for Classroom Research." In J. Kurfiss, L. Hilsen, L. Mortensen, and E. Wadsworth (eds.), *To Improve the Academy: Resources for Student, Faculty, and Institutional Development.* Professional and Organizational Development Network. Stillwater, Okla.: New Forums Press, 1987, 3–17.

Cross, K. P. "In Search of Zippers." *American Association for Higher Education Bulletin,* 1988, *40* (10), 3–7.

Cross, K. P., and Angelo, T. A. *Classroom Assessment Techniques: A Handbook for Faculty.* Technical Report No. 88-A-004.0 Ann Arbor: National Center for Research to Improve Postsecondary Teaching and Learning, University of Michigan, 1988.

Cuddy, L. "One Sentence Is Worth a Thousand: A Strategy for Improving Reading, Writing, and Thinking Skills." In J. R. Jeffrey and G. R. Erickson (eds.), *To Improve the Academy: Resources for Student, Faculty, and Institutional Development.* Professional and Organizational Development Network. Stillwater, Okla.: New Forums Press, 1985.

Cusick, P. A. *The Egalitarian Idea and the American High School.* New York: Longman, 1983.

Daniel, J. W. "Survival Cards In Math." *College Teaching,* 1988, *36* (3), 110.

Dooley, A. F. and Skinner, W. "Casting Casemethod Methods." *Academy of Management Review,* April 1977, pp. 227–288.

Ebel, R. L. *Essentials of Education Measurement.* Englewood Cliffs, N.J.: Prentice-Hall, 1972.

Eble, K. E. *The Craft of Teaching: A Guide to Mastering the Professor's Art.* (2nd ed.) San Francisco: Jossey-Bass, 1988.

Edgerton, R. "The 1987 President's Report to Members." *American Association for Higher Educational Bulletin,* 1987, *39* (9 & 10), 12-15.

Egan, P. H. "Frequent Short Writing: Motivating the Passive Reader." *College Teaching,* 1989, *37* (1), 15-16.

Embedded Figures Test. Palo Alto, Calif.: Consulting Psychologists Press, 1971.

Ericksen, S. C. *The Essence of Good Teaching: Helping Students Learn and Remember What They Learn.* San Francisco: Jossey-Bass, 1984.

Erickson, G. "A Survey of Faculty Development Practices." In M. Svinicki, J. Kurfiss, and J. Stone (eds.), *To Improve the Academy: Resources for Student, Faculty, and Institutional Development.* Professional and Organizational Development Network. Stillwater, Okla.: New Forums Press, 1986.

Estrada, L. F. "Anticipating the Demographic Future: Dramatic Changes Are on the Way." *Change,* May/June 1988, *14*, 16-19.

"Fact File: Attitudes and Characteristics of This Year's Freshmen." *The Chronicle of Higher Education,* Jan. 11, 1989, pp. A33-A34.

"Fact File: Attitudes and Characteristics of This Year's Freshmen." *The Chronicle of Higher Education,* Jan. 24, 1990, pp. A33-A34.

Farber, E. I. "Alternatives to the Term Paper." In T. G. Kirk (ed.), *New Directions for Teaching and Learning: Increasing the Teaching Role of Academic Libraries,* no. 18. San Francisco: Jossey-Bass, 1984.

Fields, C. "The Hispanic Pipeline: Narrow, Leaking, and Needing Repair." *Change,* May/June 1988, pp. 20-27.

Fincher, C. "Learning Theory and Research." In J.C. Smart (ed.), *Higher Education: Handbook of Theory and Research.* New York: Agathon Press, 1985.

Fitzgerald, J. "Research on Revision in Writing." *Review of Educational Research,* 1987, *57* (4), 481-506.

Forrest, A. "Managing the Flow of Students Through the Higher

Education System." *National Forum: Phi Kappa Phi Journal,* Fall 1987, pp. 39–42.

Fraleigh, J. B. *Calculus With Analytical Geometry.* (2nd ed.) Reading, Mass.: Addison-Wesley, 1986.

Frank, O. M. "Effect of Field Independence-Dependence and Study Technique on Learning from a Lecture." *American Educational Research Journal,* 1984, *21* (3), 669–678.

Frederick, P. "The Dreaded Discussion: Ten Ways to Start." *Improving College and University Teaching,* 1981, *29,* 109–114.

Frederick, P. "The Lively Lecture—8 Variations." *College Teaching,* 1986, *34* (2), 43–50.

Frederiksen, N. "Implications of Cognitive Theory for Instruction in Problem Solving." *Review of Educational Research,* 1984, *54* (3), 363–407.

Fuhrmann, B. S., and Grasha, A. F. *A Practical Handbook for College Teachers.* Boston: Little, Brown, 1983.

Gagné, R. M. "Learnable Aspects of Problem Solving." *Educational Psychologist,* 1980, *15* (2), 84–92.

Gallup, A. M. "The 17th Annual Gallup Poll of the Public's Attitudes Toward the Public Schools." *Phi Delta Kappan,* 1985, *67* (1), 35–47.

Gibbs, N. R. "Hail and Beware, Freshmen." *Time,* Sept. 12, 1988, pp. 62–64.

Goodlad, J. *A Place Called School.* New York: McGraw-Hill, 1984.

Gordon, V. N. *The Undecided College Student: an Academic and Career Advising Challenge.* Springfield, Ill.: Charles C. Thomas, 1984.

Green, M. F. (ed.). *Minorities on Campus: A Handbook for Enhancing Diversity.* Washington, D.C.: American Council on Education, 1989.

Griffith, M., and Connor, A. "To Extend Opportunities to All, Colleges Need to Redefine Remedial Education." *The Chronicle of Higher Education,* Sept. 27, 1989, p. B2.

Guskey, T. R. *Improving Student Learning in College Classrooms.* Springfield, Ill.: Charles C. Thomas, 1988.

Habley, W. R. (ed.). *The Status and Future of Academic Advising: Problems and Promise.* Iowa City, Iowa: American College Testing Program, 1988.

Haines, V. J., Diekhoff, G. M., LaBeff, E. E., and Clark, R. E. "College Cheating: Immaturity, Lack of Commitment, and the Neutralizing Attitude." *Research in Higher Eductation*, 1986, *25* (4), 342–354.

Hall, R. M., and Sandler, B. R. *The Classroom Climate: A Chilly One for Women?* Washington, D.C.: Association of American Colleges, Project on the Status and Education of Women, 1982.

Hall, R. M., and Sandler, B. R. *Out of the Classroom: A Chilly Campus Climate for Women?* Washington, D.C.: Association of American Colleges, Project on the Status and Education of Women, 1984.

Hazen Foundation, The Committee on the Student in Higher Education. *The Student in Higher Education.* New Haven, Conn.: Hazen Foundation, 1968.

Heermann, B. *Teaching and Learning with Computers: A Guide for College Faculty and Administrators.* San Francisco: Jossey-Bass, 1988.

Hexter, H. "Students Who Work: A Profile." *Research Briefs*, 1990, *1* (2), 1–6.

Hills, J. R. *Measurement and Evaluation in the Classroom.* Westerville, Ohio: Merrill, 1976.

Hodgkinson, H. L. "Guess Who's Coming to College?" *Academe*, March/April 1983, pp. 13–20.

Hodgkinson, H. L. *All One System.* Washington, D.C.: Institute for Educational Leadership, Inc., 1985a.

Hodgkinson, H. L. "The Changing Face of Tomorrow's Student." *Change*, May/June 1985b, pp. 38–39.

Holdaway, E. A., and Kelloway, K. R. "First Year at University: Perceptions and Experiences of Students," *The Canadian Journal of Higher Education*, 1987, *17* (1), 47–63.

Holmes, W. "Small Groups in Large Classes." In J.R. Jeffrey and G.R. Erickson (eds.), *To Improve the Academy: Resources for Student, Faculty, and Institutional Development.* Professional and Organizational Development Network. Stillwater, Okla.: New Forums Press, 1985.

Holmes, W. "Art Essays and Computer Letters." In J. Kurfiss and others (eds.), *To Improve the Academy: Resources for Student, Faculty, and Institutional Development.* Professional and Organizational Development Network. Stillwater, Okla.: New Forums Press, 1988.

Jendrek, M. P. "Faculty Reactions to Academic Dishonesty." *Journal of College Student Development*, Sept. 1989, pp. 401–406.

Jensen, G. H. "Learning Systems." In J. A. Provost and S. Anchors, *Applications of the Myers-Briggs Type Indicator in Higher Education*. Palo Alto, Calif.: Consulting Psychologists Press, 1987.

Johnson, D. W., and Johnson, F. P. *Joining Together: Group Theory and Group Skills*. Englewood Cliffs, N.J. Prentice-Hall, 1975.

Johnson, D. W., and Johnson, F. P. *Learning Together and Alone: Cooperative, Competitive, and Individualistic Learning*. Englewood Cliffs, N.J.: Prentice-Hall, 1987.

Johnson, D. W., Johnson, R. T., and Holubec, E. T. *Advanced Cooperative Learning*. Edina, Minn.: Interactive Book Co., 1988.

Johnston, J. "The Computer Revolution in Teaching." *Accent on Improving College and Learning*. Ann Arbor: National Center for Research to Improve Postsecondary Teaching and Learning, University of Michigan, 1989.

Katz, J., and Henry, M. *Turning Professors into Teachers*. New York: American Council on Education and Macmillan, 1988.

Katz, J., and Associates. *No Time for Youth*. San Francisco: Jossey-Bass, 1968.

Keimig, R. T. *Raising Academic Standards: A Guide to Learning Improvement*. ASHE-ERIC Higher Education Research Report No. 4. Washington, D.C.: Association for the Study of Higher Education, 1983.

Kibler, W. L., Nuss, E. M., Paterson, B. G., and Pavela, G. *Academic Integrity and Student Development: Legal Issues and Policy Perspectives*. The Higher Education Administration Series. Asheville, N.C.: College Administration Publications, 1988.

Kiewra, K. "Notetaking and Review: The Research and Its Implications." *Instructional Science*, 1987, *16* (3), 233–249.

Kolb, D. A. "Learning Styles and Disciplinary Differences." In A.W. Chickering and Associates (eds.), *The Modern American College: Responding to the New Realities of Diverse Students and a Changing Society*. San Francisco: Jossey-Bass, 1981.

Kolb, D. A. *Experiential Learning: Experience as the Source of Learning and Development.* New York: Prentice-Hall, 1984.

Kolb, D. A. *Learning Style Inventory.* Boston: McBer, 1985.

Kramer, H. C., and Gardner, R. E. *Advising by Faculty.* Washington, D.C.: National Education Association, 1977.

Krukowski, J. "What Do Students Want? Status." *Change,* May/June 1985, pp. 21–28.

Kurfiss, J. G. *Critical Thinking: Theory, Research, Practice, and Possibilities.* ASHE-ERIC Higher Education Report No. 2, Washington, D.C.: Association for the Study of Higher Education, 1988.

Kurfiss, J. G., and others (eds.). *To Improve the Academy: Resources for Student, Faculty, and Institutional Development.* Professional and Organizational Development Network. Stillwater, Okla.: New Forums Press, 1988.

Lawrence, R. L. Note in "When They Don't Do the Reading." *The Teaching Professor,* 1989, *3* (10), 3.

Lederman, M. J., Ribaudo, M., and Ryzewic, S. R. "Basic Skills of Entering College Freshmen: A National Survey of Policies and Perceptions." *Journal of Developmental Education,* 1985, *9* (1), 10–13.

Lemoine, L. F. "Student Perceptions and Academic Success at LSU." Unpublished paper, 1988.

Lenth, S. C., Zuniga, R. E., and Halcon, J. J. *Setting the Agenda: Reform and Renewal in Undergraduate Education.* Boulder, Colo.: Western Interstate Commission for Higher Education Publications, 1989.

Letcher, S. V. "Mastery-Learning Examination Procedure for Introductory Physics." *The Physics Teacher,* Nov. 1989, pp. 613–614.

Levine, A. *When Dreams and Heroes Died: A Portrait of Today's College Student.* San Francisco: Jossey-Bass, 1980.

Levine, A. "Who Are Today's Freshmen?" In M. L. Upcraft , J. N. Gardner, and Associates, *The Freshman Year Experience.* San Francisco: Jossey-Bass, 1989a.

Levine, A., and Associates. *Shaping Higher Education's Future: Demographic Realities and Opportunities, 1990–2000.* San Francisco: Jossey-Bass, 1989b.

Lou, R. "Model Minority? Getting Behind the Veil." *Change,* Nov./Dec. 1989, pp. 16–17.

Mabry, M. "Living in Two Worlds." *Newsweek on Campus,* April 1988, p. 52.

McCartan, A. M. "Students Who Work: Are They Paying Too High a Price?" *Change,* Sept./Oct. 1988, pp. 11–20.

McKeachie, W. J. *Teaching Tips: A Guide for the Beginning College Teacher.* (8th ed.) Lexington, Mass.: Heath, 1986.

McKeachie, W. J., Pintrich, P. R., Lin, Y., and Smith, D. A. F. *Teaching and Learning in the College Classroom: A Review of the Research Literature.* Ann Arbor, Mich.: National Center for Research to Improve Postsecondary Teaching and Learning, 1986.

Marchese, T. J. "Bitting, Bargain, Seatwork, and Finishers," *Change,* May/June 1985, pp. 6–7.

Marchese, T. J. "College: Raising a New Vision," *Change,* Nov./ Dec. 1986a, *10,* 12–17.

Marchese, T. J. "The Freshman Year: An Old Theme, A New Context." *Proceedings, 1986 Conference on the Freshman Year Experience.* Columbia: University of South Carolina, 1986b, 13–26.

Marchese, T. J. "A New Conversation About Undergraduate Teaching: An Interview with Prof. Richard J. Light, Convener of the Harvard Assessment Seminars." *AAHE Bulletin,* 1990, *42* (9), 3–8.

Martin, D., Blanc, R., and DeBuhr, L. "Supplemental Instruction— A Model for Increasing Student Performance and Persistence." In L. Noel and R. Levitz, *Academically Underprepared Students: A Catalog of Successful Practices.* Iowa City, Iowa: American College Testing Program, 1982, 75–79.

Martin, K. H. "Writing 'Microthemes' to Learn Human Biology." In P. Connolly and T. Vilardi (eds.), *Writing to Learn Mathematics and Science.* New York: Teachers College Press, 1989.

Masterton, W. L., Slowinski, E. J., and Stanitski, C. L. *Chemical Principles, Alternate Edition.* Philadelphia: Saunders College Publishing, 1983.

Maxwell, M. *Improving Student Learning Skills: A Comprehensive Guide to Successful Practices and Programs for Increasing the*

Performance of Underprepared Students. San Francisco: Jossey-Bass, 1979.

Messick, S., and Associates. *Individuality in Learning: Implications of Cognitive Styles and Creativity for Human Development.* San Francisco; Jossey-Bass, 1986.

Meyers, C. *Teaching Students to Think Critically: A Guide for Faculty in All Disciplines.* San Francisco: Jossey-Bass, 1986.

Milton, O. *Will That Be on the Final?* Springfield, Ill.: Charles C. Thomas, 1982.

Milton, O., Pollio, H. R., and Eison, J. A. *Making Sense of College Grades: Why the Grading System Does Not Work and What Can Be Done About It.* San Francisco: Jossey-Bass, 1986.

Mingis, K. "The Reluctant Freshman." *Sunday Journal Magazine* (Providence, R.I.), Aug. 30, 1987, pp. 6–13.

Moffatt, M. *Coming of Age in New Jersey.* New Brunswick, N.J.: Rutgers University Press, 1989.

Moony, C. J. "3 in 4 Professors Think Their Undergraduate Students Are Seriously Underprepared, Carnegie Study Finds." *The Chronicle of Higher Education,* Aug. 16, 1989, p. A13.

National Institute of Education. *Involvement in Learning: Realizing the Potential of American Higher Education.* Washington, D.C.: U.S. Department of Education, 1984.

Noel, L., and Levitz, R. (eds.). *Academically Underprepared Students: A Catalog of Successful Practices.* Iowa City, Iowa: American College Testing Program, 1982.

Noel, L., Levitz, R., Saluri, D. and Associates. *Increasing Student Retention: Effective Programs and Practices for Reducing the Dropout Rate.* San Francisco: Jossey-Bass, 1985.

Norman, D. A. *Learning and Memory.* New York: W.H. Freeman, 1982.

Nuss, E. M. "Academic Integrity: Comparing Faculty and Student Attitudes." *College Teaching,* Summer 1984, pp. 140–144.

Nyquist, J. D., Abbott, R. D., and Wulff, D. H. (eds.). *Teaching Assistant Training in the 1990s.* New Directions for Teaching and Learning, no. 39. San Francisco: Jossey-Bass, 1989.

Park, O. "Example Comparison Strategy Versus Attribute Identification Strategy in Concept Learning." *American Educational Research Journal,* 1984, *21* (1), 145–162.

Perotti, V., and others. "Understanding New Learners: The Role of Personality Assessment in Facilitating Learning." Paper presented at the Second International Conference on The First Year Experience, Southampton, England, 1987.

Perry, W. G., Jr. *Forms of Intellectual and Ethical Development in the College Years*. New York: Holt, Rinehart & Winston, 1970.

Perry, W. G., Jr. "Cognitive and Ethical Growth: The Making of Meaning." In A. W. Chickering and Associates, *The Modern American College: Responding to the New Realities of Diverse Students and a Changing Society*. San Francisco: Jossey-Bass, 1981.

Perry, W. G., Jr. "Notes on Scheme and Some Implications for Education." Unpublished note. Cambridge, Mass.: Bureau of Study Counsel, 1989.

Peters, C. B. "Rescue the Perishing: A New Approach to Supplemental Instruction." In J. Kurfiss (ed.), *To Improve the Academy: Resources for Students, Faculty, and Institutional Development*. Professional and Organizational Development Network. Stillwater, Okla.: New Forums Press, Inc., 1987, 183-195.

Powell, A. G., Farrar, E., and Cohen, D. K. *The Shopping Mall High School: Winners and Losers in the Educational Marketplace*. Boston: Houghton Mifflin, 1985.

Rendon, L. I. "The Lie and the Hope: Making Higher Education a Reality for At-Risk Students." *American Association for Higher Education Bulletin*, 1989, *41* (9), 4-7.

Richardson, R. C., Jr., Fisk, E. C., and Okun, M. K. *Literacy in the Open-Access College*. San Francisco: Jossey-Bass, 1983.

Robinson, F. P. *Effective Study*. New York: Harper & Row, 1961.

Ross, D. "Training Teaching Assistants to Use Active Learning Strategies." In S. F. Schomberg (ed.), *Strategies for Active Teaching and Learning in University Classrooms*. Minneapolis: Communication Services, Continuing Education and Extension, University of Minnesota, 1986.

Ruddock, M. S., and Wilkinson, C. Y. "Retention—What Happens During the Freshman Year?" Paper presented at the 23rd Annual Forum of the Association for Institutional Research, Toronto, May 1983.

Scheers, J. J., and Dayton, C. M. "Improved Estimation of Academic Cheating Behavior Using the Randomized Response Technique." *Research in Higher Education,* 1987, *26* (1), 61–69.

Schoem, D., and Knox, W. (eds.). *Students Talk About College: Essays from the Pilot Program.* Ann Arbor, Mich.: Prakken Publications, 1988.

Sedlak, M. W., Wheeler, C. W., Pullin, D. C., and Cusick, P. A. *Selling Students Short: Classroom Bargains and Academic Reform in the American High School.* New York: Teachers College Press, 1986.

Simpson, M. L. "Teaching University Freshmen to Employ, Regulate, and Transfer Study Strategies to the Content Areas." *Forum for Reading,* 1986, *17* (2), 61–71.

Skinner, E. R., and Richardson, R. C. "Making It in a Majority University." *Change,* May/June 1988, pp. 37–42.

Smith, D. *The Challenge of Diversity: Involvement or Alienation in the Academy?* ASHE-ERIC Report No. 5. Washington, D.C.: School of Education and Human Development, George Washington University, 1989.

Smith, P. *Killing the Spirit: Higher Education in America.* New York: Viking Penguin, 1990.

Snow, R. E., and Peterson, P. L. "Recognizing Difference in Student Aptitudes." In W. J. McKeachie (ed.), *Learning, Cognition, and College Teaching.* New Directions for Teaching and Learning, no. 2. San Francisco: Jossey-Bass, 1980.

Stanford, G., and Stanford, B. G. *Learning Discussion Skills Through Games.* New York: Citation Press, 1969.

Starling, R. "Professor as Student: The View from the Other Side." *College Teaching,* 1987, *35* (1), 3–7.

Stice, J. E. "Using Kolb's Learning Cycle to Improve Student Learning." *Engineering Education,* 1987, *77,* 219–96.

Suzuki, B. H. "Asian Americans as the 'Model Minority.'" *Change,* Nov./Dec. 1989, pp. 13–19.

Svinicki, M. D., and Dixon, N. M. "Kolb Model Modified for Classroom Activities." *College Teaching,* 1987, *35* (4), 141–146.

Tennyson, R. D., and Park, O. "The Teaching of Concepts: A Review of Instructional Design Research Literature." *Review of Educational Research,* 1980, *50* (1), 55–70.

Terenzini, P. T., and Wright, T. M. "Students' Personal Growth

During the First Two Years of College." *The Review of Higher Education,* 1987, *10* (3), 259-271.

Tinto, V. "The Principles of Effective Retention." Paper presented at the annual meeting of the American Association of Higher Education, March 1988a.

Tinto, V. "Stages of Student Departure." *Journal of Higher Education,* 1988b, *59* (4), 438-453.

University of Rhode Island. "Entering Students' Questionnaire." Unpublished summary of surveys. 1988.

Weimer, M. "The First Day of Class: Advice and Ideas." *The Teaching Professor,* 1989a, *3* (7), 1-2.

Weimer, M. "Office Hours." *The Teaching Professor,* 1989b, *3* (7), 7-8.

Weinstein, C. "A Metacurriculum for Remediating Deficits in Learning Strategies of Academically Underprepared Students." In L. Noel and R. Levitz (eds.), *Academically Underprepared Students: A Catalog of Successful Practices.* Ames, Iowa: American College Testing Program, 1982, 91-93.

Whipple, W. R. "Goodbye to Studenthood?" *Change,* Sept./Oct. 1988, p. 14.

White, E. M. *Teaching and Assessing Writing: Recent Advances in Understanding, Evaluating, and Improving Student Performance.* San Francisco: Jossey-Bass, 1985.

Whitman, N. A. *Peer Teaching: To Teach Is to Learn Twice.* ASHE-ERIC Higher Education Report No. 4. Washington, D.C.: Association for the Study of Higher Education, 1988.

Who's Who Among American High School Students. *Nineteenth Annual Survey of High Achievers' Views on Education, Politics, Drugs and Alcohol, Social Issues, Teen Suicide.* Lake Forest, Ill.: Educational Communications, 1988.

Winn, M. "The Plug-in Generation." *Change,* May/June 1985, *14,* 16-20.

Winston, R. B., Jr., Miller, T. K., Ender, S. C., Grites, T. J., and Associates. *Developmental Academic Advising: Addressing Students' Educational, Career, and Personal Needs.* San Francisco: Jossey-Bass, 1984.

Witkin, H. A. "Cognitive Style in Academic Performance and in

Teacher-Student Relations." In S. Messick and Associates, *Individuality in Learning*. San Francisco: Jossey-Bass, 1976.

Witkin, H. A., Oltman, P. K., Raskin, E., and Karp, S. A. *A Manual for the Embedded Figures Tests*. Palo Alto, Calif.: Consulting Psychologists Press, 1971.

Zeakes, S. J. "Case Studies in Biology." *College Teaching*, 1989, *37* (1), 33–35.

Index